Literary
Luxuries

Literary Luxuries

AMERICAN WRITING AT THE END OF THE MILLENNIUM

Joe David Bellamy

University of Missouri Press

Columbia and London

Copyright © 1995 by
Joe David Bellamy
University of Missouri Press, Columbia, Missouri 65201
Printed and bound in the United States of America
All rights reserved
5 4 3 2 1   99 98 97 96 95

Library of Congress Cataloging-in-Publication Data

Bellamy, Joe David.
    Literary luxuries : American writing at the end of the
    millennium / Joe David Bellamy.
        p.   cm.
    Includes index.
    ISBN 0-8262-1029-5 (cloth : alk. paper)
    1. American fiction—20th century—History and criticism.
    2. United States—Intellectual life—20th century.   3. Bellamy, Joe
    David—Authorship.   I. Title.
    PS379.B424   1995
    813'.5409—dc20   95-20790
                                                                CIP

∞ This paper meets the requirements of the
American National Standard for Permanence of Paper
for Printed Library Materials, Z39.48, 1984.

TEXT DESIGN: ELIZABETH K. FETT
JACKET DESIGN: KRISTIE LEE
TYPESETTER: BOOKCOMP
PRINTER AND BINDER: THOMSON-SHORE, INC.
TYPEFACES: PALATINO, TRIUMVERATE EXTENDED

FOR ALL MY STUDENTS

especially Lorrie Moore, Elizabeth Inness-Brown, Susan Dodd, Jerry Doland, Tom Chiarella, Elizabeth Cox, Phyllis Barber, Steve Amick, Emily Hammond, Arni Sabatelli, Alma Villanueva, Christopher Williams, Rhonda Strickland, Stephen Kirk, Stacy Freed, Emily Zukerberg, Andy Dephtereos, Maudy Benz, Nini Diana, Bob Zock, Kelli Sheehan, Caitlin Gross, Sarah Mosher, Katie Zock, Erica Foley, Peter Girard, Dan Conaway, Martha Watterson, Krissy Bonin, Karen Hoberg, Jen McGregor, Mary Ann O'Grady, Elizabeth McDowell, Cristan Tamminga, Erik Atwell, Kerry O'Connell, Kevin Wright, Karin Schneider, Shawn Lambert, Terese Mattil, Margaret Newberry, Eric Scola, Bill Black, Amie Carroll, Kristen Peters, Raouf Gangjee, Jeff Graf, Aimee Minbiole, Dawn Montanye, Malora Mathis, Scott Judd, Brendan Jones, Wendy Button, Andrew Albanese, Vicki Flick, Scott Pomfret, Matt Soden, Deborah Peryea, Nicolle Hall, Elizabeth Burrows, Gail Yngve, Bill Lennertz, Anne Sanow, Mary Hart, Rick Henry, Mitch Meyer, Diana Newton, Eleanor Funk, Daryl DeBerto, Nancy Edmondson, Amy Oliver, Carol Gooding, Laura Sparling, Richard Beusman, Lauren Church, Anne Gray, Alan Meeker, Barry Davis, Susan Aasen, Elsa Kellstrom, Katherine Hershey, George Hughes, John Fitzsimons, Holly Haas, Seth Denning, Scott Conroe, Barbara Goldberg, Lynne Wighton, Ted Williams, Abby Heed, Elizabeth Denton, Eldonna Shepard, Jody Dixon, Kam Ghaffari, Carol O'Connor, Sonya Cunningham, Lynne Basler, John O'Connor, Colin Irving, Lael Bellamy, Donna Laskowski, Jane Jervis, Pam Dahlstrom, Robert Mirsky, Ellen Dodd, Lauri Fritzinger, Anne Deutsch, Ann Douglas, Susan Ryan, Cathy White, Lisa Faulkner, Kathy Klingenstein, John McCormick, Rebecca Savage, Beth Anton Dooley, Cameron Noble, Joe Nunez, Hal Stokes, John Clogston, Pat Broikow, Leslie Moore, Craig Gibson, Chuck Burrall, Bonnie Legro, Meredith Keller, Rick Klingman, Anne White, Carol Rushin, Robert Snyder, Tony Ross, Janis Glickstein, Mindy Ross, Roberta Agley, Rod Baird, Jennifer Knapp, Bob Vilas, Kathy Krablin, Susie Knap, Michael Mascioni, Laurie Marsh, Doug Collum, Kirsten Halvorsen, Melissa Shaw, Mary Zimmerman, Kessa Raymond, Mary Foster, Elizabeth

Soloman, Hillary Elmer, Sam Bellamy, Kirsten Scheer, Bill Purdy, Paul Castron, Jennie Ellis, David Schelle, Carolyn Dahm, Jayne Billinson, Julie Gilbert, Darcy Lane, Connie Johnson, Nina McHale, Kathleen Dunn, K. C. Cerio, Dina Casciola, Barbara McNeice, John DiBello, Sally Barker, Marge Benoit, Julia Carlisle, Judy Abbate, Linda Pooler, Gigi Peterson, Dan Rusanowsky, Kathy Eustis, Louise Evans, Carolyn Stutz, Diana McDaniel, Nancy Schwalenstocker, Cindy Habeeb, Juliette Sweet, Ray Shero, Steve Rich, Steve Rhodes, Suzanne Kent, Sue Schultz, Laura Roscoe, Tamsen Olver, Nancy Start, Chandler Dumaine, Arnold Beerman, Jamie Forton, Lisa Powers, Sharon Clark, Connie Wood, Dennis Miller, Steve Peters, Donna Ronchi, Beth Edwards, Bill Losinger, Bill Robertson, Kathy Evans, Kathy Coombs, Wesley Skillings, Debbie Harer, Linda Hixson, Dennis Shattuck, Stephanie Garman, Mike Holland, Martha Colton, Steve Van Nuys, Paige Leichner, Tammie Lewis, Dan Notkin, Cindy Daniels, Alisha Laramee, Angela Sass, Liesl Taylor, Moray Fleming, Jenny Foulke, Britt Richards, Christine Scott, Chris Wood, Lisa Beech Hartz, Tully Beatty, Priscilla Brown, Kim Hill, and Celeste Schell.

OTHER BOOKS BY JOE DAVID BELLAMY

FICTION
Suzi Sinzinnati
Atomic Love

POETRY
Olympic Gold Medalist
The Frozen Sea

INTERVIEWS
The New Fiction
American Poetry Observed

ANTHOLOGIES
Apocalypse
Superfiction, or the American Story Transformed
Moral Fiction: An Anthology
New Writers for the Eighties
Love Stories/Love Poems

CONTENTS

Acknowledgments   *xi*

Introduction   *1*

LITERARY LUXURIES

Literary Luxuries: Of Pens and Swords   13

LITERARY OCCASIONS

The Magazine Wars   27

The Bread Loaf Experience   39

A Star in the Wilderness: Six Years at Saranac Lake   48

LITERARY METEOROLOGY

Superfiction: Fiction in an Age of Excess   63

Lifestyle Fiction: A Downpour
of Literary Republicanism   75

Muscular Fiction: A Postscript   83

LITERARY EDUCATION

The Theory of Creative Writing I:
Keeping the Frog Alive   87

The Theory of Creative Writing II:
The Uses of the Imagination and
the Revenge of the Pink Typewriter   99

The Iowa Mystique and Those Who Loathe It   108

Finding One's True Voice   115

LITERARY SATIRISTS

T. Coraghessan Boyle and the Renaissance of the Short Story *121*

Tom Wolfe as Visiting Martian   *126*

Kurt Vonnegut for President:
   The Making of a Literary Reputation   *137*

LITERARY VICES

The Autobiographical Trap   *153*

Still Arguing about Moral Fiction   *156*

Five Sex Acts and Wild Thing:
   John Frohnmayer's Last Days at the NEA, and Mine   *163*

CONTEMPORARIES

Max Apple   *179*

Russell Banks   *183*

Donald Barthelme   *186*

Raymond Carver   *191*

John Casey   *193*

Don DeLillo   *196*

Frederick Exley   *199*

John Gardner   *201*

Beverly Lowry   *204*

Mailer/Miller   *206*

Joyce Carol Oates   *209*

George Plimpton   *211*

Ishmael Reed   *214*

Kurt Vonnegut   *216*

Dan Wakefield   *219*

Paul West   *220*

Index   *223*

ACKNOWLEDGMENTS

Grateful acknowledgment is made to the following publications in which some of these essays (some in different form) first appeared: *Antioch Review, Chicago Review, Chicago Sun Times Book Week, Harper's, Michigan Quarterly Review, Mississippi Review, The Nation, New York Times Book Review, North American Review, Other Voices, Saturday Review, Washington Post Book World,* and *Witness.* Grateful acknowledgment is also made to *The Contemporary Literary Scene,* edited by David Madden; *The Purple Decades,* by Tom Wolfe; *The Vonnegut Statement,* edited by Jerome Klinkowitz and John Somer; and *Writers and Their Craft,* edited by Nicholas Delbanco and Laurence Goldstein.

I would also like to give special thanks to St. Lawrence University for sabbaticals, for leave-time, and for generous ongoing support over more than twenty years that helped me to complete much of the work presented here.

Literary
Luxuries

INTRODUCTION

The literary life in the United States in the last decades of the twentieth century—if one could find it—was a far different experience than it had been for any previous generation of Americans. This book is the record of one person's search for a literary life in the United States, from the sixties to the nineties, and some of the contretemps, personages, fashions, and institutions encountered along the way.

Somewhat by accident, I seem to have showed up in most of the likely locales and done what any aspiring literary citizen of my time might have tried and many did. In that sense, looking back, I feel very much like a literary Everyman. I attended the Iowa Writers Workshop and survived to tell the tale. I taught creative writing for a living and did battle for territorial rights within the bizarre realm of the late-twentieth-century American English department. I set out to understand and describe a literary movement and was accused by some of having caused it—and thus became an "expert" in the highly inexact science of literary meteorology. I was a reader and reviewer, as well as a writer, and I read as many of the important books of my time as I could find the time for and pondered their significance and wrote about some of them and wondered which ones would last. All in all, during the course of my travels, I founded three literary magazines and a small press and a literary prize and a writers' conference and a bookstore.

Again, somewhat by accident, I ended up, in middle age—largely because no one else wanted the job—as a spokesman and institutional representative from my generation of writers: president of the Coordinating Council of Literary Magazines, then president of Associated Writing Programs, then director of the literature program of the National Endowment for the Arts during the most divisive and controversial period in its brief history. I testified before Congress and before the National Council on the Arts concerning literary matters, and I provided literary advice that, unwittingly, led to the firing of John Frohnmayer as chairman of the Arts Endowment.

Whatever its status as memoir, literary criticism, or social commentary, I see the work collected here as the record of an odyssey;

1

whatever other function it might perform, my hope is that it might serve my fellow habitués as a source of comparative recollection, that it might help interested onlookers to understand the vicissitudes of the writer's life and of the American literary experience at large and focus new attention on some of the problems thereof—since the fate of our writers is important to our national well-being—and that it might eventually serve future historians who may wish to reflect upon the aspirations and peculiarities of our time and place.

It all started because, in 1967, it began to seem impossible to me to write a realistic coming-of-age novel that didn't seem unspeakably gauche, and, at the Iowa Writers Workshop, that is what I was trying to do. This novel was about a woman I had been in love with several years before who had one day, inexplicably, told me she was going to marry someone else; and I was determined to turn this poignant fact into a tragic masterpiece of monumental proportions and never to forget it.

The main obstacle to completing this project was that the sensibility of the times was rapidly turning against this sort of book. Far more consequential issues were on people's minds and on the national agenda. Not that it would ever be an easy matter to transform a love story between eighteen-year-olds—where neither lover dies—into the stuff of immortal tragedy, but, in normal times, it was a goal that one might have aspired to without seeming quite so foolish. It was certainly the most tragic personal event that had ever happened in my lifetime up to that moment, and what was literature *for,* I wondered, if it wasn't to help a person comprehend the subtleties of tragic events and thus to find a way to cope with them?

Thus blocked from what I actually wished to accomplish and in a self-imposed state of some misery, morosity, and confusion, I started reading some of the contemporary writers who seemed to be speaking for the times, writers such as Kurt Vonnegut, Joyce Carol Oates, John Hawkes, Donald Barthelme, John Barth, John Gardner, Susan Sontag, Ishmael Reed, Ronald Sukenick, Tom Wolfe, and wondering how *they* might treat the kind of tragedy I was attempting to deal with, how they might treat *anything,* since something quite strange seemed to be happening to American writing and nobody seemed to be able to say exactly what it was.

As it turned out, I invested some years interviewing these pivotal writers, asking them a number of the pressing questions that were on my mind, traveling from place to place like a literary Diogenes and holding up the lantern (and my microphone) and staring into the faces of these future immortals and asking them, earnestly, "Why?" and "How?" and "What is the way?"

After completing the work that made up my book *The New Fiction: Interviews with Innovative American Writers*, I certainly understood more of the questions and some of the answers. But I was still feeling perplexed and no closer to a solution for my own languishing novel. The launching of the literary magazine *Fiction International* in 1972–1973 enabled me to continue plying some of these same waters, and I set to work on a definitive anthology that would describe and clarify, once and for all, the modes of experimentation that were still bouncing around the literary landscape like so many unpredictable balls of light inside the new video games of the time.

The anthology was called *Superfiction,* and when it appeared from Random House in 1975 I had no idea that it would stay in print for the next fifteen years and become a seminal anthology of what was to become postmodernism in American fiction. I also had no idea that simply by trying to complete my literary education in a reasonably honorable way and explore this singular new way of writing, I would become identified with it. I would become, in the eyes of the world, a postmodernist, an advocate of experimental writing, and a critic! But, at least for a time, that is what happened: "Barth, Barthelme & Co. is neither very old nor very philanthropic," Gordon Lish proclaimed in the forword to *his* definitive anthology. "It is rigorous and vigorous and franchising like crazy. With the result that we now have outlets called Sukenick . . . or Bellamy doing fire-sale business on every campus. . . . Of course there is no crisis in the hygiene of the national literature, but this will do until we get a real one."

But there *was*, of course, a crisis in the hygiene of the national literature, not to mention the national mind and body—that was just the problem. Between 1963 and 1968, the freight train of history had gone off the tracks perhaps for good and was spinning itself into a deeper and deeper rut, and American writers were attempting to delineate the scope and shape and feel of cataclysm and change. American writing was in a full-scale flight from realism because realism no longer seemed real enough, no longer seemed adaptable to the madness of the day-to-day. My essay on "Superfiction," circa 1975, conveys the full argument and a broader description of that dangerous stretch in American life when a certain innocence no longer seemed possible.

It wasn't long before the rampant experimentalism of the late sixties and early seventies was taken to task, however, and, in some cases, by some of those writers who had been closely identified with it. The most notable and controversial attack was in 1978 by the novelist John Gardner in his book *On Moral Fiction*. Gardner wanted to remind writers of their historical responsibilities because he felt that American writing had become too decadent and nihilistic. He was worried that if not even the writers could find redemption in American life, what about the rest of the country? He wanted our literature to provide moral perspectives and reasons to live. Some of his arguments, however, seemed both murky and strident; worse yet, Gardner felt his case would be stronger if he showed the courage to point out the specific failings of a number of his contemporaries. His close readings and analyses were often peculiar or wrongheaded, and the book created instantaneous outrage. Thus, many rejected *On Moral Fiction* as simply a hatchet job and dismissed it out of hand. Max Apple's response in the Writers' Forum sponsored by *Fiction International* was more generous than most: "When Gardner is making the grandiose claims of art in simple language, he is most eloquent. . . . [B]ut when Gardner moves from the general to the specific, it is sometimes as easy to say no to him as it is to the missionary on the street corner."

However, in spite of what seemed to be an overwhelmingly unsympathetic response to *On Moral Fiction*, and perhaps for reasons entirely unrelated to the book, over the next several years American fiction seemed bent on further change, much of it not that remote from some of the principles John Gardner had enunciated. By the early years of the Reagan administration, a full-scale retreat from innovative modes and stylistic flourishes seemed to be in progress. Almost overnight, it seemed, superfiction had become superfluous. Almost overnight, the most imitated short-fiction writer of the seventies, Donald Barthelme, was deposed by the most imitated short-fiction writer of the eighties, Raymond Carver.

Carver established very quickly, by the example of his work, that one of the chief arguments against "realism"—that everything had been *done*—was bogus. All of American experience had *not* yet been written about. New content, and a new attitude toward it, was still possible. Carver knew corners of American life that had never been seen by the light of day. He was direct and emotional, never cerebral. Carver's style was a throwback to Hemingway's—the most imitated style of the first half of the century—and Carver's way of saying that style was not his main concern. The very accessibility of Carver's work seemed to be staking out an aesthetic position in opposition to the complexity, indirectness, and opacity of the narratives of his contemporaries. Suddenly critics were talking about the advent of "blue-collar realism" and "lifestyle fiction" and "minimalism," and, just as suddenly, the short story was apparently back in vogue with readers who had nearly given up on it out of frustration with the difficulties of the experimentalists. Here was fiction that one could read without the need for exegesis.

Of course, Carver's differences with superfiction were not merely stylistic, as my essay on "Lifestyle Fiction," included here, attempts to articulate. Superfiction was about "the inner" and the nature of the imagination and its relationship to "the real"—and other heavy-duty philosophical matters. Carver's fiction was about mimesis all over again and about suffering and injustice-collecting and the difficulty of communication and the nature of evil.

But so many writers jumped aboard the bandwagon with such apparent relief (and some with much less stunning results than those of Raymond Carver) that by the mid-eighties "minimalism" had already moved from the status of the dangerously fashionable to that of the pallid and predictable. A "Minimalist Fiction" issue of the *Mississippi Review* in 1985—which invited critics to comment and writers such as Raymond Carver and Lee K. Abbott (never a minimalist) to take their own pulses and try to say what was afoot—is an early sampling of the misgivings that were in the air. Since then, the stock of minimalism has continued to plunge. Minimalism has now been blamed for everything from divorce to child abuse and presented as further hard evidence of "the dumbing of America."

In 1987–1988, the *Michigan Quarterly Review* devoted two special issues to "A Symposium on Contemporary American Fiction," which included comments from over eighty writers and the last of my three definitive statements (among those included here) on "which way the winds are blowing" for American fiction. If it's all right with you, I think I will pass on this opportunity for a further update. If pressed, I suppose I would have to agree with Sven Birkerts that we have entered a lull or a period of pluralism where "everything is permitted. Where there is no one necessary artistic style," all possible styles might flourish. But I am not as ready as Birkerts seems to be in *American Energies* or in *The Gutenberg Elegies* to assume a shrinking-violet attitude toward the condition of our literary culture and to throw in the towel in behalf of literacy, creative writing, or the phonetic alphabet—because I think we must resist these easygoing capitulations to the power and influence of the media and the philistinism of American life and the abysmal failures of education.

In the mid-seventies, writers workshops were blamed for producing superfiction. In the mid-nineties, writers workshops have recently been blamed for creating and perpetuating minimalism, as if it were a kind of disease limited primarily to writers workshops. To begin to blame writers workshops for a particular kind of writing is, perhaps, a sign that a new age and a new literary manner are already at hand.

During the eighties, by the way, I did finally figure out a way to finish my long-festering novel—the cause of it all—which I had continued to work on sporadically and despondently over the years. One day it suddenly dawned on me that I was, in fact, writing a comedy, not a tragedy! Sometimes the simplest discoveries are the hardest to make, but when they do occur, they have the force of revelation. I only had to throw away about 500 pages.

If any literary label or hard core of memory adheres to the present moment, it is less likely to be that of a particular aesthetic movement, perhaps, than that of the "culture wars" in general, and the "culture of complaint" and the atmosphere of intolerance and confrontation that helped cause these wars. All the arts have become a part of the fin de siècle discussion—or vehement disagreement—about how Americans want to live and express themselves in the twenty-first century, of what shall be private and what shall be permitted to be public, of what value we should place in art and how much we are willing to pay for it. Politics has infected art as never before in American experience, and ignorance, prudery, bigotry, and fanaticism have too often carried the day. How well we understand the passage we are currently going through, and what we are willing to do about it, will surely have enormous consequences for art, for parlance, and for our national integrity.

It was 1964 when a wild-eyed English professor, Marshall McLuhan, told us that the phonetic alphabet was doomed and that literacy, as we had known it, would be dead by the year 2000.

Well, the year 2000 is almost here, and literacy is undoubtedly suffering, but I don't yet see how we can possibly do without it.

Upon first reading McLuhan, I remember feeling a terrible sense of foreboding. There I was, trying to make literature my life's work, teaching it at least and writing it if possible, and I didn't look forward to the prospect of becoming an antiquarian by the end of the century—someone with an obsolete specialty living unhappily in a world of booming electronic gadgets and mindless electronic celebrities—and hardly anybody left with any semblance of an inner life.

In 1973, in my introduction to the inaugural issue of *Fiction International*, I was still arguing with McLuhan, seeing the launching of a new, engaged, literary magazine—a quixotic activity if there ever was one and one of the last forms of martyrdom—as one way to help subvert the dawning of a new era of the Idiot Box. How could one possibly win even a small victory against so monolithic a scourge?—especially since I was hooked on television myself! "TV creates an irresistible kind of hypnotic/narcotic trance," I told my students, "for creatures so attuned—conditioned by eons of evolutionary development—to hand-eye coordination activities as a primary focus of survival. . . . But we must resist it, if we can."

In many ways, for me, I now realize, the three decades 1964 to 1994 have been an ongoing dialogue, argument, and holding action against what I see as the forces of McLuhanism and catatonic death. I have now spent the better part of thirty years, in the classroom, arguing with McLuhan and, outside of it, trying to cause his prophesies to go seriously awry. Luckily, McLuhan had more than just the timetable wrong, because this is not a battle that anyone could hope to win alone, or even with the collective forces of all our English departments and creative writing programs behind him.

It does seem clear that books are not cultural events anymore—the way they were even thirty years ago. Is this because no books of overriding cultural significance are being written anymore? Of course not! If one believes critic Bruce Bawer, all of our serious novelists have failed simultaneously, so, of course no one wants to read them. Or, at least Bruce Bawer doesn't want to read them, which is, I think, *his* problem. In "The Theory of Creative Writing" I look into some of the possible explanations for this misunderstanding, which is not by any means only Bawer's.

The more common explanation for the failure of audiences is, of course, the failure of our educational system. As Alvin Kernan has commented: "People who can't read well, or don't need to read very much, are not going to be very interested in the very complicated books and ways of reading that are central to literature. The literacy crisis therefore is a very fundamental threat to literature." It is also true that the crisis for literature is a fundamental threat to literacy. Readers need the incentive and the promise of the higher-level rewards of literacy in order to persist in the rote and the rudimentary paths that lead to that end.

Certainly, literature that aspires to art, if it is any good, does not often entertain the same audiences that respond enthusiastically to *Terminator II*, nor is it likely to have the same earning potential, which is the only real argument against it (and not a very good one). But *Terminator II* and serious art can certainly coexist. If one believes, as I do, that there *must* be a place for literary art in our culture—which is, after all, the historical record of our country, of our time, of the main concerns of our people, "the national memory" as Solzhenitsyn has said, and *our main bead on the truth*—then something more must be done, as I argue in my title essay, "Literary Luxuries." If literature becomes too great a luxury, then literacy can't survive; and if literacy can't survive, then I doubt that civilization can.

In spite of what may seem a bleak prognosis for our abused alphabet, the electronic media will *not* be replacing the magnificent technology of literacy any time soon—in spite of all the dismal prophesies to the contrary and plenty of evidence of the powerful effects of the media. It is important to remember that all of television, whether drama, news, or commercial, is based on a written text, so it is *not at all* a medium that is exclusively "visual" or "electronic." It ends up as visual, *but it starts out as language on a page* or computer screen. If it doesn't start out as language, it ends up in some kind of irritating disorder. And the same is true of film.

After *Star Wars* and its sequels made hundreds of millions of dollars, the filmmaker George Lucas built himself a self-contained, state-of-the-art studio with all the most advanced special-effects technology. The core of this studio, both architecturally and spiritually, according to Lucas himself, is the *library*.

McLuhan was correct in his perception that world culture is passing through some sort of visual/electronic transformation of consciousness that affects all of us. This may be somewhat more far-reaching than Robert Hughes's apt characterization in *Culture of Complaint* that "network television is mostly junk designed to produce reality-shortage." But we are still attached very strongly to the phonetic alphabet, and our powerful electronic media are *utterly dependent* upon it. We are nowhere near a point when we might be able to leave literacy behind or expect that jettisoning the phonetic alphabet (and the skills of literacy) might be a blessing.

Bill McKibben's experiment in television-viewing, which he recounts in *The Age of Missing Information*, is further proof of this, if we need it. With the help of videotape, McKibben watched and evaluated twenty-four hours of television on every channel of one of the largest cable systems in the country—ninety-three channels in all—and found that the content of those hours and hours of viewing was essentially eye candy, pointless distraction, absurdly useless information, and little else.

"We believe that we live in the 'age of information,'" McKibben remarks, "that there has been an information 'explosion,' an information 'revolution.' While in a certain narrow sense, this is the case, in many important ways, just the opposite is true. We also live at a moment of deep ignorance, when vital knowledge that humans have always possessed about who we are and where we live seems beyond our reach. An unenlightenment. An age of missing information."

I would say it is an Age of Eye Candy suffering from tooth decay of the soul, and it is a time badly in need of the redeeming powers of the imagination and of great writing—all the literary sorts of luxuries that we simply can't do without.

LITERARY
LUXURIES

LITERARY LUXURIES

Of Pens and Swords

The ten winners of the National Medal of the Arts were finishing their White House luncheon when President Bush, who was seated next to Isaac Stern, sprang to his feet and announced: "All right, you artists! Now I want you to meet some real artists!" He made a sweeping gesture, the door opened, and there in the doorway stood Joe DiMaggio, and next to him was Ted Williams. (They were there to accompany the president to the All-Star Game in Toronto that evening.)

My job, as I understood it, was to cast my gaze out beyond the Washington Monument, which stood like a sentinel outside my window beyond the IRS Building, and to survey the condition of American literary culture. Across the mountains and prairies, the cities and rivers and baseball diamonds, I would have to decide what the literary culture needed to ensure its good health—and how writers could be helped—when judged from a completely benign perspective. Since I had nothing to "sell" but literature itself, I sometimes had the feeling that I was the only person in the country with the lonely assignment of assessing and safeguarding the literary realm in this peculiar way.

As director of the literature program of the National Endowment for the Arts, I was presumably in a position to do something about what I saw: with government funds allocated for that purpose (almost $5 million per year as I began my term in 1990) and through the force of influence and persuasion; with Congress and private citizens, who badly needed persuading of the worth of what the Endowment was trying to accomplish; with members of the literary community; and with artistic and bureaucratic personnel within the Endowment itself.

As I began to learn the territory, especially the relative stature of literature as an art form in comparison to the other art forms within the Endowment, and the place that literature has managed to carve out for itself across the land in over two hundred years of American civilization, in an institutional sense—a mighty small place—I began to feel an overpowering sense of disappointment. "You mean this is it?" I felt like saying. What became obvious to me over the course of my two years at the Arts Endowment is that literature has fallen on unreasonably tough times and that the literary culture needs help—wherever that help can be found.

How to promote literacy at the highest levels and to sustain a viable literary culture under conditions where most serious writers must "buy time" away from their culturally approved work in order to do their writing, where approximately 96 percent of talented, well-qualified applicants for individual fellowship support at the NEA each year must be turned away because of lack of funds, where publication is often difficult and demoralizing (if it can be attained at all), where the core literary organizations are relatively small and undercapitalized? How to encourage great writing in a country where potential audiences of readers must first find a way to unglue themselves from the tube and then show real persistence to locate good work within the mountains of well-hyped, name-brand, subliterary glut that fill the bookstore windows? The sheer volume of our marketplace has outstripped the capability of our cultural institutions to manage it or make sense of it.

Add to these difficulties the recent assault on the arts by groups representing the religious and political right and the pressure they have managed to exert on Congress and the administration and you have a situation that is completely out of hand—and one that is especially dangerous for literature, though, in most instances, literature has not been the source of consternation or controversy within the Endowment or the culture at large. If one believes, as I do, that there must be a legitimate place for literary art in our culture, which is, after all, the human record of our country, of our time, of the main concerns of our people—"the national memory," as Solzhenitsyn says—then something more must be done. If literature becomes too great a luxury, then literacy itself cannot survive.

The abuse suffered by the arts and by the Arts Endowment in the United States is so radically out of proportion to the provocation that it seems amazing to me that so few supporters of the arts have spoken up, in a convincing way, to defend them. I suppose there are a number of reasons for this. Some of the attacks are based on such staggering ignorance or misinformation that they seem, perhaps, not worthy of a reply. But one begins to wonder if we have forgotten what art is good for, or if we ever knew.

With the discovery by the right that the issue of censorship of art could be a big political winner, the Bush administration felt it necessary to appease the art-bashers instead of defending the arts, greatly exacerbating the predicament of the arts, and placing the office of the chairman of the Arts Endowment under incredible pressure. "When the scuds were fired at the NEA," in the words of John Brademas, "no Patriots were fired from the White House." Some of the NEA-thrashing that followed is a reaction of concerned citizens appalled by a society that seems out of control, who have been led to believe, incorrectly, that the arts are to blame for a lot of random bad behavior and the profligate misuse of taxpayers' hard-earned dollars. Some of it has come from disgruntled artists and artists' groups peeved at the contortions of the NEA and its administrators in the face of the onslaught. But I do believe there has been a general failure to articulate art's benefits and the rationale for the establishment of an Arts Endowment in the first place.

While at the Endowment, I heard three frequently reiterated arguments in defense of federal support for the arts: the economic argument, the social benefits argument, and the arts-in-education argument, all of which have some degree of credibility.

The economic argument is that the arts are good for business, the arts stimulate tourism and civic energy, the arts can lead to rehabilitation of the inner city. Cuts to the arts do not represent money saved but economic stimulation of a high order lost. The social benefits argument is that the arts can be used for social programming to ameliorate the effects of poverty, poor education, old age, racial inequality. Let poets read their work at senior citizens' centers, for example. This gives the poets something to do, and it entertains the senior citizens. Never mind that the senior citizens may not know what the poets are talking about. Enlist the poor in the arts. It keeps them off the streets, helps them get their troubles off their chests, and persuades them that they have something to contribute to society. The arts-in-education argument is that an exposure to the arts in the public schools leads students to perform better in science and math.

The one argument I seldom, if ever, heard at the Endowment, except as I tried to make it myself, or as then-chairman John Frohnmayer made it, quite eloquently, was that the arts deserve support because they are the arts; that great art is important to a culture and deserves, therefore, to be nurtured. The goals of great art are so much more important to us then the alleged dangers of obscenity, even if obscenity were a serious side effect of arts support, which it is not, that the present predicament of the arts seems all the more absurd and destructive—enough to make a strong man weep.

John Frohnmayer wept when he first viewed the ten-minute video clip narrated by Walter Cronkite and produced by the Endowment to present a defense of the arts, and Frohnmayer had once been a Naval officer and a quarterback of the Stanford football team. I suspect he was moved to tears in this case because it was one of the very few instances during his tenure at the NEA that anyone with the appearance of authority had said anything positive in a public forum about the power and glory of the arts, of their ability to transform, inspire, and transcend, of their potential importance to us all—simply by themselves, because of their human shape and intent, because of the ways they give meaning to our lives.

Real art is about imagination, empathy, emotion, and aesthetic and poetic truths, and it teaches us how to become more skillful in these domains. Real art is about getting through life and finding meaning in it and trying to understand and remember it. We need the literary artist because he or she reminds us of ancient truths, pricks our consciences, and, by creating scenes from the present, showing who we are, helps create the national memory. As Lady Murasaki says in her *Tale of Genji* when she's asked by the prince why she writes, "So there will never be a time when people don't know these things happened." Literature is our national treasury of language and style and our best reckoning about human life, as it is lived in this time and place.

John Updike explains why societies need writers in his recent book of essays, *Odd Jobs:* "The poet and his song served as a memory bank, supplying the outlines of the determinative tribal struggles and instances of warrior valor. Who we are, who our heroic fathers [and mothers] were, how we got where we are, why we believe what we believe and act the way we do—the bard illuminates these essential questions, as the firelight flickers and the mead flows and the listeners in their hearts renew their pact with the past. . . . The author is not only himself but his predecessors, and simultaneously he is part of the living tribal fabric, the part that voices what all know, or should know, and need to hear again."

Robert Motherwell, testifying in 1970 in support of legislation to encourage education about the environment, said: "I am sure that scientists have or will testify to the relevant facts here and know them far better than I. I speak only as an artist. But to speak as an artist is no small thing. Most people ignorantly suppose that artists are the decorators of our human existence, the esthetes to whom the cultivated may turn when the real business of the day is done. But actually what an artist is, is a person skilled in expressing human feeling. Far from being merely decorative, the artist's awareness . . . is one . . . of the few guardians of the inherent sanity and equilibrium of the human spirit that we have."

If the NEA had gone down, which it was very close to doing, it would have been a catastrophe of unimaginable proportions for our culture, and certainly for our literature and for literacy. When I think of those great pundits, David Brinkley, Sam Donaldson, George Will, and Cokie Roberts—who ought to have known better—sitting around before the credits rolled on yet another edition of *This Week with David Brinkley* and concluding in their collective wisdom that, yes, because of all the controversy, it was probably time for the NEA to fold up its tent, I still want to beat on the nearest wall.

The truth is that if we want to have a culture worthy of the name, we need to support it—by supporting its practitioners—and not abandon the effort and the principle because of partisan politics or the noisy protests of the uninformed with their false assumptions, their shocked rectitude, and their seventh-grade educations. The Arts Endowment is an important cultural resource, and we have to assume that a great nation deserves to have great art and great literature. How can we use this relatively modest resource to serve that purpose as best we can?

The United States already gives less for the arts than many civilized nations—and a great deal less for literature. The United States spends about $50 million more each year for military bands through the Defense Department budget than it spends for the entire Arts Endowment, which is intended to nurture everything from symphonies, museums, and theaters to architecture, painting, ballet, film, and the literary arts.

For 1987, which was the most recent figure available, the Germans spent the equivalent of $5.154 billion for the arts. This equals over

$190 per capita, while we spend sixty-eight cents per capita. A visiting German novelist told me that the city of Munich alone gives more for literature than does the entire United States government. The German contribution to the arts is surely the world's largest, an awesome investment that simply dwarfs the amount—$176 million—contributed by the United States to the National Endowment for the Arts. But at $585 million annually, the French are also ambitious contributors to the arts. The Japanese recently decided to begin an Arts Endowment modeled on ours but with a budget twice as large.

The total Canada Council budget for literature is $22 million, which is approximately 20 percent of Canada's total annual arts budget of $110 million. The United States budget for literature (because of the Congressionally mandated set-aside to the states) is now down to $4 million, which is less than 2.5 percent of the total. The province of Ontario alone now has an annual budget of $8 million for literature, which is twice as much as the entire United States. In other words, not even counting Ontario and the other provinces, the Canada Council allocation for literature is more than five times larger than the United States amount, in a country with less than 9 percent of our population.

I asked the Canadians how they came up with these percentages and amounts, and they said they based them on a comparison to other countries (obviously not ours), on expressed need based on the numbers of applications for support received, and on reach—the potential effect on the largest number of citizens able to understand and make some use of the art form. Literature, they concluded, turned out to be their "most cost-effective cultural product." They actually studied this question in depth in order to find a reasonable answer. The Canadians care about building a cultural identity and having a national memory. We, on the other hand, seem to feel that our cultural identity, our national memory (if it is likely to be longer than a sound bite), will take care of itself.

Another partial explanation for the commitment to arts-spending around the world is, of course, that other countries are trying to protect themselves from the influence of American pop culture. It may not be entirely altruistic on their parts; it may not be that they love writers and artists so much more than we do, though that may be part of it. I don't think one can explain these policies, finally, in any other way, however, than that leaders in these countries believe in the power and importance of culture, of literacy, and of a strong national literature. Someone of influence in Canada, in Germany, in France, in Japan, has considered these issues and believes, perhaps more enthusiastically than we do, in regard to their own countries, some of these fine words from the enabling legislation for the National Endowment for the Arts:

> The Congress hereby finds and declares: . . . that the practice of art . . . requires constant dedication and devotion and that, while no government can call a great artist into existence, it is necessary and appropriate for the Federal Government to help create and sustain not only a climate encouraging freedom of thought, imagination, and inquiry, but also the material conditions facilitating the release of this creative talent. . . . That the world leadership which has come to the United States cannot rest solely upon superior power, wealth, and technology, but must be solidly founded upon worldwide respect and admiration for the Nation's high qualities as a leader in the realm of ideas and the spirit. . . . To fulfill its educational mission, achieve an orderly continuation of free society, and provide models of excellence to the American people, the Federal Government must transmit the achievement and values of civilization from the past via the present to the future, and make widely available the greatest achievements of art.

Canadians, apparently, want to accomplish these goals quite a bit more strenuously than we do. Canadians crave a national identity separate from the United States, and they believe this is a goal worthy of the investment of large sums; and, quite intelligently, they believe they are going to accomplish this end most expeditiously through supporting Canadian literature.

We've already begun to see some of the results. Margaret Atwood and Alice Munro—to name two writers who spring immediately to mind—are Canadians and among the most splendid writers in the English-speaking world. I suspect that over the next ten or twenty or thirty years, you will find great Canadian writers emerging who will speak for all English-speaking peoples, in a sense; and who will become the Nobel laureates of the future. One of the explanations for that will be the devout way the Canadians have supported their literary artists.

I believe the mistake we are making, aside from the relatively pathetic sums we are willing to contribute to cultural development, is that we are basing our funding for the disciplines within the NEA on historical precedent rather than on an intelligent assessment of need and scale—in a world that has changed drastically since the precedents were set.

Literature's cut of the pie at the NEA has been based on other factors entirely than the ones mentioned by the Canadians, mainly unconsidered historical precedent. The "big" art-form programs (film, music, museums) and the well-intentioned people and vested interests associated with them helped found the Endowment to see that their own interests and art forms would receive the attention and support they deserve. Literature was a poor stepchild who came along for the ride. Literature was associated with commerce, which made it seem, perhaps, less aristocratic; and literature, it was probably felt, didn't need the levels of support of the other art forms because it was better able to make its own way in the marketplace. Also, literature, I suspect, simply did not have many persuasive advocates on the scene at that time. (Maybe twenty-five years ago it didn't need them quite so badly.)

The writer's life in America is somewhat different from that of other artists because literature is the only art form (except for some of the visual arts) that is both conceived and received in solitude. This condition affects the entire literary culture, because literature is in competition for support with art forms that are much more public, well developed, sociable, and socially rewarding. The consequence is that writers do not have a lot of friends of the philanthropic sort, and they are the least well organized of all the artistic communities.

The ten or twelve largest and most important organizations for writers, the core of the literary culture in the institutional sense, are extremely fragile. Nearly all of these organizations are dependent upon the NEA for program support, and, without it, they would be on the verge of insolvency within a year or two. So if Jesse Helms and Philip Crane (and Sam Donaldson and Cokie Roberts, and the others) were to succeed in having the NEA abolished, or if all the arts money were shipped out to the state arts councils for disbursement, as has been proposed, the literary culture as represented by these service organizations for writers would just about evaporate within a year or two.

I'm impressed by the sense of aloneness that writers already feel in our country, the difficulty they have in connecting with any sort of institution or entity to support them. Certainly, this is one reason writers often feel abandoned or unappreciated—because their work must be done alone, and they are, in fact, largely unappreciated, though most of them are enormously grateful for any encouragement they do receive, and they work hard to earn it. How extraordinarily isolated writers would be without these organizations—with no source of news about writing, no sense of a culture or a community that they are a part of.

But life is tough all over, right? Where are the service organizations for plumbers? Well, the difference between writers and plumbers is that if the literary culture were to sustain a blow of this sort, it would have serious consequences for literacy itself. (And plumbers are paid well for their work and do quite well without federal help.) As writing affects literacy it should be of vital importance to all of us, whether or not we identify with the literary culture, or the arts in general, or make a habit of reading the latest novel by Joyce Carol Oates.

Literacy is increasingly at risk in the United States. There are dire reports on this subject from many sources. Congress has recently allocated $150 million to throw at the problem. A notable young New York trade editor who served on one of the recent literature program panels at the NEA exclaimed that one reason it is harder and harder for literary editors in New York to acquire serious books is that literary books that used to sell 7,000 now sell 4,000, and books that used to sell 4,000 sell 1,500; the publishers don't know why this is happening, but they are worried about it.

One reason it is happening, of course, is that New York publishing, which used to be about what was good, what mattered, what should guide us, and what was worth saving, is, increasingly, only about money—it is only about what will sell—like so much else in American life since the greedy eighties. The American marketplace does not adequately support the most serious and talented American writers—except those who have already become famous; it primarily supports entertainment.

Some of the critics of the NEA seem to believe that all art should be able to make its own way in the marketplace—otherwise it is, by definition, trivial. This is the most simplistic idea of capitalism gone astray, used by people who either despise art or who don't know the facts of art patronage over the centuries. Every country in the history of civilization that has aspired to greatness, except this one, has seen it as an important government function to support artists. It's true through history. It's true now.

Unfortunately, many in the literary field itself believed that literature could make its own way in the marketplace, or did not know of any alternative; hence, there was very little effort made to establish a support system for literature comparable to the support systems of the other art forms—based, that is, on private philanthropy, foundation support, and federal and state support. As commercial publishing became more and more commercial and bottom-line oriented over the last thirty-five years, literature was left swinging in the breeze, with inadequate commercial support, a weak organizational structure, and the lowest of profiles for support from state and federal agencies.

Literature has been ignored for years by private philanthropy. Certainly the main reason for this is that no one representing literature was knocking on foundation doors. Literary organizations have only recently become strong enough and stable enough to engender support. Even at their present levels, literary organizations are so small that, recently, when the Lila Wallace-Reader's Digest Fund started its ambitious program of support for the literary culture, it had to make several concessions to past practices because it had never before in its history given to such tiny organizations.

Now foundations are discovering that literature is an area deeply in need of help and an area that affects the level of discourse within the culture (which may be at an all-time low) and the level of literacy—simply because we are verbal creatures and our civilization is *conducted* through language. If our citizens become dead to language, it is not healthy for our democracy. There are plenty of broad-based reasons—reasons that go beyond art, that is—for support of the literary culture; and this message is finally getting through in a few places.

Not long ago, when John Updike appeared at Carnegie Hall to receive the American Book Award for Fiction for *Rabbit Is Rich,* he modestly declined to read his prepared speech and said simply, "Thank you," and hurried from the podium. But one of the things he was going to say, according to a report that later appeared in *Publishers Weekly,* was: "The poets and fiction writers among us are in the retrograde business of spinning clouds, syntactical filament by filament, in an age when clouds can be had at the twist of a knob or the push of a button on an aerosol can."

But these literary sorts of clouds, he might have added, though fragile, are ultimately far more important to us than most of the electronic or chemical variety. If literature is our national memory, as Solzhenitsyn believes, we are in some immediate danger of experiencing a prolonged period of national forgetfulness and oblivion if we cannot continue and intensify the sort of support provided to writers by the Arts Endowment, which is truly indispensable to the minimal health of the field. This is especially true now— with the disarray in the traditional sources of publishing support for writers and the scramble to establish a new national publishing network of literary presses and magazines and university presses, more aesthetically, geographically, and culturally diverse, to replace what has been lost.

If we are to leave any memory behind us as a culture, any memory worth having, we must take some pains to help nourish literary art. Without writers, there can be no words. Without publishers, there can be no books. Without literary organizations, there can be no literary culture. Without audiences, does any of it matter? We have to hope that if good books are written, produced, and offered to the public, some audience somewhere will find them. But enlightened citizens must eventually come to terms with the jeopardy of the literary culture and the implications for us all if we allow McLuhan's predictions about the death of the phonetic alphabet to come true.

This argument is not about preserving elites, not about whether or not we will continue to have high culture in this country, but about whether or not we want to have any culture at all—other than pop culture.

As we approach the end of the twentieth century and the end of the millennium, I think we should look with great alarm at the condition of American culture and American literature because market forces are putting it out of business. Our best young writers are largely anonymous; our best films are technically very advanced comic books. If Ernest Hemingway were a young writer today with the manuscript of *In Our Time* under his arm, would any commercial publisher give him the time of day?

Literature is in an especially precarious condition because it is the last of the arts to realize that it cannot pay its own way in the marketplace. It is the farthest behind in building an organizational infrastructure to support itself, so it is the most dependent on public support and philanthropy.

The literary culture doesn't own the buildings in which it lives, and so the very real danger exists that one of these days the people who own the buildings that literature is now borrowing are going to say: "Sorry, but there are more entertaining and lucrative things for us to be doing here. You'll have to get out." And if that occurs, what will happen to the national memory? Do we want our legacy as a nation to be *Terminator II* and *Wayne's World*? At what point will literature become a luxury we can no longer afford?

LITERARY
OCCASIONS

THE MAGAZINE WARS

The chairman of the English department at the state college where I held my first teaching job (and was grateful to be in 1969) had the idea that a magazine might be a terrific ornament under his regime. We would call it *The Falcon*, since the students already published a magazine by that name, and thus our launching would be less conspicuous to the state's auditors, not to mention our learned colleagues in other departments who were competing for funds and likely to cause an uproar. (In fairness to the students, the chairman thought we might simply rename the student magazine or let them choose their own name.)

By the time any of our detractors caught wind of this shrewd plan, the chairman reasoned, we would be too far along to stop, perhaps already in print and basking in praise from the new dean, who already had a hand in these machinations. The dean thought a magazine would be a terrific ornament too.

When the chairman invited interested parties from the department to speak to him about these suggestions, no one volunteered for this mission except me and one other naïve fellow, my office mate, who was the other "creative" member of our department, an unpublished poet and teacher of poetry. So *The Falcon* would have to be a "creative" magazine. The chairman was somewhat disappointed—he was hoping for something along the lines of *PMLA*—but he was willing to follow what energy there was to its natural fulfillment.

I felt I was absolutely right for this assignment. In the early sixties at Antioch, as an undergraduate working as a student assistant, I had been so impressed by the simple technology of a hand-crank ditto machine that I had started my own literary magazine once before. I had experience. My friends and I had hawked the *Jewel Weed* outside the Antioch cafeteria and made enough at a quarter per issue to cover printing and production expenses, even with offset-produced covers and text pages printed from erasable stencils and an IBM film ribbon. I was already an expert, I wanted the chairman to know—I had had ink on my hands. I had seen the impact a literary magazine could have on the consciousness of a community.

"Capacity for the nobler feelings is in most natures a very tender plant, easily killed, not only by hostile influences, but by mere want of sustenance"—an epigraph chosen from John Stuart Mill—had served as a sort of personal manifesto for our first issue of the *Jewel Weed*. The jewel weed, a stately plant with smooth leaves and stem, often found in wild places in that corner of Ohio, and whose juices were thought to be a cure for poison ivy, seemed a fitting symbol for the tender plant of Mill's sentiment and the fragile artifact we hoped to create in order to provide sustenance for the nobler feelings. Whether a bird of prey could fulfill the same function for this new magazine at "Felicity" State College, especially considering its secretive and hypocritical origins, was a risk I was more than willing to accept.

When we began to collect material for that debut issue of *The Falcon*, we were deluged with submissions, but not many of them were what you would call first-rate or even publishable. We knew we would probably have to go out and get the really good work. One of our first difficult decisions, I remember, was what to do about a batch of doggerel that arrived after we had solicited work from a famous poet. We were delighted and surprised when we saw the fat envelope with his name on it, but our elation soon turned to chagrin when we realized he must have sent us the contents of his wastebasket. Of course, we could always return it and ask for more, but was it a good idea to take a chance of offending such a man? This could be the end of us; after all, we had asked for this work. Wasn't it true that even his worst poetry would be worth a footnote in history? In the end, we simply couldn't rationalize the prospect of publishing work we thought inferior. As a matter of policy we decided to trust our instincts and publish only the best work, no matter who had written it. We might be wrong but at least we would have clear consciences. We returned the poems and never heard from the great man again. Still, we had settled on an important matter of principle that would often help govern our decisions. We had navigated through the first dangerous waters and made it safely home.

In scouting for fiction, I tried to remember some of the stories I had read, mulled over, and argued about in classes during the years I had spent at the Iowa Writers Workshop not long before. I remembered one story in particular that had impressed me: first, because I had thought it was an original and well-written story, and second, because it had been, unmercifully and, I thought, unfairly trashed when it was presented in our workshop. I had tried to defend the story at the time, but the group had pounced on me as well as upon the story and its author so relentlessly that I almost doubted my own judgment.

In any case, I decided to telephone the author, whose name I still remembered, and find out if his story had ever been published. I still recall his sense of surprise at hearing from me, followed by some embarrassment at mention of the story in question. He had been so traumatized by that day in the workshop that he must have believed the story was a disgrace. He had put it into a drawer and hadn't looked at it since, hadn't sent it out, and hadn't written a whole hellava lot either. He wasn't at all sure that he wanted now to have it considered for publication, in fact, even if it was some unknown magazine where no one of any importance would ever read it. But he finally said okay, he would send it along.

What happened after that was that we did indeed publish the story, and it was eventually chosen for mention in Martha Foley's *Best American Short Stories*. I was probably as astonished as the author. By accident, you might say, or dumb luck, or by trusting my instincts, I had taken an unknown, lost story out of someone's drawer and helped transform it—simply by publishing it—into one of the best, most admired stories of the year and brought its author some long overdue attention. Somehow it didn't seem right that it should have to happen in quite that way—because of so many accidental occurrences, rather than because the story's merit should have been plain from the beginning—but it gave me stronger evidence, if I needed it, of the relative worth of what I was doing, of the surprising power in even this brand-new backwoods-variety magazine that had been inappropriately named after a bird that was not even indigenous to the region.

Now comes the sad part of the story. Several years later, after I had moved on to another magazine, *Fiction International*, this same author sent me a long story that I reluctantly declined to publish, though I encouraged him to send other work whenever he was able. He replied with a letter so full of insults, I thought at first it must be a joke. Not a trace of any gratitude for the earlier miracle (not that I had asked for any), just one vicious slander after another upon my character and the rectitude of my ancestors. It was the sort of response that made me a little leery of licking the return flaps of future rejection envelopes for fear they might be coated with cyanide. Still, I understood. He had had more than his share of rejection. For him, I was in league with the scores of mindless fools who had rejected his work and wished to see him fail. But I didn't wish that. Bill, if you are still out there somewhere, I swear to God I would never wish such a thing for you.

The trouble with editing magazines, committing yourself to recognizing good work and giving it a place in the world, is that most of the time what you are actually doing is rejecting manuscripts, taking a chance at ruining someone's dream and hurting his or her feelings; and there is no help for it, and it is the absolute worst part of the job.

A thorny fact that faces a new editor almost immediately is that he may often be forced to reject perfectly competent, even excellent, work, simply because of limitations of space or his own taste. The strong suit of the small magazine process is that the editor's taste is freer to dictate selection—that is, taste alone, rather than the demands of the marketplace, the expectations of any board of overseers, or the lowest common denominator of mass appeal. But this forces the conscientious editor to come to terms with all the vices and virtues of his tastes, and his sometimes elusive motives and motivations for choosing one thing over another, in ways he may never have contemplated.

Tastes in literature are about as difficult to describe or explain as tastes in eating or clothing or the opposite sex. But I do know this: Just any taste will not do—there is good taste and bad taste. Good manuscripts are often rejected, even by editors with good taste. And also: Tastes change. Tastes are influenced and evolve.

Some of what goes into making up good taste is improved by a familiarity with and a responsiveness to old verities and universal principles, upon which a consensus may be said to exist among the enlightened. But beyond that, you are on your own, relying on whatever intelligence, whatever innate sense of form and grace and order and understanding you can muster, and depending sometimes on perceptions and values that may not be primarily verbal or rational but rooted in a complexity of emotion, sensory experience, muscular habits, or the identity of one's grandmother.

Among all those fictions I might recognize as competent, well written, even accomplished, there are many that I am not moved to admire in a special way, to want to "make my own"—as the editor inevitably does. There is a sense I am talking about in which an editor signs his own name by the works he chooses to publish just as clearly as any person expresses an identity by the favorite objects he or she chooses to place in his or her living room or bedroom.

Of course, there is also such a thing as trying to be responsible about one's taste. There are many pressures at work in an editor's life, including the most obvious and crass sorts of threats and blandishments (accompanied by irrelevant punishments for crimes not committed) calculated to influence him to publish work he may not like. But if he allows himself to give in to these extraliterary pressures, he proves he is in the wrong line of work. He might just as well spend his time as some other, better paid, kind of whore.

Gordon Lish has said that good editing "ignores the technology of literature as well as the philosophies of social good—and listens only to the sounds the heart makes." His own editorial decisions are made, he claims, according to whether or not a "buzzy feeling" is aroused "from the long muscle that runs down the inside of my thigh." When "you've got a reliable muscle," Lish says, "you don't need anything else. Indeed, you are a very lucky fellow, never mind where that muscle is situated."

I like that idea well enough—call it Lish's theory of coronary-auditory and muscular editing. A good editor will have faith in the relative infallibility of his muscle, of his complex relation to a text, and will be able to act in each instance on the force so generated, which is an instinct closer to the Zen art of dart-throwing or divining for water than to traditional critical analysis.

For the next two and one-half years, for the duration of my stay in Felicity, Pennsylvania, I and my coeditor edited and produced *The Falcon,* which was, from the moment we took it on, an entirely new magazine, of course, publishing no undergraduate work, inviting submissions from everywhere, and mailing our issues everywhere—a "national" magazine. As editors, we were bent on making an impression by publishing the best fiction and poetry we could find and working hard to locate and encourage first-rate work. Once having produced our semiannual jewel, I was determined to see that it landed where it should, in the red-hot center of the literary culture. I felt it was our role to see that the hard-won victories of our writers were paraded before the eyes of the generals. I imagined the magazines landing like bombs in the mailboxes of powerful editors, publishers, and agents in New York, time bombs that might carry explosive potential for imaginative change, the power to transform vision and the lives of the writers offering that vision.

It was a hectic life. I taught four courses—all writing courses with a heavy load of papers and as many as 125 students in all, all furiously churning out themes and stories and research papers and essays on *The Great Gatsby*. If I didn't grade a batch of thirty-five papers or so every single night of the week, I would get hopelessly behind. When I was not grading papers, I was busily reading manuscripts or writing letters for the magazine, preparing for classes, or eating, or sleeping, or reading bedtime stories to my kids, who were still babies then.

I was also in charge of the assembly committee, which was a euphemism of sorts. The committee consisted of one man, me. I had twenty thousand dollars to unload each year and had to organize and coordinate the entire year's slate of visiting speakers, including everything from arranging for rooms and seating to picking them up at the airport, to harassing Harrisburg when their honoraria were two months late in passing through the state's bureaucratic machinery. I was constantly on the telephone, dealing with velvet-voiced booking agents or trying to track down Jane Fonda.

An accidental consequence of this responsibility was a series of interviews that I began in order to occupy the visiting celebrities while they were in town and to provide fodder for *The Falcon*. The *Paris Review* had made a valuable tradition of the literary interview; those anthologized interviews had served as a part of my own education; so, I decided, there was no reason at all why we should not march through the streets of Felicity, PA, holding the lantern up before the faces of visiting writers and questioning them unmercifully, imitating the *Paris Review*. Before very long, I had recorded John Barth, Tom Wolfe, and Susan Sontag in my own living room.

During the presidential campaign of 1971, I came close to landing George McGovern, the Democratic candidate for president, for our little corner of the commonwealth. "How many people are likely to be in attendance?" the advance man wanted to know. We negotiated for days. Some days it was a sure thing; other days, he was less certain. Finally I received an emergency phone call—he wanted to know if we would take Leonard Nimoy instead. McGovern was over-committed; he was sorry. As I imagined escorting a Vulcan around campus, listening to his views on the presidency, interviewing him for *The Falcon*, my life in Felicity began to seem particularly surreal. But ten minutes later the agent called back and said that Leonard Nimoy couldn't make it either. How would we like to have Marlo Thomas? I told him to go to hell.

In 1970 I had my first contact with members of the small press community at a meeting of the Committee of Small Magazine Editors and Publishers (COSMEP) in Buffalo. It was an eye-opening experience, partly because George Plimpton was scheduled to appear and did. It was a strange mix of people: motorcycle jockeys in rivet-studded vests and ammo belts, wild-eyed poet-professors, bourgeois sorts in drip-dry suits, students. Several of them were very worked up about whether or not we should accept money from the government for our publications through the National Endowment for the Arts (NEA) and the Coordinating Council of Literary Magazines (CCLM), which was at that time the sole dispenser of magazine grants from the NEA. It was nothing but blood money, they said, which had been used to kill innocent children in Vietnam; and by associating ourselves with it, we were collaborating with murderers. Others argued that if we accepted the money we were, in fact, helping to prevent further conflict by draining away resources that might be spent on napalm or bombers. People stood up, one after another, in this large airy room at the student union at the State University of New York at Buffalo and screamed at one another.

Once the rage started flying around the room, other targets came in for abuse. One group created a fuss about George Plimpton's impending appearance. Who was George Plimpton, they wanted to know, but some rich guy in a Brooks Brothers suit and an expensive haircut who liked to hang around in locker rooms? What did he have to do with literature?

Another notion bandied about in various forms was the theory that we assembled few, in our motley agony, wrongheaded as some of us so obviously were, were nonetheless the only hope for the survival of literature. Big-time publishing in New York had sold out to the entertainment industry and no longer had any interest in publishing the serious work of the most important writers of the period, some of them assembled at this very meeting. So it was up to us to take on this responsibility ourselves, as some already had; because if we didn't do it, no one else would.

I must admit I liked the idealistic ring of that sort of talk. Even though I knew it to be a gross distortion in 1970, some of it began to seem like prophecy just ten years later. But before I had started to feel at all comfortable with the missionary rhetoric, I learned that I was myself a member of the enemy camp: the professors! I was part of the conspiracy, it seemed, part of the privileged elite.

I was making eight thousand dollars a year, living in a crummy rented house with nothing but dried milky spots of baby upchuck decorating the ratty, secondhand furniture; and I was working my head off, working weekends and late at night; and as far as I could tell, I was doing a credible job of trying to teach half the eighteen-year-olds in Pennsylvania to write an interesting English sentence and of trying to edit a magazine that would make some small difference in the world. But because I worked at "a college," I was considered by many of the small press folk there assembled to be a creature of unspeakable loathing and decadence, an agent of oppression, a pawn of the Establishment, which was a word still used in those days. I was ready to turn in my membership card. Ironically, it seemed to me, back in Felicity, the "professors" regarded me as an interloper too, someone who didn't even have a Ph.D. and who was making them all uncomfortable by publishing too often and too conspicuously, and editing this goddamned magazine all the time and trying to get more attention than I deserved.

That night we all went to a party where Allen Ginsberg played the piano in his stars-and-stripes Uncle Sam hat and sang in his incredible bass voice and pretended he was a concert pianist, and several of my fellow COSMEP members passed around funny cigarettes and sang along with Allen and hoped aloud they wouldn't get busted.

The next day when George Plimpton arrived, he was wearing a navy blazer and a red tie; and he was taller than everyone else, and he did a remarkable thing. He waded into the audience and began to shake hands with every person up and down the rows, one after the other, like a candidate for the presidency; and he seemed to want everyone to know that he felt, in a sense, like one of us, even if most of us had not, as he had, escorted Jacqueline Onassis to the opera; and by the time he had been introduced and approached the podium, he had shaken hands with every person in the room and there was a sudden swell of affection for Mr. Plimpton and all the hostility that had been there before he came had melted away.

We were invited to Leslie Fiedler's house, which was a gargantuan Victorian mansion on a street of gargantuan Victorian mansions. Leslie was on the phone, chewing on his cigar, as we passed
through on our way to the pool. In the bathhouse there was an
awkward moment while George Plimpton and I, who seemed to be
the only people in the bathhouse just then, undressed next to adjacent
benches. George said it reminded him of the time he and Bill Cosby
had gone swimming, and he told a Bill Cosby joke. Outside some
people were talking and hooting so loudly I missed the punch line,
but I laughed anyway. George was lean and well tanned and in great
shape for a man his age. He pulled on his red skintight bathing suit,
and we toddled out together and sat down on the edge of the pool
and dangled our legs in the water and talked about the *Paris Review*
for a while.

Allen Ginsberg was taking a swim in his Jockey underpants. I
guess he had forgotten to bring a bathing suit. A few minutes later, he
dripped his way to the side and sprawled out on a canvas hammock,
which collapsed loudly. Allen tried to move but got tangled in the
intricacies of the hammock and slumped over and acted injured.
Several people rushed to his rescue.

After a while, Leslie came out, cigar in teeth, and checked on us
and wanted to know if anyone was hungry or thirsty. My colleague
from *The Falcon* was sitting in a corner next to the wire fence—as far
away as he could get from anyone famous—looking miserable and
as if he was ready to head for home.

During my third year at Felicity, I was able to find a better job at
another school. Without giving it a great deal of thought, I assumed
that I would either continue to help edit *The Falcon* via the mailbox
and long distance or, quite possibly, since I was the one person clearly
obsessed with the work, move *The Falcon* to where I was going. After
all, I was the coeditor and cofounder. My optimism was accelerated
by news of a grant of two thousand dollars for *The Falcon* from CCLM.
But much to my surprise, the chairman of the English department at
Felicity did not see it my way at all.

His opinion was that *The Falcon* was an organ of the English department and of Felicity State College. The college had financed the
magazine, and the contents of the magazine had been copyrighted in
the name of the college. I was merely an employee of the college, and
since I was no longer going to be an employee of the college, someone

else would be found to take my place. One of the senior members of the department (whose specialty was nineteenth-century drama) had already volunteered. The grant from CCLM was also the property of the college, in his opinion, even though I had been the one who had secured it and even though it had been given largely on the basis of my work. But didn't he realize that I was indispensable, I wanted to say, that without me there wouldn't even be a magazine? Apparently, this thought had never occurred to him. Lest he appear to be too autocratic about his position, he offered to send it up for a vote to the department.

I should have known what was to come, but, in my naïveté, I expected to be able to make a case in support of my continuing. What is a magazine, after all, I reasoned, but an artifact of the minds and energies of the persons who edit it? Who cared, really, who had paid for it? Money buys any number of worthless commodities. Vision, on the other hand, is a much rarer medium of exchange. Hadn't I shared in creating *The Falcon* out of nothing, out of the air? Therefore, it seemed to me that it was, at least partly, mine. I felt as if one of my children was being unfairly wrested from my grasp.

At the meeting, several members mentioned that *The Falcon*, after all, had been at Felicity long before I had ever appeared. Never mind that it had been a student magazine of no real consequence. Many of these same persons were those who had expressed no interest whatsoever in *The Falcon* three years before, but they were now suddenly excited by the possibility of participating as associate editors and at seeing me banished from the flock—or so it seemed to me at the time. They had no doubt that they could do the job as well or better than I had—after all, every one of them was the possessor of a Ph.D. in literature. Except for my coworkers on the magazine, who gave their loyal support, and my wife, no one quite understood my attachment to *The Falcon* or appreciated the amount of time and effort I had expended on its behalf. The vote went lopsidedly against me.

I vowed that I would never let anything like this happen to me ever again. And I would find some way to go on.

The next morning I woke up with a great plan, the product of sleeplessness and despair. "Who is *The Falcon* after all?" a voice in my head wanted to know. "I am *The Falcon!*" I could almost feel the huge dark wings folded behind me on the chair or shadowed against the wall. I'll simply start another magazine, I decided, and call it *The Falcon!* And we'll see, soon enough, who the world decides is the real Falcon. "Will the real *Falcon* please stand up?" the voice in my head intoned, and I rose quickly to my feet and saluted my birdlike profile reflected in the nearby windowpanes.

I spent that day and the next looking into copyright law and the legal background on titles and trademarks. What was I going to do when the Commonwealth of Pennsylvania filed the first lawsuit? I began to get excited about the possibilities of a new magazine with monumental legal problems. After all, I had started magazines twice before. I could do it again and face the consequences. The new *Falcon* would make the old one look feeble and inept. The English department, if they thought about it at all, would be eternally sorry they had voted to cast me out.

A few days later, in a somewhat saner frame of mind, a further elaboration occurred to me. Why did I even need a name I had never liked anyway, a name that sounded like a not-very-good junior high school yearbook? Surely I could come up with a better name than that and leave *The Falcon* behind forever. Turn the other cheek, give them what they wanted, and be free. Living well is the best revenge. So that is what I did.

The following fall, when Martha Foley's *Best American Short Stories 1973* appeared, my lowly *Falcon* received five mentions for distinctive stories published in 1972, my last year as editor. During that one year, in other words, *The Falcon* (in two issues) had apparently published more fiction of lasting literary significance—according to Martha Foley—than had *The Yale Review, The Hudson Review, Partisan Review, The Antioch Review,* or *Paris Review* (with their four issues each) or *Harper's* and *McCall's* (with their twelve issues each); and, if counting mentions of American writers only (in other words, stretching it a bit and not counting writers like Sean O'Faolain, who were classified as foreign), we had tied with *Playboy* (which had had twelve issues to beat us and hadn't managed it, not to mention hundreds of thousands of dollars at its disposal and a somewhat higher profile). *The Falcon,* I calculated, had spent $125 for this work—not that I was proud of paying only twenty-five dollars per story, but it was all we could afford. *Playboy,* on the other hand, had spent possibly a thousand times as much—but even if somewhat less, say, a hundred times as much, it seemed a staggering amount, more than we had ever dreamed of. If Martha Foley was right, *The Falcon* had certainly gotten its money's worth.

If I needed any further evidence of the potential of the little magazine and the value of having spent so much of my time and effort on something apparently so small, Martha Foley settled it for me; and I will be forever grateful to her for that. Not that I was bombarded by engraved invitations to join the staffs of *Esquire* or *The New Yorker* or *Playboy*, or even *The Falcon*, or that I expected to be. I know it probably didn't matter to anyone in America but to me, but to me it mattered a lot. Well, it mattered to the writers and probably to their mothers.

Although the elderly scholarly gentleman who was my immediate replacement as editor of *The Falcon* quit after the first issue, *The Falcon* did manage to keep going for most of the next decade after I left, proving that I was not at all as indispensable as I had thought. Hardly anyone ever is. The magazine had had the good luck to fall back into the hands of my able coeditor and former staff. When I occasionally discovered a new issue in my mailbox, *The Falcon* began to seem like an old and well-intentioned friend or relation. After all, it was still performing the thankless, important task for which it had been created. After all, I had helped to give it birth and could hardly be blamed for feeling some of the pride of fatherhood. It was still alive, and by God, there it was, chirping right along without me.

THE BREAD LOAF
EXPERIENCE

It was named after the highest mountain in that vista of the Green Mountains, a bizarre mesa some thirty-eight hundred feet high, shaped like a loaf of Pepperidge Farm stone-ground whole wheat and covered with wild forest. As you saunter up the walk to the Bread Loaf Inn—in your sunglasses in the warm August light—you see the same mountain there on the sign with the likeness of a hot steaming loaf superimposed upon the high plain where you stand, on what looks, on the sign, like the launching pad for a whole fleet of flying saucers and a real wooden eagle flapping up above the signpost as if he had just flown in from the nearest Trinity Methodist Church pulpit. Just about then you realize—my God!—the walk you are walking on is solid white marble, and suddenly you feel a little stagestruck thinking of all the people who have walked on that same sidewalk before you, and then a little ethereal too, jumping up on the porch and ducking under the Virginia creepers and through the front door, where so many writers before you have also passed.

Robert Frost and Willa Cather. Sinclair Lewis, Saul Bellow, Bernard DeVoto. William Carlos Williams, John Crowe Ransom, Cornelia Otis Skinner. Archibald MacLeish. Hamlin Garland—for God's sake— Edwin Markham! This is it. You have finally made it—this pilgrimage and ritual initiation you have been waiting for all these years—into the American literary mainstream. No matter that no one seems to recognize you yet once you enter the lobby.

This same sense of ghosts-in-the-shrubbery is evoked that night by director Robert Pack during his welcoming talk in the Little Theater. Referring to Frost's historic relationship to Bread Loaf, Pack comments that even the highway department has taken note of the importance of Frost's ghost by placing any number of yellow signs along the road inscribed "Frost Heaves." Bunched together in our creaky wooden chairs, we chortle over this and are grateful that the Bread Loaf brass is big enough to make light of the Bread Loaf past; but the ghosts, of course, are still caterwauling about the rafters, and luckily they are in no way dispelled or offended. They will be with us for our entire stay.

This is our first good look at our fellow initiates, and they are an odd lot, from hip kids with electric hair to little old ladies in orthopedic shoes. Our median age, we are told, is thirty-two. We are mostly from the eastern megalopolis (ninety-seven of us), we learn; there is, however, a strong southern contingent (forty-six); forty-one are from "other places" in the United States; and we have two from Canada and one from (think of it!) New Zealand. Occupationally, our crew is described as: sixty-five teachers, twenty-four "writers," thirty-seven students, ten housewives, two doctors, and, variously, actresses, a ski instructor, a museum curator, and a stunt pilot.

Already we are trying hard to figure out where the writers are in the crowd. No sign of Harry Crews yet, but over there we see Seymour Epstein, looking like a middle-aged stockbroker; and there's Mark Strand in a navy blue polo shirt, sitting next to benevolent, mischievous-looking Marvin Bell in his Dutch Boy painter's hat. The real trick is to figure out who the fellows and scholars are, since the faculty, we reason, will be showing themselves soon enough. The fellows, the elite among the students, are all young writers who have published, or are about to publish, first novels or books of poetry or, in some few cases, are already working on second, third, or fourth books. They are more like resident sages or shamans than students; they are made much of by the staff; they live in preferred cottages; they receive a free ride and an open invitation to hobnob at Treman—the exclusive faculty retreat, hangout, and private drinking cottage. There are also six Bread Loaf "scholars," who attend tuition-free and have also published fairly widely—though perhaps not so impressively as the fellows—and have edited a textbook or two maybe or seem to hold promise as critics or reviewers. A third class of special students are the waiters, about twenty kids in their late teens or early twenties, who tend table in the Inn as a way of making ends meet. They live together, work together, and, over the course of the conference, come to develop a distinct group identity and loyalty, united in adversity and the hysterical energy necessary to keep up with the schedule of lectures, workshops, and readings and still fulfill their kitchen and serving duties.

After Pack's welcoming address, we wander out across the dewy lawns, eyeing the shadows of pines and the dreamy glow of lights in the Inn. Some few are already headed back to their rooms and their neat row of sharpened pencils, having come to Bread Loaf with the notion that a writers' conference is a place you go where you're supposed to write a lot. Most of the rest of us head out to the Barn.

The Barn is an enormous frame building with classrooms on one side (dark at this hour), and on the other side a monstrous room the size of three basketball courts. The room is full of wicker furniture, has a snack bar and a flagstone fireplace, and is the off-hours congregating place of the rabble (for example, someone who is not on the faculty, a fellow, a scholar, or a gate-crasher at Treman), though it is patronized at times by almost anyone, especially those sipping juice with their English muffins, doggedly nursing hangovers on bright sunshiny mornings at 10:45 A.M. The Barn has the two largest screen doors ever seen in the state of Vermont or anywhere, and when you push through them you have the sensation of entering a saloon in Dodge City, and just then the door spring goes tweek-tweek-tweek, the door bangs, and everybody inside looks up at you across two acres of floor to find out if you are anybody worth looking at.

At this hour, the Barn is pretty full of all sorts of people trying to size up other people, the lights are all turned on, and the women are coy and noncommittal. Everybody is playing it close to the vest. After a couple of low-key skirmishes, you spot a really interesting-looking young woman over to the side sitting all by herself and just two chairs over from one of your dorm buddies. So you saunter on over and say a few cheerful words to good ol' Jerry, and then you just sort of ease into the next chair; and there you are sitting right next to this beautiful woman, and you say, "Hi, what do you write?" and she says, "Hi, what do you write?" and she's very nice and friendly with great big ice-blue eyes, even if her mascara is flaking a bit, and you can't figure out why she's sitting here all by herself—it doesn't make sense. And just then she touches you on the arm and she says, "Look, one thing you should know is I'm Harry Crews's girlfriend, and we just spent two months hiking up here from Georgia along the Appalachian Trail, and don't look now but that's Harry right over there and I think he's coming this way." You look up and, sure enough, there's Harry Crews now, with a big gold earring in his left ear, looking just like his picture from the brochure, only close up a little bit less like a Comanche and a little bit more like a tight end for the Miami Dolphins and he's saying: "Hiya, Jack! Now what can I do-you-for?"

*   *   *

Bright and early the next morning you are off for an eight o'clock breakfast, ready for anything. Three lectures before lunch, a gargantuan seminar in the afternoon; after dinner a reading by some member of the staff or a visiting dignitary. Except for Sunday morning, Bread Loaf is packed full of scheduled events day after day. At first, you are likely to gloat in this richness and take in every event, but very soon you develop an acute case of sitter's cramps and the body resists. You begin to pick and choose—and worry about missing something. During the second week—after you have just about had it with lectures and seminars—workshops and panels take over. In the workshops, you get sectioned off with one of your top three choices of mentors and a group of fifteen or twenty others. You sit around on the lawn or in the classrooms on the left-hand side of the Barn and carry on as your mentor sees fit, usually reading and discussing work the members have submitted for criticism.

This year is the first year of "the new regime" at Bread Loaf, so you keep your ears open to find out what, if anything, has changed since the Ciardi years. You have read all about the Ciardi years in Rust Hills's entertaining article, "We Believe in the Maestro System," and you wonder how much of that stuff is really on the up-and-up.

You ask ol' Jerry, for instance, about the new regime; and he says, "What new regime?" So you explain that this is actually the first year the conference has been run by Pack and Martin, that before it was run with an iron fist by poet-translator John Ciardi and that rumor has it that Ciardi's departure may not have been a planned or a happy occasion. You are looking around for signs of hurt feelings, bad tempers, sour dispositions, and vengeance.

One night at Treman, for instance, you are talking to Joy Anderson, a holdover from the Ciardi days who teaches writing for children at the conference, and she says Lord, how much she misses big John sitting there at the table in the living room and just holding forth the way he used to do, but she is careful to add: "Even though things are different this year, it's still a good Conference."

Seymour Epstein complains about having to work so bloody hard this year—it's cutting into his tennis time—the seminars, it turns out, are an innovation of Pack's to try to overcome the accusation leveled in years past that there wasn't enough teacher-student contact. Another Pack effort has been to bring the podium down off the stage in the Little Theater to produce a sort of "theater-in-the-round" effect and thus reduce the impression that the lecturer might be "above" those in the audience, a highhanded presumption of the Ciardi years. Ciardi's "maestro system" was apparently full of such rigid status distinctions, and certain people just didn't take to it very kindly.

Well, I feel obliged to report that in spite of Robert Pack's best and most earnest efforts—statuswise—Bread Loaf is still something of a jungle. There's just no way around some of it. You get over two hundred people together on a landlocked cruise and nobody is in uniform or wearing name tags or chevrons to tell them apart, and before you know it status confusion is running rampant. Nobody knows who to be nice to and who to snub. Then someone starts thinking he is better than you are because he has published one poem in *The Green Groad,* and the dumb klutz is too stupid to even care that you have published three poems in *The Green Groad* and you are too proud to tell him. So you both suffer. And then there are the faculty, and you start noticing that they think they are better than you are just because they may have published six novels or won a Pulitzer Prize or some damned thing, and that starts to gall you just a bit—especially when you've only had three hours of sleep and you're a little lonely and homesick and can't find anyone you know to sit with in the dining hall, and there they are at some other table, laughing their heads off at some probably tasteless joke just out of earshot. Yes, me brithers and sisters, there is some of that at Bread Loaf, and I'm afraid there's just no way of avoiding it or helping it.

But, of course, Bread Loaf is a great deal more than a pecking contest. Perhaps the most impressive aspect of the experience is the incredible parade of talented people the directors run through the place. This particular year, in addition to fourteen full-time faculty members—in fiction, Vance Bourjaily, Harry Crews, George P. Elliot, and Seymour Epstein; in poetry, Marvin Bell, Anthony Hecht, Maxine Kumin, Pack himself, and Mark Strand; in nonfiction, Walter Goodman and Peter Schrag; in writing for children, Joy Anderson and Lore Segal; plus the ubiquitous administrative director, Sandy Martin—one never knows who else might turn up. Anatole Broyard of the *New York Times,* for instance, appears one morning and delivers the best lecture at the conference on love and poetry: "What is poetry but a kind of perceptual tenderness. . . ." Poet William Meredith, a fine man, talks convincingly about "Teaching Poetry Writing." One night at Treman, I am puzzled by a vaguely familiar woman I had not recalled seeing before; she has been sitting quietly on the couch for a long time and I keep wondering: "Who is that woman? Who is that woman?" I think she is someone I should sit down and talk to, but something stops me. Finally I ask someone who she is. They look over at her. "Oh, that woman over there? Why, that's Anne Sexton."

Trying to define the "Bread Loaf experience" that first night, Robert Pack had referred to it as "this two-week eternity." It is not until somewhere around midvoyage that we begin to get an inkling of what he meant. First, you hear a lot of people talking about being hungrier than usual "up here" ("My God, I am really packing it in—this has got to stop"). Maxine Kumin is heard to say, "Well, you don't have to eat up here," implying that the spiritual food at Bread Loaf is more than adequate for physical needs. In these prosaic ways, people are starting to feel the need to define the experience, most not entirely sure what it is but fairly certain that it is something special. Some very close friendships are developing—Pack has warned us that we might be in danger of forming some lifelong friendships. Some of these people are at least shacking up, you can bet on it. On the other hand, the two telephone booths are constantly filled with people calling home. One evening I wait for forty-five minutes outside the Inn phone booth while some poor, distraught hausfrau breaks into tears over her child's promise to "hug my teddy bear for you, Mommy." I can tell she must be in the writing-for-children group.

Far and away the biggest personality cult of this year's conference is growing up around poet Mark Strand, who is one handsome fellow at six feet six inches tall and who looks the way a poet ought to look. Every time he passes through the Inn lobby with his tennis racket, sighs are heard. One evening at sunset, Mark Strand is spotted trekking slowly off across the distant cow pasture with one of the actresses, a hot-looking snooty young blond-haired chick from L.A., and hearts break all along the veranda. "Aren't they beautiful," someone says. "Someone should write a poem about that."

Time passes and more and more people are taking longer and longer walks. Tales leak out about increasingly rampant skinny-dipping high jinks at Ye Olde Pond at three o'clock in the morning. Starved for exercise, you decide to cut classes one afternoon; and donning your jogging shorts and Converse All-Stars, you head out among the "vast stretches of uplands, pastures, and timberland, covered in season with yarrow, devil's paintbrush, vetch, goldenrod, steeplebush, gentians of many kinds, wild orchids," not to mention "stands of various pines, spruce, tamarack, maples, oaks, birches, and occasional sycamores and beeches." The air is good, the sun is streaming down, and you are really zooming along. Every time you come to a fork in the path, you wait until the last instant to decide which branch you are taking. The woods are lovely, dark, and deep, and full of raspberry bushes. You are running down old lumber roads grown over with grass, vines, and stickers. You are running so fast that any snakes or spiders down there where your feet are landing will be too startled to do anything and by the time they figure out who you are, you will be gone. Slowly it dawns on you that this couldn't possibly be the place you think you are, as pictured on the map in the Bread Loaf literature. You stop and look around. You are at least three miles out; the sun is waning; already it seems darker; the path has dead-ended twenty feet ahead in a fallen log the size of a Brontosaurus carcass, and something stirs in the bushes. Holy Toledo! You spin around like lightning and start sprinting back the way you came.

Ever since your run, you have been sneezing like a hayfever victim, a condition that is definitely aggravated by the long walk back and forth from your distant cottage, Brandy Brook. (Advice: Don't tell them you may have your car there if there's a chance you won't—you'll find yourself with a more distant cottage and extra long walks to the Inn, the Little Theater, the Barn.) So you decide to ask a favor of the Bread Loaf brass and see about getting your room changed. This is Sandy Martin's department. Sandy Martin listens to your problem something like your high school principal might, with his ear cocked toward you but not meeting your eyes; and you can tell he figures you are the first case in a possible insurrection that must be squelched. You are informed that such a room change would not be possible because all the rooms are filled. You find this hard to believe; you are a little disappointed with the administrative director. During the next several days each time you sneeze you consider whether or not you should bear him a lifelong grudge. You consider your friend Bernie Kaplan's advice (a fellow during a previous summer): "Relax." Good advice but impossible to follow.

*　　*　　*

You meet an agent, Wendy Weil, with the Julian Bach Agency. She is a big-boned, loose-jointed Radcliffe type with owl-rimmed glasses and a disarming manner—a really appealing person. So you decide to take in her afternoon spiel on "The Agent" scheduled for the Barn. When you get there, you find the audience is made up predominantly of little old ladies. You sit down next to Wendy Weil and try to keep from sneezing. One little old lady with painted-on eyebrows, blue stockings, and wattles comes over:

"Oh, where is the agent?" she says.

"She is right here," someone says.

She squeezes Wendy on the wrist. "Oh, let me touch you!" she says.

As Wendy begins to describe the agenting process, it becomes evident she is unwittingly dramatizing the most active fantasies of this audience. Their eyes are glowing like hens on a roost, just waking up. They begin to ask questions. They are all so cheerful in their desperation, false teeth, and furious crimson lipstick.

"But what if they want to buy 'all rights'?" one of them asks. Wendy describes.

"Well, I guess that's about everything," Wendy says finally, "except movie rights. But you probably already know about movie rights."

"Oh no. Go ahead," says the little lady with the painted-on eyebrows. "Tell us about that too!"

It is nearing the end. The cigarette machines are all running out. The lines are getting longer outside the telephone booths. You are sitting in a white lawn chair in front of the Barn, watching the people go in and out and up the dusty trail toward the Inn. The surrounding grandeur of the countryside and the Bread Loaf Mountain massif are overwhelming. You decide it really has been . . . an experience. Some of what has transpired here . . . you won't ever forget. You even decide to forgive Sandy Martin. Someone walks by and you hear them say: "Oh, I'm so tired of this blasted place," and you smile knowingly. "Hey, you wanna go down the road and see Robert Frost's cabin," someone yells. You go.

You get out of the van and walk up a long stony road through the woods. When you reach a white farmhouse, there is a rock obelisk with a bronze plaque and in front of the obelisk is the most beautiful and carefully cultivated thistle in North America. You walk on up through the yard past the thistle, on up past a field of long-stemmed grass and yarrow? vetch? wild wheat? and past some apple trees, and there is the cabin. You go in. You look carefully into each room. You can see the chair Frost sat in beside the fireplace. You try it out. You walk back out and look down the hill through the orchard and across the valley at the mountains, as Frost must have done. Something magical is happening. Hoping no one will notice, you wade out into the tall grass to the apple trees and you pick two of Frost's apples. You are eating these apples all the way back to the Bread Loaf Inn, feeling ghostly in the turquoise van, staring out across the empty fields. Already you are missing Bread Loaf.

A STAR IN THE WILDERNESS

Six Years at Saranac Lake

Next morn, we swept with oars the Saranac with skies of benediction. . . .
—Ralph Waldo Emerson

Among the early campers in the Saranac region was a group of ten distinguished Cambridge intellectuals, which included Ralph Waldo Emerson, James Russell Lowell, and Louis Agassiz, who founded what they called a "Philosophers Camp" there in 1858. Longfellow had been invited, but he declined to join the group when he heard that Emerson was bringing a gun. They were attracted to the Adirondacks because of the great natural beauty and wildness of the place and because the lakes and forest encouraged contemplation.

David Madden confided to the assembled dinner crowd of writers and students the first year at the St. Lawrence Writers Conference at Saranac Lake that he had been so affected by the beauty of one of the small, deserted islands out in the middle of the mist on the lake that morning that he had rowed all the way out there, taken off all his clothes, and stormed about through the rough forest and rocky wastes like a wild man. A few eyebrows went up, but those of us who had been there even a day—and had walked through the woods, inhaling the balsam, and had seen the eerie way the sunlight fell through the enormous branches of virgin trees four and five and six feet thick—*understood.*

In spite of our disappointment that our headliner Erica Jong failed to show up that year—because, she told me tearfully over the phone, she was simply too afraid to climb aboard the airplane—there was, from the beginning, something special and magical about the place and what happened there. Over the six years of the conference, nearly everyone associated with Saranac noticed and commented about its uniqueness and felt its mysterious power.

Gail Godwin said she thought it had to do with "the spirit of the place (the landscape) combined with the intensities of the various people." Saranac veteran Robie Macauley said: "Saranac is like a week in the country in the company of friends carrying on an informal, continuous, frequently brilliant conversation about the creation of literature. . . . And that Saranac conversation is very hard to leave at the end of the week. All year long, I have letters, snapshots, short story manuscripts, telephone calls from writers I first met there. They have a feeling of community and stimulation that is just astounding. . . . St. Lawrence has added something new and original to American literary life and the teaching of writing."

It all started in 1974, the year following my Bread Loaf experience, when, full of youthful hubris and ignorance, I decided to start my own writers' conference, modeled after the famous Bread Loaf conference but with certain strategic "improvements" I hoped to make. With a smaller conference and the advantage of a lovely and intimate lakefront conference center called Canaras owned by St. Lawrence University at Upper Saranac Lake in upstate New York, I thought it might be possible to bring students and faculty together without some of the rigid status distinctions that had sometimes gotten in the way of interactions at Bread Loaf. I wanted the ambience to be cordial and upbeat, an atmosphere that would convey the message: "You can do this too—if you work at it," rather than the usual: "No matter what you do, you can never walk among gods like these, except at a place like this."

Whatever secret chemistry there *was* came about, so far as I could tell, from luring people to the middle of an almost pristine wilderness to talk about literary and spiritual matters, just as Emerson had done in almost the same location a century earlier, and we were attracting some of the best literary talent in North America to do it, in case anybody noticed, and, increasingly, people did notice. But I think an additional reason for the radiance of Saranac and the fondness participants felt about the experience is the fact that, outside of New York and Boston and a few cultural meccas, there are *so few literary crossroads* in this country that *any* coming together of talent and energy and the right people with the time to get to know one another would have been valuable.

My philosophy was to try to bring the right people together, to create what I perceived to be the appropriate mood, and to let the fireworks begin, and what resulted was almost always interesting: whether it was education, new books written or discovered, jobs offered, marriages, friendship, love—all the basic human transactions, though we assiduously avoided murder and—very much on purpose—we discouraged opportunities for hatred, greed, or envy. In general, we encouraged people. We showed them that writers are human and that they can be kind and generous to one another. With instantaneous good results, we pushed onward in spite of the black flies and in spite of the fact that the weather is often unpredictable and erratic in the Adirondacks in June.

Our second year, it rained continuously for six days running, and everyone huddled in front of the flagstone fireplaces and drank Cutty Sark and talked and talked, and all the readings that year— in the main lodge surrounded by the heads of moose and elk, and the full-feathered bodies of mounted owls and loons—were full of rainy-day emotions. Clark Blaise won the St. Lawrence Award for Fiction and read from *Tribal Justice*. Bharati Mukherjee introduced us to India, and Asa Baber, to *The Land of a Million Elephants*. On the last two days of the conference, the sun came out like a beacon, and I remember Diane Wakoski doing deep-knee-bends for the longest time and Michael Benedikt sitting quietly at a rattan table in front of the Jackson Lodge boathouse in the sunshine, writing poetry in his bathing trunks.

In 1976 the weather was fine. John Hawkes talked with great eloquence about "aesthetic bliss" and argued against the autobiographical impulse in fiction, and Gail Godwin defended autobiography as the sine qua non and the ne plus ultra. Russell Banks won the St. Lawrence Award for Fiction for *Searching for Survivors*, and Jim Tate and Robie Macauley gave the funniest readings ever heard in the Northeast.

In 1977 three major women writers were among the faculty at Saranac: Joyce Carol Oates, Gail Godwin, and Ann Beattie. Oates did not travel much in those days and, so far as I know, had never before served as a faculty member at a writers' conference. Luckily, my friend Gail Godwin was her friend too and helped me persuade her to come to Saranac, and what a coup it was to have landed her!

In those days, and for many years before, I admired Joyce Carol Oates, though I had never met her, with a degree of passion, commitment, and wild and reckless enthusiasm that could only be described as a literary crush. To my mind she was a celebrity roughly equivalent in stature to Marilyn Monroe, the Virgin Mary, Joan Baez, and the goddess Athena all rolled into one, far beyond mere mortal queens, movie stars, or presidents. I had written to her, I had published her work, I had taught her work, I was one of the few people who had read everything in print that she had written, and I had imagined meeting her, and had actually dreamed about it, on several occasions as a version of divine communion. So far I had met two others who had actually seen Oates in the flesh, and one had described her as "tiny" and the other had described her as "tall and imposing." Somehow these conflicting descriptions had fed my imagination and made Oates seem even more ethereal. And now I was actually going to have the opportunity to meet her firsthand.

Oates was reputed to be shy and emotional and unpredictable, and so I was quite concerned that she be made to feel comfortable. I was willing to go to whatever lengths might be required. I assigned her the best room at the conference center and had it specially cleaned, and I rearranged the furniture and placed a bouquet of wildflowers on the dresser. The conference schedule had worked out in such a way that Oates would not be arriving until the second day of the conference at a late afternoon hour when I would be teaching, so I had alerted my assistants to be on the lookout for her and her husband, who were driving down from Windsor, Ontario, and I had told my assistants to escort Oates and her husband to her room as soon as they arrived, and I would catch up with them later.

That day as my class was ending one of my assistants ran up with a stricken look on her face and said that Oates had arrived all right, but that things had gone badly and now she was talking about leaving. Apparently the trip had been longer and more arduous than expected and she was very tired, and then when they had taken her to her room to rest, she had stumbled into a room filled up with noisy people and flailing bottles! An hour or so earlier a bunch of students had seen this lovely empty room and had decided to have a party in there. So what Oates had seen when they opened the door for her was a bacchanalia-in-progress, and she had reeled back across the threshold with her limp wrist across her forehead as if this was simply more than anyone should be asked to endure after so long a journey, and she was now sitting dejectedly with her solicitous husband in the otherwise empty dining hall trying to decide what to do next.

I hurried along the path beside the lake and through the forest on my way to the dining hall and went in, and there they were. Oates was staring down into a plate of cold mashed potatoes and congealing gravy that the cook had rustled up quickly in hopes of cheering her up and staving off starvation, and Oates had not touched one bite of it; and her husband, Ray, was sitting by her side with a look of grave concern and consternation on his face.

I sat down and introduced myself and apologized for the misunderstanding regarding her room. The students would be terribly embarrassed, I said, when they found out what difficulties they had caused by their rampant partying. I told her we would have the room cleared out and cleaned up instantaneously. She said she thought perhaps it would just be better if she got back in the car and went home. I said, "Oh no, please don't do that. We can work this out." We were so glad to have her here, I said, and we would do whatever was necessary to make her comfortable. All she had to do was whistle. She said that if she was going to be able to stay, she would have to have a room with quite a bit more privacy. I said I knew of just the room, and if she would like to come along with me now, I would show it to her.

We walked along the lakefront and through the lush forest, and we stopped off at Jackson cottage, where Gail Godwin was staying, and Oates and Godwin embraced; and Gail immediately began to regale Oates with rhapsodies about Saranac, and Joyce began to relax. Within five minutes, she was having such a good time she didn't want to leave, so Ray and I walked on down to the room I had in mind at the far end of the camp facing into the deep woods. Ray looked it over and pronounced it suitable, and so it was settled.

After a good night's sleep, Joyce Carol Oates assumed her teaching duties the next day, and the students who had been lucky enough to gain admission to her workshop progressed quickly from awe and amazement to admiration and rapport and cordiality. I realized that the person who had described her as "tiny" must have meant "slender," and the person who had described her as "tall and imposing" must have been talking about her mind and her teaching abilities as well as her physique. That week Gail Godwin and Ted and Renée Weiss and I went searching through the woods for a "lost" lake—and found it—and Oates met Ted and Renée Weiss, and soon after that she was offered a job at Princeton, where Ted was a senior member of the creative writing faculty. Joyce and Ray left western Ontario, and she has been a fixture at Princeton ever since.

Ann Beattie was not yet famous in 1977, not so famous as Oates and Godwin at least. She had written for *The New Yorker,* and she had published two books, a novel, *Distortions,* and a collection of stories, *Chilly Scenes of Winter,* on the same day—her publisher's idea for a splashy debut, which indeed it was. Her picture in *Newsweek* had made her seem childlike, even "tiny," so I was a bit surprised when she turned out to be tall, long-legged, flamboyant, and buxom, with the longest set of real fingernails I had ever seen on a living human being, though I had seen pictures of the Genghis Khan, who had even longer ones. That year Ann wore black T-shirts and tight jeans that quietly scandalized several of the more sedate, middle-aged women in attendance and, in general, Ann was so unselfconscious and young and full of herself that she inspired great cattiness. One evening at our get-acquainted cocktail party, one of the middle-aged women stalked up to Ann and without batting an eyelash said pointedly: "I hear you published two books on the same day. Who did you *sleep* with?" Ann looked at her in horror and disbelief and without saying a word spun around and walked straight out of the room.

That night, for her reading, Ann read the short story "Shifting," which was a story about an alienated young woman who takes driving lessons from a teenage boy. The next day Ann consented to be interviewed for the local college radio station by one of my undergraduate students—call him John. John was one of the shyest kids I had ever seen. As a freshman, his face would turn beet red whenever he was called upon in class, and he had a minor but quite noticeable stutter. At some point during his sophomore year this gentle and shy fellow had the bright idea that he would pursue a career as a radio personality, and he began the project of transforming himself into the sort of person who can talk about any subject with glibness, frankness, and dispassion and who can manipulate a microphone. He experimented on me for one of his early interviews, and he had one of those handheld mikes that had to be shoveled under the nose of whoever was speaking whenever they opened their mouths and then returned to the mouth of the inquisitor. John was remarkably inept. Before we were finished, John's face was so red I was worried about his health and I was certainly worried about his choice of career—it seemed so completely out of character.

At any rate, after her interview with John, Ann and I happened to have lunch and she told me in elaborate detail, complete with handheld mike gestures, about her interview with John, which had climaxed with John asking her: "Ms. Beattie, can you reveal to me now, somewhat more clearly perhaps, exactly *why you slept* with the boy in the story." John turned dangerously red in the face at that point, and, after stifling her laughter, Ann had given him a stern little lecture about how first-person narrators in fiction are not necessarily the same as the author. Some writers would have been offended, I'm sure, but Ann thought it was a great joke and turned it instantly into a comical anecdote. She was especially pleased when I told her what a triumph of machismo it must have been for John, ignorant though he was, to have asked her such a question. And I'm happy to be able to report that—against all odds—John went on to quite a successful career in the media. Ann, of course, went on to become Ann Beattie.

Later that same week, Ann gave a talk during which she revealed the "secret" of how she managed to break into print in *The New Yorker*. Early on in one of the rejection letters she had received from *New Yorker* editor Roger Angell, he had conveyed the information that he was quite certain her work would eventually be acceptable for *The New Yorker*. His advice was to keep working and to keep sending him new work, and he predicted that by the time she submitted her twentieth story, she would be ready. For some reason, Ann found this enormously encouraging. She worked and worked; she submitted each new story to Roger Angell, one after the other; and each new story was returned with a kind note and a rejection until she finally submitted the twentieth story—and the twentieth story was accepted! She didn't know whether she had simply gotten better or whether she had worn him down.

One of the "fellows" in the audience that day was an unpublished fiction writer who was extremely impressed with Ann's story because she had been corresponding with Roger Angell lately too, and he had been rejecting her work with a series of kind notes. She said at dinner that night that she didn't know if she could write twenty stories in her lifetime, but if that's what it took, she would certainly try to do it—because she wanted to be in *The New Yorker* more than almost anything. I hope you will not think I am making this up if I tell you that, in fact, this particular writer, after many rejections, eventually had her twentieth submission accepted by *The New Yorker*, and quite a few since. Her name is Bobbie Ann Mason.

Other students and fellows who first attended Saranac as unpublished or slightly published writers and who later published work of some note include: Dianne Benedict, Elizabeth Cox, Ursula Hegi, Elizabeth Inness-Brown, Jayne Anne Phillips, Pamela Painter, C. E. Poverman, Tess Gallagher, G. E. Murray, and Kelly Cherry—not a bad record for six years of meetings.

*   *   *

In 1978, about two weeks before the conference was to begin, I received a phone call from someone who said he was Seymour Lawrence. Of course I recognized his name immediately—he was a legend as a publisher. If he was who he said he was, then I was talking to *the* Seymour Lawrence of Seymour Lawrence/Delacorte, but I had never spoken to him before and it was a little difficult to imagine what he might want with me.

He said he had recently received my conference flyer in the mail and he had, of course, followed the progress of *Fiction International* for several years, and he just wondered if I would mind too awfully much if he stopped by the conference for a few days. I could hardly believe my ears. "I wouldn't mind at all, Mr. Lawrence," I said. "In fact, we would love to have you. The only problem is it's so late in the game, I'm afraid I've committed all of my budget, so I won't be able to pay you anything."

"Oh, for heaven's sake," Seymour Lawrence said. "I just want to come up for the fun of it. I don't expect you to *pay* me anything. I'm rich!"

"Wonderful," I said. "Say, how would you like to be part of a panel discussion on—oh . . . the future of publishing . . . or something like that?"

"Oh, I think I could manage that," he said. "By the way, everyone calls me Sam."

"Okay."

"Is Margaret Atwood still on your program?"

I confirmed that she was.

"Good—I'd like to meet her while I'm there."

I assured him that if he came to Saranac I would personally introduce him to Margaret Atwood, and I kept my promise.

It is my theory that Sam's primary reason for wanting to come to Saranac in the first place was to try to recruit Margaret Atwood for his list, which at that time, except for Tillie Olsen, showed a notable absence of significant women writers. With Sam's nose for literary talent, he recognized that Atwood was a major writer, and I think he wanted to sign her up for his team, or at least to find out firsthand if she was available.

Atwood had just finished *Lady Oracle,* and she had decided that nothing was going to stop her from starting her next novel (which eventually became *Life Before Man)* during the week of the conference. We made elaborate arrangements, in advance, so that she could accomplish this. Her schedule was arranged so that she would have every afternoon free to write, and I agreed to provide expert childcare assistance for her two-year-old daughter, Jess, in the form of a young woman who needed scholarship assistance in order to attend the conference.

Margaret Atwood was unfailingly polite to everyone, and she performed all of her teaching duties with care. But perhaps because of the hunkering-down-to-start-a-new-book mood she was in, or simply because of a clash of temperaments, she appeared to be not the least bit impressed that Sam Lawrence had come all the way from Manhattan into the wilds of the Adirondack Park to meet her. She wanted peace and quiet in order to think and write, and every time Sam Lawrence came around and wanted to talk it was like someone had turned the radio up to a station playing loud, offensive music. Sam was so jolly, goofy, gregarious, and down-to-earth that everyone loved him, but Atwood fled in apparent horror whenever he entered the room as if he was some annoying buffoon ready to twist her arm to sell her more life insurance.

Sam Lawrence was not a man to despair, however. He was having a big time trying to beat Annie Dillard at Ping-Pong and tennis. Both of them hated to lose at anything, and their matches were so ferocious and hard fought that they drew crowds. Annie looked like a gangly fifteen-year-old, but, as soon as she got a racket in her hand, any kind of racket, she was a giant-killer with the heart of a champion, and no one could beat her at anything, Sam included.

Another visitor that year was Jayne Anne Phillips, whom I had invited as a fellowship participant. Jayne Anne had been sending me stories that were knockouts, and I was determined to get her together with Sam, if I could, because I knew she was looking for a publisher. Jayne Anne wore nothing that year but diaphanous white dresses with little filigrees of embroidery along the bodice, and she resembled a particularly lovely angel. Jayne Anne was so sweet and hip and beautiful it was difficult to believe she was a literary genius, but I already knew that she was.

One night, on a lark, a big group of us from the conference got together and we all went down to the village of Saranac Lake to go bowling. Annie, Sam, Rob Wilson, Rosellen Brown, and Jayne Anne Phillips were all there; and Sam had never gone bowling before in his life. So every time his turn came, he rolled a gutter ball. Not that any of us was that great, but Sam was by far the worst, and the harder he tried, the more humiliated he became. We kept saying things like,

"Never before in human history has so much literary talent been so embarrassed on one bowling alley," to make Sam feel better.

Finally, on our way home in the car, with everyone in a totally exhausted state, I told Sam quietly that I thought it was probably destiny that had brought him to that bowling alley on this particular night to be so completely humiliated because it had actually been his golden opportunity to get to know his next great literary discovery, Jayne Anne Phillips.

"Jayne Anne is good?" he said, with an astonished look on his face.

"Jayne Anne is very good," I said.

"I'll ask her to send me something."

"You definitely should. If you don't publish her, I will," I said. "But something tells me, you can do a better job."

The next time I walked into Brentano's on Fifth Avenue in New York my visit happened to coincide with the publication date of Jayne Anne Phillips's *Black Tickets* from Seymour Lawrence/Delacorte. Just inside the glass doors was a monumental column of Jayne Anne's lavender-covered volumes that measured six feet across and floor to ceiling. There was also a review and an interview with Jayne Anne in *Newsweek*—this kind of exposure for a first book of literary short stories from a previously unknown author! Well, she wasn't unknown for long. Staring up at that gigantic column of books, I thought, *Is Sam Lawrence a great publisher or what?* Sam knew how to get the job done.

Far across the glassy surface of Upper Saranac Lake from the Canaras Center was the wreckage of a once-great hotel, the Saranac Inn, whose remaining walls and chimneys caused it to resemble a magnificent white palace in the distance. Guests at the writers' conference often gazed across to the distant shore and inquired about it. It was only close up that one could see it was a derelict structure, its roof destroyed in many places with birds flying in and out, its once graceful parquet buckling, and its spacious rooms and corridors haunted by ghosts from the balls and banquets and romances and quiet teatime talks of an earlier time. In the quiet of the mountains, it was easy to imagine that one could almost hear the clinking of the china. America does not have many authentic ruins, but this was one; and over the years of the conference our writers and students visited the place because there was something ineffable there that was unspeakably sad and that pressed upon the heart.

On a bright June afternoon in 1978 several of us were standing out on the sundeck above the water at Canaras, and Annie Dillard glanced across the lake and suddenly Annie said: "Look! It's on fire!" We all stared off in the direction she was pointing in, and all could see that the beautiful white hull of the hotel was bright with orange flames. "Oh, my God," someone yelled. "What a sight." Ted Stratford, the camp director, ran down to the boathouse and leaped into his speedboat, and Jayne Anne Phillips and Rosellen Brown and I leaped in behind him, and we all went streaking out across the lake straight toward the fiery hotel. When we got close, we could see it was hopeless. An enormous wall of heat kept us at a distance, bobbing and listing in the boat, while embers floated down around us and hissed on the water. I suppose there wasn't much there of real practical value worth saving, even if the fire department could have gotten to such a remote location quickly, but it felt as if history itself was being destroyed in front of our eyes. The fire was an electrifying spectacle, more exciting than I could have imagined. We sat there watching it burn and collapse, hypnotized by its beauty and strangeness, until the sun started to set and the air began to grow darker and the burning hotel warmed us against the chill approach of evening. "What does this mean?" I kept thinking. "Does it mean anything?" It seemed so full of dramatic import that it should surely be the climax of something or perhaps the end.

Well, it was nearly the end of the writers' conference. We went on one more year, a year that gave us E. L. Doctorow reading from his novel *Loon Lake* and Carolyn Forché reading her poems from El Salvador, and Dan Halpern lecturing on the "The Rhetoric and Pursuit of Suffering." Bill Kittredge and Jayne Anne Phillips were cowinners of the St. Lawrence Award for Fiction. Whitley Streiber attended as a modest student hoping to work with E. L. Doctorow, and, so far as I know, had not yet encountered either werewolves or extraterrestrials. Carolyn Forché didn't sleep for six straight days, so far as I could tell, and, like a gypsy, she hung her sexy underwear out on bushes to dry, and she insulted the dean's wife, and she led a secret invasion party on a sneak attack of the kitchen facilities at 3 A.M. one night and made off with a chocolate cake and the next day's dessert for the whole camp.

One of the best writers' conferences in the history of the republic ended in 1980 because a new director of summer sessions was appointed who wanted to usurp our time slot at Saranac in order to organize a wonderful new conference devoted to "midlevel academic administrators." It was decreed that we would have to hold our writers' conference on campus instead of at the Canaras conference center at Saranac Lake, where we had always held it previously. I was opposed to this change, though, without any apparent choice, I was willing to consider it, and I even accompanied the new director of summer sessions on a fact-finding tour of the dormitories, which we would now have to utilize if we were to continue.

I was having a hard time imagining where John Updike might be willing to sleep. I had been trying for years to persuade Updike to attend, and I thought this might be the year he would finally say yes. One triple on the top floor of one of the dorms seemed as if it might be possible, but when I asked the new director of summer sessions if some of the extra furniture could be removed for the duration of the conference—I thought it might seem a little strange to Updike to be staying in a room with three beds, three dressers, and three desks—the director flew into a rage. No, it would not be possible to move any furniture! Who did these people think they were anyway? John Updike, whoever the hell *he* was, would just have to rough it!

LITERARY
METEOROLOGY

SUPERFICTION

Fiction in an Age of Excess

In the mid-sixties the rules of the game of American fiction writing changed so quickly that the transition all but cost fiction its life. A number of the most serious American fiction writers—faced with encroachments from other media, a depleted pantheon haunted by dead giants, and bothersome aesthetic prophecies—turned away from so-called realism toward a variety of new modes and attitudes. How are we to understand this sweeping change in the literary climate? A number of explanations have been offered.

Just as photography helped turn painters away from representationalism, one argument goes, so film, television, and the new journalism conspired to deflect serious fiction writers away from realism. When it comes to representing *things,* the argument goes, one picture is worth a thousand words, and one movie may be worth a trillion. Having lost out in the contest to "represent reality," fiction could survive only if it abandoned "reality" altogether and turned instead to the power of words to stimulate the imagination.

How else to account for the parade of droll and murderous visions that began to take shape in American fiction of the mid-sixties? Gathering in momentum and frenzied imaginative energy through the seventies, such visions seemed the most conspicuous aspect of a bewildering range of experimentation with the forms of "the short story" that would have stunned early-twentieth-century masters of the genre.

A weariness with worn-out fictional conventions was partly responsible, some critics believe; the new writing indicated that fiction was at last catching up with the waves of innovation and consolidation that had already taken place decades before in other, less refractory arts such as painting, music, or film.

But perhaps the most revealing explanation for this obsession with forms and visions can be located in the vagaries and intense dislocations of contemporary American experience. As early as 1961, that erstwhile American realist Philip Roth began saying that the substance of the American experience itself was so abnormally and fantastically strange, it had become an "embarrassment to one's own meager imagination."[1] Suddenly fiction writers were struggling to discover modes equivalent to their emotional and imaginative perception of this strangeness.

This was approximately the point, in other words, at which American experience itself began to seem surreal. The apocalyptical ambience of the sixties was gearing up. What followed—Vietnam, assassinations, the new drug culture, continuing national fragmentation and embarrassment, an increasing sense of the loss of a shared reality, real people becoming more and more disposable, social relations becoming more and more businesslike and ritualized and compartmentalized—only accelerated the process. There was less and less need to relate personally to the vast horde of strangers—mass murderers, junkies, hard hats, mad bombers, sadists, perverts, freaks of all kinds—and more and more desire for intimate relations with Walter Cronkite and Jane Fonda, the Beatles and Howard Cosell, Archie Bunker and Iron Butterfly, the Playmate of the Month and the Lord of the Rings—all disembodied personalities reaching fingers of light, shape, print, or sound directly into our brains with new immediacy, yet dispensing with the old social ratios, requiring hardly more than passive, dumb attentiveness from us to mold a relationship.

If reality becomes surrealistic, what must fiction do to be realistic? Critic Robert Scholes predicted a "return to a more verbal kind of fiction, . . . a less realistic and more artistic kind of narrative: more shapely, more evocative; more concerned with ideas and ideals, less concerned with things." And he called this new direction "fabulation."[2]

Whatever one calls it—fabulation, fantasy, or irrealism (John Barth's word for it via Borges)—the fiction of the sixties was suddenly full of worlds where fantasies are allowed to get up and walk around; where little green spacemen may be "real"; where a man on his way home from a quiet visit to the zoo, as in Kurt Vonnegut's "Unready to Wear,"[3] accidentally learns how to walk

1. Philip Roth, "Writing American Fiction," *Commentary* 31 (March 1961): 224.
2. Robert Scholes, "Preliminaries," *The Fabulators* (New York: Oxford University Press, 1967), 12.
3. Aesthetic change is seldom perfectly monolithic. Though Vonnegut's "Unready to Wear" did not receive wide circulation or serious attention until the

right out of his body, and the discovery changes human life "more than the invention of fire, numbers, the alphabet, agriculture, or the wheel." Or a character may wake up, as in Rudolph Wurlitzer's "Quake," to find himself being abruptly herded into a crumbling football stadium with a mass of naked maniacs to await the end of the world—and it ain't no joke. Although sometimes it might be—as in Robert Coover's "The Elevator," where the narrator-protagonist sifts playfully through the collective fictive detritus covering the important (if widely overlooked) subject of public elevators. Involved in an elaborate fantasy of plunging to his death locked in erotic embrace with the elevator operator, Coover's hero still exercises the artistic freedom to step neatly out of his fantasized structure at the last instant and take the stairs, allowing the elevator to whiz down the shaft and crash without him. In this kind of fiction, the laws of nature are sometimes quietly suspended, as in Ursule Molinaro's "Chiaroscuro," where a third eye erupts in the middle of a woman's forehead as the most startling symptom of the awakening of hideous insights about her life that she cannot face. In all these cases, in exchange for a sense of prosaic reality we get a dreamlike world with big horrors and big jokes—but generally full of surprises.

What was developing during the sixties was a growing awareness, among new journalists and fiction writers alike, that the old conventions based on the probabilities of the experiential world, which had supposedly guaranteed "objectivity," weren't adequate to new experience, on the one hand; and that, on the other, they were faulty— since even a modest understanding of the way language works led to the realization that selection, arrangement, and attitudinal investment affect every "realistic" account. The new fiction was thus the expression of radical new doubts about the nature of "reality" and the validity of the fiction-making process in relation to "reality."

---

publication of his retrospective collection *Welcome to the Monkey House* in 1968, the story was originally published by Galaxy Science Fiction in 1953! (For more detailed comment on the special vagaries of Vonnegut's career, see *The Vonnegut Statement,* edited by Klinkowitz and Somer.) Similarly, William Gass's story "Order of Insects" appeared originally in 1961 in *The Minnesota Review* but did not see wider circulation until the publication of his collection *In the Heart of the Heart of the Country and Other Stories* in 1968. That events seemed to come to a head in the mid-sixties does not, of course, argue against the likelihood of such isolated, slightly earlier examples in similar modes.

ORIGINS AND ANTECEDENTS

In attempting to make sense of American fiction of the late sixties and of the seventies, our understanding is decidedly enhanced if we adopt the view that the history of fiction from Defoe and Richardson to the present embodies a series of advances toward greater and greater inwardness and individuation, or at least a series of different but effectively more intense ventures in that direction: forays inward. Forays *inward* over the course of nearly three centuries, I would argue, led logically to the genesis of the mental processes that account for the evolution of the dominant inward-turning modes of this period: fantasy/fabulation/irrealism, neo-gothic, myth/parable, metafiction, and parody/put-on—the varieties of what I will call, in general, "superfiction."

In speaking of the "new concept of inwardness" that characterized the rise of the novel, critic and novelist Leslie Fiedler described that revolution as one marked by "the invention of a new kind of self, a new level of mind; for what has been happening since the eighteenth century seems more like the development of a new organ than the mere finding of a new way to describe old experience."[4] Careful study of the origins of prose fiction in the eighteenth century reveals the important historical connection between the birth of the genre and a unique set of economic, political, social, and philosophical features—industrial capitalism, Puritanism, and, especially, the emergence of individualism—an ideology primarily based *not* on the tradition of the past but on the autonomy and ascendancy of the individual within society. Literary scholar Ian Watt has shown what an unprecedented leap Samuel Richardson's narrative mode represented, for example, with its interest in the "minute-by-minute content of consciousness," and how it reflected a much larger change in outlook, "the transition from the objective, social and public orientation of the classical world to the subjective, individualist and private orientation of the life and literature of the last two hundred years."[5]

Implicit in Leslie Fiedler's discussion of the novel throughout his monumental study *Love and Death in the American Novel* is his

4. Leslie Fiedler, *Love and Death in the American Novel* (Cleveland and New York: World Publishing, 1962), xxviii.
5. Ian Watt, *The Rise of the Novel* (Berkeley and Los Angeles: University of California Press, 1962), 176.

belief that the history of American fiction continues the snowballing effect of individuation and inwardness that began with Richardson: "For the novel must continue to carry the torch to the back of the cave . . . or surrender its birthright, its essential function."[6] The hallmarks of the new age of the novel were mass production and lonely consumption, a process that still goes on.

In the early twentieth century, when modernist writers, from Virginia Woolf to William Faulkner, revamped the idea of "character" and "retreated" into consciousness, traditional critics bemoaned the loss of authorial authority and the absence of "memorable" characters. "There is something burglarious about these silent entries into a private and alien consciousness," Mary McCarthy complained.[7] Erich Auerbach, W. J. Harvey, and others seemed inclined to dismiss the whole modern tradition as closet drama. The crucial insight that many such readers overlooked was that emphasis on consciousness—a significant turn toward greater inwardness— was an abandonment not of character but of the idea of self *as other*. Instead of *looking at* the characters in a piece of fiction, the twentieth-century reader was *feeling through* them. Even though the effect of this change was a diminution of the reader's ability to "remember" these bodies as "characters," he was still quite capable of experiencing a novel or a story vividly and memorably. It was really merely the external and social aspects of character that were falling away as common social meanings became so dubious for some writers that only an affirmation of inner meanings seemed possible.

To put it another way, in traditional fiction we meet "characters" who are looking out—at society, manners, plots; in the early-twentieth-century novel of consciousness or modernist short fiction, we are *inside* a character (or characters) looking out. In the world of the contemporary superfictionist, we are most frequently inside a character (or characters) looking *in*—or these inner phantasms are projected outward, and in a sometimes frightening, sometimes comical reversal, the outside "reality" begins to look more and more like a mirror of the inner landscape—there is so little difference between the two.

6. Fiedler, *Love and Death*, 42.
7. Mary McCarthy, "Characters in Fiction," in *Critical Approaches to Fiction*, ed. Kumar and McKean (New York: McGraw-Hill, 1968), 87–88.

NEO-GOTHIC

"Through a dream landscape . . . a girl flees in terror and [is] alone amid crumbling castles, antique dungeons, and ghosts. . . . She nearly escapes her terrible persecutors, who seek her out of lust and greed, but is caught; escapes again and is caught; escapes once more and is caught . . . ; finally [she may break] free altogether and . . . [be] married to the virtuous lover who has all along worked . . . to save her."[8] This is the classic gothic plot as it comes down to us from the eighteenth century.

At the center of the story is the "virgin" in flight, the Persecuted Maiden who, under one name or another, has been fleeing violation ever since Pamela took off at a frantic clip through Richardson's novel, and even before. But one significant difference between the Richardsonian and early gothic treatments of the pursuit of the maiden was that in the former, virtue was invariably triumphant, while in the latter the emphasis was upon portraying the powers of darkness. Incest was often the underlying sin, the archetypal root of the gothic tradition, a breach of the primal taboo, and frequently involved some offense committed against the father.[9]

Neo-gothic modes in contemporary American fiction offer bizarre variants and interpolations on this basic prototype. In Joyce Carol Oates's "By the River," for example, a "sinful" young woman is shockingly punished by her deranged father. In John Hawkes's "The Universal Fears," the sinful "daughters" unexpectedly assault and inflict incredible physical damage, near castration, upon the "father." The "maiden in flight" in Leonard Michaels's "Manikin" is dated, cornered, and raped by the dark, brooding stranger and later hangs herself in guilt and humiliation. In Thomas Pynchon's "In Which Esther Gets a Nose Job," the maiden, frightfully, though symbolically, molested by the aggressive seducer, returns to the scene of the crime enthusiastically to act out her literal "fall from virtue"— thus "fleeing" into the very arms of the villain.

The neo-gothic aspects of this fiction—its extreme, obsessive, sometimes arbitrary or perverse violence; its macabre, grotesque, or terrifying events—exemplify what Herman Kahn and Anthony J. Wiener would call "Late Sensate" art, the art of a culture in a

8. Fiedler, *Love and Death*, 107.
9. Ibid., 108–9.

state of decline.[10] The simplest explanation for neo-gothic is that it reflects the violence of American life. This mood or mode is not, after all, limited to fiction. During the period of the emergence of the neo-gothic in fiction, we had Roman Polanski and Sam Peckinpah and Ken Russell knocking them dead in the movie theaters, and what used to be called teenyboppers dancing kinky dances to Alice Cooper's necrophilic rock operas. If nothing else, the neo-gothic phenomenon in fiction is an escalation brought about to attract audiences jaded by the routine of real horror on the evening news.

Whether or not we accept Kahn's pessimistic attitude toward it, this inward-turning, which makes manifest the hyperviolence of dreams, has been around in one form or another in American fiction for a long time. It may be less an expression of cultural degeneration than of a logical progression in the American imaginative tradition. To borrow again from Fiedler's *Love and Death in the American Novel*, "Our fiction is essentially and at its best nonrealistic, even anti-realistic, . . . not merely in flight from the physical data of the actual world, in search of a (sexless and dim) Ideal; from Charles Brockden Brown to William Faulkner or Eudora Welty, Paul Bowles and John Hawkes, it is, bewilderingly and embarrassingly, a gothic fiction, nonrealistic and negative, sadist and melodramatic."[11] Other critics, among them Richard Chase and Irving Malin, have, of course, pointed out that the gothic and the romance—as opposed to the realistic novel—are the most characteristic works of the American imagination.

One could argue that American experience has always seemed violent, surreal, gothic. And possibly we have always been degenerating! In any case, the neo-gothic, with its predilection for the ferocity of dreams, is a natural bedfellow of irrealist impulses and interiority. Whatever the influence of contemporary culture and the literary tradition upon neo-gothicism, one must always bear in mind that nightmares antedate and are the true prototype of all gothic forms.

MYTH/PARABLE

Myth is a way of making up or organizing the world that antedates philosophy or the realistic novel, and therefore a logical resource to

10. Herman Kahn and Anthony J. Wiener, *The Year 2000* (New York: Macmillan, 1967), 40–41.
11. Fiedler, *Love and Death*, xxiv.

explore in a period of acute introspection, aggravated sensibilities, historical awareness, and formal experimentation. Deeply rooted in inner consciousness, myths, according to Jungian definition, are still a primary means by which archetypes, essentially unconscious forms, become articulate to the conscious mind—a complex version of the idea that the truth of the world is buried within. A parable, of course, is usually a simple story illustrating a moral or religious lesson, and it may contain mythical or archetypal elements.

Experiments with myth and parable in American fiction of the sixties and seventies reflect many of the same attitudes, premises, and disillusionments as the other forms we have discussed: loss of faith in mimetic methods, turning inward, the search for deeper meanings, the projection of fantasy creatures ("characters") into the "outside" world as a way of dramatizing experience. In addition, the use of character as archetype holds out the promise of finding universality in seeming particularity—a unitive strategy in the face of cultural dissolution.

A rich example of recent experimentation with myth and parable, John Gardner's "Queen Louisa," incorporates many of the most characteristic aspects of superfiction: the fairy-tale form, in which the heroine may change from an "enormous toad to a magnificently beautiful redheaded woman with a pale, freckled nose"; the use of deliberately anti-illusionist devices in the midst of the tallest of tales; and the droll tone of the put-on. But even more crucial to an understanding of this story is the historical echo of the chivalric love tradition and the didactic use of the parable of the rosebush at the end of the story. Here we have, in an ancient and venerable setting, a battle of ideas made tangible: a classic battle between good and evil. The forces of evil do exist in the world, Gardner seems to be saying, but just as the rosebush blooms more brightly with each swing of the witch's ax against it, so the forces of evil in real life may be thwarted and *are* by the end of the story. Queen Louisa, the good queen, is victorious. Gardner cleverly saves himself, however, from an ending too simplistically affirmative—and makes a shrewd metaphysical observation at the same time—by commenting that, well, maybe the rosebush *was* cut down after all, since the queen is insane and "can never know anything for sure, and perhaps the whole story was taking place in a hotel in Philadelphia."

William Gass's "Order of Insects," on the other hand, is clearly intended as an answer to Kafka's "Metamorphosis." In contrast to the anguish and bitter ignominy of Gregor Samsa's life as a gigantic cockroach, Gass's heroine (who identifies with an insect even if she does not literally become one) is so awed by the absurd discovery of beauty in the grace and order of insects that it seems to her to epitomize the orderliness of a universe that all living things share. This is a story heavy with wonder and meditation and, once again, simple, but not simple-minded, affirmation.

The use of myth and parable in fiction could be seen as part of the wave of reaction in American culture to the apparent failure of objective science to solve human problems and improve the human condition. It represents a yearning for ritualistic satisfactions and a search for a new kind of ordering principle—a viable American mythology. Also, perhaps, it is an expression of nostalgia for a literature of charismatic wisdom and authority, for tribal solidarity, for the fabled restorative magic of the oracle.

Of course, many writers of the modernist era, including Eliot, Joyce, Kazantzakis, Yeats, and Pound had been preoccupied with myth too. The theories of Freud, Jung, Frazer, and others provided a natural impetus. What was new to the superfictionists was the sudden spate of writers (Updike, Barth, Gardner, Katz) inviting their readers to interpret "the way we live now" in the light of traditional sources of archetypal patterns. John Updike in *The Centaur* could thus present a modern situation, for instance, and refer the reader to a familiar (or not so familiar) analogy, hoping, with luck, to revitalize the old mythological resonance on the one hand and capture some of the mystical reverberations for his modern situation on the other.

Like Barton Midwood in "One's Ship," the writer could satirize an archetypal human situation—in this case, the mating ritual as seen from a quirky masculine viewpoint—by placing his generalized characters in a timeless primeval setting. Or, like Robley Wilson Jr., in "Saying Good-bye to the President," he could take a crack at trying to discover or create new mythical material especially significant for our time and place—through, for instance, a dramatization of the ancient theme of "the fall of the king." By concentrating on our then-recent national trauma of leadership, this peculiarly powerful little fiction suggests both the eagerness and the pathos with which the United States followed the downfall of Richard Nixon. (It was written, incidentally, prior to the impeachment hearings and resignation.) A variation of this sort of experimentation has been attempted by writers (for example, Steve Katz in "Mythology: Plastic Man") who believe that new sources of myths may be unearthed from pop culture: sports, songs, comic books, and so on. According to Leslie Fiedler, this is just the place to look for them. It is high time for writers to "cancel out those long overdue accounts to Greece and Rome."[12]

METAFICTION/PARODY/PUT-ON

Fiction in which the conventions or techniques of the story itself became the subject matter developed as a commonplace practice for superfictional experimenters—an inward turning toward pure theory. Among the many motivations for this sort of self-conscious but sometimes entertaining game-playing have been an impulse toward joking and parody, now that the rules of the game are so clearly understood and mastered; a yen for "new" subject matter free of clichés and old bugaboos; and sometimes simply a voguish parading of intellect brought about by the historical fact that most writers these days hang out in universities where they are apt to pick up critical baggage, perspective, and sophistication that eventually find their way into writers' work in one way or another.

In a willful mass revolt against the Jamesian prescription of author self-effacement, many practitioners called for the "truth of the page" and set out to write deliberately anti-illusionist fiction, to defy all the verities and still try to keep the old ball rolling. One way to subvert a willing suspension of disbelief is to call attention to the conventions of the fiction one is in the process of creating, or to comment on or parody the form—as, for example, Ishmael Reed and Judith Rascoe attempt with the western in "The Loop Garoo Kid" and "A Lot of Cowboys." Sometimes this sort of parody has even taken potshots at the literary culture itself, as in John Updike's "Under the Microscope" or in John Batki's "At the National Festival." The joy of invention apparent in this work may seem to be its greatest virtue. The serious effect of such horseplay, however, is to undergird the rightness of the individual and idiosyncratic vision of experience as against the implicit attitude of much conventional fiction that reality is a thing, essence, landscape we can all agree upon and wish fervently for art to imitate.

The most important impetus for this sort of fiction had been the expression of anxiety over the epistemological validity of the fiction-making process, plus an intensified concern with the forms, ideas,

12. In a lecture.

and language that might revitalize it. It was more than sheer frivolity, for instance, that motivated John Barth in "Life-Story" to attempt to write a story against apparently impossible odds by deliberately setting up nearly insurmountable technical obstacles to his own success; and more than defiant virtuosity that motivated Donald Barthelme in "Sentence" to attempt to do the same by cramming a whole story into one sentence and then omitting the period. While Barth's "Life-Story" is a self-conscious satiric "story" about the process of writing a self-conscious satiric story, it is, more important, a sophisticated essay on the state of the art. The ironic clincher in "Life-Story" is that, despite Barth's narrator's cantankerous will to make his creation unlike any story ever written, it does meet many of the standard definitions of what a conventional story should do: that is, something happens; the protagonist's experience in the story leads to a basic change in his viewpoint—but, paradoxically, while conforming with superficial accuracy to these definitions, "Life-Story" mocks them mercilessly.

What Barthelme gives us, in a sentence . . . about itself . . . is, in fact, a study of the peculiar nature of sentences that concretizes William H. Gass's dictum that there "are no events but words in fiction."[13] Or, as Barthelme's sentence itself reminds us toward the end: "the sentence itself is a man-made object."

Through the use of similar techniques, Gilbert Sorrentino's love story "The Moon in Its Flight" offers an answer to the question "How do you write a love story in an age when all love stories have become sentimental?" Turning on a risky theme—youth, alas, cannot be recaptured; lost love, lost opportunities are forever lost—the story is saved from sentimentality by an impatient narrator who keeps distracting the reader with reminders that this is only a story and yet enticing the reader by his disclaimers into believing it to be an intimate autobiographical confession.

In Ronald Sukenick's story "What's Your Story," the narrator says: "I sit at my desk, making this up. . . ." His use of "strike" makes the reader conscious of his ongoing revisions. A parody of Mafia and espionage "thrillers" is in progress, but the unifying focus is upon the writer sitting at his desk and his relationship with his desk and his imagination—and other desks he has written on, views out his

13. William H. Gass, *Fiction and the Figures of Life* (New York: Alfred A. Knopf, 1970), 30.

window from these various desks, or pictures on various walls near these various desks. If Joan comes into his room while he is writing, she goes into the story. Since a story is a man-made object, Sukenick, Barth, Barthelme, and Sorrentino seem to be saying, you can put anything in or leave anything out (for example, note the comical way Sukenick puts *in* Ruby Geranium's tie).

Why should writers insist on emphasizing in their stories: "This is just a story. These are just words. This is all made up"? "Adequate adjustment to the present can be achieved only through ever-fresh perception of it," Sukenick says.[14] These fictions all dramatize the sweeping perception that art and language help create reality rather than serving as inert vehicles through which a self-evidently recognizable external reality is made manifest—a major ideological split between this new fiction and the old. Language, these writers are saying, *helps to constitute our reality*. Imagination (making things up) is a major form of perception, not a mere literary luxury but an absolutely necessary means of getting from one moment to the next. Fiction-making is seen, therefore, not only as a way of making up the world but also as an indispensable way of making sense of it.

What, then, is the upshot of these developments?

The world, both of ideas and of facts, has changed drastically; and the artistic ethos must be expected to change with it. Readers have sometimes been troubled by these radical experiments—fictions within which conflicts are not conventionally resolved and expectations are not conventionally satisfied. Precisely because many of these stories attempted to speak for a new order of existence, and a new perception of that existence, they offer new and special difficulties as well as heightened pleasures. However, if one reads the history of prose fiction as, among other things, a history of increasingly bold and complicated forays inward, toward a confrontation with human consciousness and unconsciousness, then, whatever its changes, American superfiction carries on the same tradition with impressive fidelity to this original and ancient impulse.

14. Ronald Sukenick, *Wallace Stevens: Musing the Obscure* (New York: New York University Press, 1967), 3.

LIFESTYLE FICTION

A Downpour of Literary Republicanism

With very little fanfare, a new kind of serious fiction seems to have swept into the American literary consciousness. Like an erratic tropical storm gathering force just offshore, it now threatens to blow inland, striking major population centers. For want of a better name, it has been called the "minimalist/realist" tendency, and there is considerable evidence that it may be yet another symptom of the neoconservative or Republican tide.

Some critics have espoused the idea that the minimalist/realist impulse in recent American writing is actually a part of what came to be called postmodernism, that every kind of new and somewhat strange fiction written in the United States since about 1967 is, by definition, an example of postmodern consciousness, or of "superfiction." I doubt it. I believe the current minimalist/realist tendency is, like "moral fiction" before it, a reaction against the complexity, intellectuality, self-consciousness, the presumed moral evasiveness, and the polymorphous formalism of the postmodern consciousness—although not without immediately worrying about several qualifications that would take into account the widespread hybridization of influence, the tendency toward the subsuming of all modes in the voracious maw of the infolding, unfolding, and refolding of the American literary consciousness.

Alas, in such vast realms of speculation, analytical and pigeon-holing behavior ultimately may be worthless, the temptation to overgeneralization is sometimes overpowering, and nothing is pure. The conscientious observer may, in plain fact, be no more able to describe, predict, or account for the literary climate than the local weatherman can the next day's cloud cover or probability of rainfall. But just as weather forecasting is worth attempting, even though it is not yet an exact science, so literary meteorology may also have a place in human affairs, if only to ease our anxiety about what the skies portend.

Symptoms of mutiny in the postmodernist camp were visible as early as 1978 with the publication of John Gardner's controversial book, *On Moral Fiction*. "Moral fiction" became a much maligned catchphrase, largely because of Gardner's well-meaning but sometimes barbaric treatment of fellow writers under its banner and because few readers quite understood or agreed with Gardner's definition of moral fiction. However, moral fiction is still useful as a label for certain impulses that undoubtedly began to be expressed by the late seventies, including a restlessness with the idea of the postmodern. The trouble with contemporary writing, Gardner argued, is that "texture is king in all the arts." Two of the "common mistakes in bad art," Gardner said, are "overemphasis of texture" and "manipulative structure"—exactly those areas that postmodernists or superfictionists were especially interested in exploring. "The term 'post-modernism,' " Gardner claimed, "not only isolates a few writers and praises them beyond their due, depressing the stock of others or willfully misreading them; it judges cynical or nihilistic writers as characteristic of the age, and therefore significant, and thus supports, even celebrates ideas no father would willingly teach his children."

Whether or not they had read and heeded Gardner's book, or vehemently disagreed with it, many younger writers began to rebel against the theories and practice of the superfictionists. Perhaps this was because they too felt a moral vacuum opening up, or because they wished to address a wider audience and felt the elitist notions of the superfictionists would preclude that possibility, or because they felt the superfictionists were simply oblivious to questions about the proper conduct of life or any kind of straightforward human conduct presented representationally.

More often, blatant evidence of improper conduct could be seen everywhere around them—as it always is and had been—begging to be described and cataloged, even if, unlike John Gardner, some writers did not feel particularly compelled to state a philosophical position on it. Sometimes, simply pointing it out was felt to be enough. Perhaps the limits of innovative game-playing, parading of intellect, and esoteric posturing of the kind associated with superfiction had been reached—some of the same traits, incidentally, that have made academic criticism useless to the general reader.

Of course, even the sixties innovators believed they were creating fiction that served a moral purpose, that might, for instance, save the audience from the restricted and restrictive perspective of so-called realistic vision, just as the dadaists, early in the century, believed they were right in attacking limited bourgeois sensibilities and perceptions and offering a more accurate (and therefore moral) response to the "true" nature of the world. Another "moral" idea implicit in both superfiction and dadaism is the wisdom of exploring the "inner," and the assumption that the key to the mystery of life or of character lies within, so that that is where one must go to unlock such mysteries—obviously a fairly popular idea since Freud, but one that has been around in one form or another much longer.

A significant difference, however, between the American experimentalists of the late sixties and seventies and the minimalist/realists writing now—that is, an essential difference between what came to be called the "postmodern aura," "the new fiction," "superfiction," "innovative fiction," "surfiction," or what have you, and what some are now calling "minimalist/realist" fiction or, in some cases, "white trash fiction" or "coke fiction"—is that creators of the former were chiefly interested in a search for new form, while writers of the latter still believe it is possible to discover new content.

In *The New Fiction*, a book of literary interviews that sampled the barometric pressure of the early seventies in American writing, only one literary Republican, only one staunch supporter of "realism" and "content," that is, spoke up: Tom Wolfe. (Although Wolfe has remained a realist, he was, of course, not then a fiction writer, and he has never been a minimalist.) Wolfe complained, in the midst of the groundswell of support for formal experimentation, about the postmodern tendency to view form as the last frontier. "It's true in every branch of the arts," he said, "that the only frontier artists *believe* exists is the frontier of manipulating form. . . . The fact that there might be something new in content, or new in *comment*, is not anything that impresses people once they get into this frame of mind that the avant-garde is on the frontier sheerly of form." Wolfe went on to argue that the then fashionable writers had tricked themselves into believing that "Because Proust did this much, and Henry James did this much, and James Joyce did this much, I can't do those things. They're not available to me."

In opposition to this viewpoint, Wolfe strongly defended the "newsbearing" function of fiction, its capacity to tell us "the way we live now," the importance of focusing on "external reality" as well as "internal reality" as part of the fiction writer's duty. So much terra incognita of the social fabric, the social tableau, was ignored, he believed, by writers committed to the subjective and the push for formal change. But content changes too, according to Wolfe, particularly lifestyle-content, and Wolfe believed it especially important to document those changes in lifestyle, including regional or subcultural differences within a socially fragmented society. "I imagine the most serious subject now," he said, "is changes in the way people live, not politics, not wars. I think it's just the changes in the way people live, the changes in the way they look at the world. Perhaps that's always been the most serious subject." He could have been defending Jane Austen. In fact, he did have several kind words for Dickens, Thackeray, Balzac, and Tolstoy. In his nonfiction, of course, Tom Wolfe was busily putting these convictions into practice.

Now, oddly enough, Tom Wolfe's conservative diatribe and defense of traditional values, circa 1972, seems prophetic. It is almost as if several of the best new fiction writers have taken a solemn secret pledge in support of Wolfe's views, and vowed further to promulgate these views in their work—adopting an attitude that would have seemed anathema twenty years ago to a possible majority of serious writers who took such concerns into account.

Consider this: Whatever *else* they do, all these "hot" writers are interested in lifestyle, and they take us to places and lives we have never seen before, or have never seen with quite so much up-to-date detail and verisimilitude: Raymond Carver and Richard Ford and, sometimes, Tobias Wolff, to the blue-collar northwest; Frederick Barthelme, to condo life in the New South; Bobbie Ann Mason, into the lives of farm and working-class people in western Kentucky; Jayne Anne Phillips, to seedy rural West Virginia (and several other places: El Paso, heroin addiction, rock and roll, any place she wants to go); Alice Adams, to San Francisco now (and even Alaska); Elizabeth Tallent, and sometimes Tobias Wolff, to the southwestern Sun Belt; Russell Banks, to rural New England; Ann Beattie, to upscale life in the northeastern corridor; Lorrie Moore, to northeastern yuppie mating rituals seen satirically from a kookie female point of view; Jay McInerney, also into northeastern yuppiedom, snorting too much coke and moving behind-the-scenes at a highbrow magazine that every reader eventually figures out, though it is never mentioned by name, is *The New Yorker*; Bret Easton Ellis, to the decadent, blah life of the rich kids in coked-out Hollywood.

Some of this fiction—that of, say, Raymond Carver, Jayne Anne Phillips, Bobbie Ann Mason, Russell Banks, Richard Ford, or Frederick Barthelme—has been dubbed, in certain quarters, blue-collar fiction or white-trash fiction, leading to the assumption that a new fascination with working-class lives is part of the minimalist/realist phenomenon. Maybe so. Certainly the material of these writers does offer insight into the lives of the lower and middle classes and circumstantial proof to readers of *The New Yorker*, which has published a quantity of this work, that such people aren't having any more fun than the upper classes. In fact, at times these characters' suffering and their lives may seem so positively gauche, they may offer some jaded consolation to *New Yorker* readers, who, though they may also be suffering, may at least be doing so in a manner they consider more stylish.

However, in the work of Ann Beattie, and considering the emergence of writers such as Jay McInerney, David Leavitt, Lorrie Moore, and Bret Easton Ellis, it is fairly clear by now that the well-heeled youth culture, the upper and yuppie classes, have their young chroniclers of decadence as well, some of whom seem equally committed to a minimalist/realist aesthetic. Social documentary would seem to be the key attraction then, not exclusive focus on one class or another. Perhaps someone should call it, simply, "lifestyle fiction" in the realist/minimalist mode.

Another obvious aspect of the newest fiction that tends to differentiate it from the postmodern is its emphasis on suffering or feeling rather than on intellect. While the absence of interest in game-playing, metafictional interpolations, parody, and formal high jinks (all primarily "intellectual" or academic concerns associated with the postmodern) may be easy to document, the return to an interest in emotion may be more difficult to accept or substantiate. Some readers have grumbled about the flatness, equanimity of surface, or deadpan tone of certain of these recent lifestyle narratives, terms that would seem to belie an interest in feeling. Yet, as in Hemingway, this surface calm or spare, laconic style often seems to be a strategy for leading the reader to a deeper emotional response. The contemporary persona is often a sensibility anesthetized by suffering or experience. The silences, the lacunae, are telling; the events, often gruesome or tragic or morally troublesome. As in Hemingway, the understatement of feeling often leads the reader to a deeper empathetic response, or at least, that is the intention—to create fiction of apparent simplicity but which reveals understated or unstated emotional depths that tug at the reader from that, now notorious, seven-eighths of the iceberg plowing along beneath the surface.

Charles Newman complains in *The Post-Modern Aura* that some of the new minimalism fails at this task because it is "not the minimalism of [Donald] Barthelme, whose omissions are based on the circumspect demonstration that he knows what he is leaving out. These are the elisions of inadvertency and circumscription, an obdurate unsurprised and unsurprising plainstyle which takes that famous 'meaning between the lines' to its absurd conclusion, and makes the middle ground mimesis of an Updike or Cheever seem rococo by comparison." Newman continues: "It is the classic conservative response to inflation—underutilization of capacity, reduction of inventory, and verbal joblessness."

Whether or not it is actually verbal joblessness, such rapid and apparently monolithic change does invite one to consider some old-fashioned problematic questions: How much does the fiction of a particular epoch reflect the social and political currents of its time? How much does it foreshadow or influence or predict these currents? Are the artistic sensibilities of a culture galvanized by a change in the political climate? Do writers respond to a new leader like a school of fish swimming furiously after a passing morsel? These are always difficult questions to answer, of course. But, clearly, a case can be made that the latest fiction is nothing so much as a kind of literary Republicanism, a kind of mid-eighties undulation of the conservative groundswell.

Whereas postmodern writers such as John Barth, John Hawkes, or Ronald Sukenick (to mention three) might be described as liberal or Dionysian, both in the matter and in the manner of their fictions, are not Raymond Carver, Frederick Barthelme, and Bobbie Ann Mason, let's say, conservative, Apollonian? I am not speaking so much of politics, per se, as of aesthetic leanings toward particular modes of discourse: the interest of the former group in fantasy, in the "inner," in formal innovation and experimentation for its own sake, in a husky Faulknerian attitude toward style, plot, and sentence-building; in contrast to the distinct interest of the latter group in "reality," in social documentary, in the "outer," in recourse to largely traditional techniques, and in a leaner, more Hemingwayesque treatment of style and method.

Such comparisons can be taken only so far. Barth has proven he can "do" realism any time he feels like it. Frederick Barthelme, often a minimalist/realist, is a reformed experimentalist with an uncanny ability to wring eerie surrealistic moods and sensations out of the banality of so-called real life in recognizably real locales. Jayne Anne Phillips, Mary Robison, Lorrie Moore, Elizabeth Inness-Brown, Max Apple, Russell Banks, T. Coraghessan Boyle, Robley Wilson Jr., and others sometimes identified with the latest heat wave have written some first-rate fiction that seems strongly influenced by postmodern sensibilities; and Hemingway is not the only important precursor, of course, to have developed and used a minimalist aesthetic. Minimalism has also been a favored mode of postmodern sensibilities such as Samuel Beckett or Donald Barthelme. Minimalism, that is, is not always coupled with realism, as it often seems to be lately.

Still, there may be something to be said for the idea that what we are dealing with in minimalist/realist writing is, for better or worse, the inevitable—some would say, timely—flowering or showering of literary Republicanism. Conservative aesthetics are perhaps more in keeping with the time, which is increasingly traditional, authoritarian, literal-minded, grim, repressive, strict constructionist, and less playful, less indulgent, less permissive. Postmodern fiction had become too much a medium for the cacophonous voices of the intellect in too inaccessible and inconsequential a task. However, the new generation, in its flight from information overload and the tedium of theory and abstraction, in its embrace of a simpler and more documentary form of storytelling, may be abandoning certain opportunities—the beauties of amplitude, the excitement and profusion of the baroque, the ambitious conceptions that lead to great art.

Coda: Another factor that cannot be discounted, which might have been nearly enough to have propelled writers toward literary Republicanism single-handedly, has been the favor shown to the minimalist/realist impulse by two of our most important literary institutions: *The New Yorker* and Gordon Lish.

The New Yorker is often criticized by writers who have not appeared in its pages, usually for the alleged bias of its tastes; sometimes this is seen as aesthetic bias, sometimes, even, as class bias. Presumably, there is a type of story that is a *New Yorker* story, and there is a type of writer who is a *New Yorker* writer, and several types who are not. Whatever the reasons, I think it fair to say that, recently, *The New Yorker* has contributed to the minimalist/realist attitude, though this may be simply because the best fiction is now being written by writers working in that mode. Over the years, it may be shown quite conclusively, I think, that *The New Yorker* has been broadly eclectic; and, so far as class bias goes, judging from a number of recent examples, a case could be made that editors of *The New Yorker* are at least as interested in the problems and lifestyles of blue-collar characters and of characters from out-of-the-way regions of the country as in those of members of the country club set living in exclusive suburbs or in Manhattan or along the eastern seaboard. The overriding truth about *The New Yorker* is that it is open to new writers and that it is the last of the mass circulation magazines in the United States that publishes what may be described as a critical mass or volume of serious fiction and pays its contributors generously and confers instantaneous credibility and prestige upon them that is sometimes staggering. Whatever its faults, it is all we have. Whatever its faults, it is the most influential and powerful fiction magazine in the history of the world. In a sense, whatever it likes *is* what is happening. Whatever it rejects, in a sense, ceases to exist. What it likes right now fits in well with the minimalist/realist agenda.

As I see it, Gordon Lish, who published some of the now famous postmodernists while he was fiction editor of *Esquire*, has made Alfred Knopf, or at least his corner of it, a citadel of literary Republicanism during his tenure there. Lish has sponsored the books of Raymond Carver, perhaps the most influential stylist since Donald Barthelme. Also, Mary Robison and Barry Hannah. Also, Bette Howland, Bette Pesetsky, and Michael Martone. His students include writers such as David Leavitt, Richard Selzer, and Amy Hempel. And these days, Gordon Lish, Captain Fiction, likes short sentences. I mention this fact, not to pay homage to Lish's status as a cultural commissar, but to point out the possibility that one person, in this case, one man, if he is shrewd and lucky and well placed, may be responsible for imposing his own evolving tastes on an unsuspecting public. Forget, for a minute, about the effects of Reaganism and cable and satellite television and yuppieism and the deficit; forget about George Will and Jerry Falwell and the failure of the liberal arts. Forget about the possibility that Lish himself *hasn't* forgotten these things, that one reason for his power may be in his extraordinary sensitivity to cultural change. We are still speaking about the vast influence that one man may have on the literary climate—possibly enough to make it rain if he wants it to rain.

MUSCULAR FICTION

A Postscript

"A Symposium on Contemporary American Fiction" was conducted by the Michigan Quarterly Review *and appeared during 1987 and 1988. Contributors were asked to respond to the following: "Granted that contemporary American fiction is a variety of things, what kind of recent writing interests you especially and, in your opinion, is most deserving of more attention and more readers?"*

In the last thirty years, it seems to me, we have witnessed an astonishing turnaround in the kinds of fiction that our leading writers are writing. This is partly because we have several new leading writers, but also because the spirit of the times is so utterly transformed. Not surprisingly, we have also seen radical changes in the favorite aesthetic theories that writers subscribe to—when they wish to deal, self-consciously, in theories at all. Recent developments tend to reveal a wholesale escape from theorizing, since it was theory, some feel, that was the bane of the recently deposed superfictionists.

To portray the evolution of American fiction from, say, 1960 to 1990, one might describe it as a movement from middlebrow realism or modernist realism to superfiction—a radical departure that captured center stage for a few brief years—followed by a return to a different sort of realism, minimalist realism or dirty realism or designer realism or lifestyle fiction. Lifestyle fiction is not merely a return to the modernist realism of the early sixties or a sort of attenuated or watered-down version of modernist realism, as some seem to feel. The best of the newest fiction we have now, it seems to me—the work of writers such as Frederick Barthelme, Tobias Wolff, Jayne Anne Phillips, Richard Ford, Richard Bausch, Dianne Benedict, Denis Johnson, Lorrie Moore, Gish Jen, T. Coraghessan Boyle, Jane Smiley, Louise Erdrich, Rick Bass, Kaye Gibbons, Valerie Martin, Charles Baxter, Bharati Mukherjee, Ellen Gilchrist, Xam Cartiér, Kate Braverman—consolidates some of the bizarre moods and diverse discoveries and errant experiments of the superfictionists and makes them more accessible and sometimes plugs them into the realistic tradition in ways we couldn't have imagined—and it defies most attempts at labeling.

But, to my taste, some of the newest work that has gotten a lot of attention—not any of the writers mentioned above—is a little thin. Some of the so-called minimalists have sacrificed stylistic richness or sophistication in search of other values. Of course, pure styles can be conceived and delivered in six-word sentences and in fiction that more or less eliminates exposition, as Hemingway sometimes tried to do. But it isn't easy. It isn't the sort of feat everyone should be trying for at once.

For those able to find it, *new content* is undoubtedly still out there in the American vastness—somewhere between California and the New York island—or certainly within each writer's private channel to the Collective Unconscious.

I strongly suspect that much of the best American writing of the immediate future may come from women writers since, compared to most American men, most American women are emotional and aesthetic geniuses; and I believe women also have more unexplored terrain in their lives, aspects that have yet to be described, let alone understood by men (or even themselves); and this is a decided asset for women as writers.

I also feel we may see a further blossoming of new Asian American, Hispanic American, African American, and Native American writing because there is so much open territory for these writers, so much fresh talent, and a greater cultural readiness than ever before.

Whatever else the newest American fiction might try to do in the years ahead, my hope is that, stylistically and imagistically, it will strive for more robust, more muscular, more ambitious performances —a swing of the pendulum back in the direction of William Faulkner and Flannery O'Connor. That would be the sort of writing I would like to read (and write) and the kind that I imagine might even be therapeutic (consciousness-expanding) for readers with six-word attention spans too.

LITERARY
EDUCATION

THE THEORY OF
CREATIVE WRITING I
Keeping the Frog Alive

After nearly sixty years of trying it, what are we to make of the peculiar American experiment of permitting creative writers to teach in English departments? If you wanted to know about an automobile, Ezra Pound asked, would you go to a man who had merely read about an automobile, or to a man who had made one and driven it? Most Americans, I feel sure—and most students—would rather talk to the second man. But most English professors in my experience would probably agree with Harvard professor Roman Jacobson, who remarked upon hearing that Vladimir Nabokov might be appointed to the faculty that he had nothing against elephants but he would not appoint one professor of zoology.

It is a sad fact that many of my scholarly colleagues—even some of those who are not theorists—seem to think that creative writing is a frill or a waste of time. In the ongoing battle over college and university airtime, neither traditional English professors nor theorists seem willing to agree wholeheartedly that the teaching of creative writing properly embodies many of their guiding principles, or even supplements them adequately. Observers will have noted a great deal of heated debate about what English departments should or should not be doing and considerable hostility directed toward theory, or toward creative writing in particular.

The critic Gerald Graff maintains, however, that to "attack theory as such is equivalent to attacking thinking," since theory "denotes nothing more than *philosophy*, the sort of reflection on our assumptions and practices without which any person or institution goes brain dead." Very well. If that is the case—since, above all, I hope to discourage further brain death, which seems to be closing in around our necks like so much toxic waste—then I suggest that we badly need a *theory* of creative writing, because it is clear to me that many of these "camps" within English departments truly don't understand one another.

My hypothesis is that this is an ancient and inevitable misunderstanding, but one that we should make every effort to alleviate. The dispute goes back several thousand years: Plato, you may recall, claimed that there was an ancient argument between philosophy and poetry. If it was an ancient argument in Plato's time, then it must be very ancient indeed; and Plato, you may remember, made the strange and unforgivable mistake of siding with the philosophers when he decided to ostracize the poets from his ideal republic, fearing, apparently, that poets represented a dangerous potential for arousing passion, discord, and insurrection. Like good fascists everywhere, Plato apparently wanted a nation of sheep, or perhaps, sheep who enjoy chess.

I will proceed to the matter of defining *the theory of creative writing* momentarily, but first . . . some additional thoughts.

Even before the current debates, there were problems in the English department. One complaint I used to have as an undergraduate was that most of the English professors I knew wanted us to dissect literature as if it were a frog in a lab experiment. My objection to the intense analytical process of what was then called "the new criticism," especially before I learned how to perform it, was that *it killed the frog.* I thought I wanted to find a way to study literature that would keep the frog alive.

What I valued in the study of literature, as a naïve undergraduate, was the energy of art, the emotional power, the effortless release into worlds of the imagination and pure language, and, even then, I think, the potential for what John Hawkes has called "aesthetic bliss." I believed that literature was—far and away—the most important field of study because it was, for me, the most meaningful way of understanding the world and my own life. I was willing to put up with almost any silliness my English professors devised for us because I thought it would lead me to greater levels of understanding.

But then I had had a most unusual introduction to the English department and to what the study of literature might have to offer. Completely by chance, my freshman English instructor at Duke University was a young man named Reynolds Price—a creative writer, we understood, though no one had ever read or heard of anything written by him, since in 1959 he had not yet written very much, although he was, at that time, working on his first novel, *A Long and Happy Life.*

We all referred to him as Mr. Price. In like manner, he referred to me as Mr. Bellamy and to each of his men's-campus charges as Mr. Somebody. Mr. Price was twenty-six years old and had just returned from Oxford University in England, where he had attended as a Rhodes scholar. His accent was an ear-catching mixture of a North Carolina dialect and aristocratic British.

I must say I soon discovered that this Mr. Price was the most interesting teacher, and one of the most interesting persons, I had ever encountered. All my professors were good, and they were all demanding. But this Mr. Price was almost magical. Everything he said was fascinating, and he talked about everything from British politics, which I knew nothing about and cared nothing about, to literature, to the nature of art, to writing. He assigned a series of essays that we were required to bring, in hand, to his office; and there, on the spot, while we stared at the Modigliani nude above his desk, he would read our handiwork and inscribe comments and corrections and discuss the work as if it were of the utmost importance. No one had ever read my work this closely and with such intensity and had such surprising things to say about it. Nearly everything he said came as a revelation to me.

Not everyone has the luck to study with a genius who is also a great teacher. Perhaps I can be forgiven if my prejudices all seem to fall on one side of the arguments that need to be made here. But I think it safe to say, over thirty years later—and absolutely true— that I have never been the same since I accidentally walked into that freshman English class in 1959. Such is the power of art. Such is the persuasive influence of great teaching.

In contrast, I ask you to consider the experience of most students today in our colleges and universities. How many of these students emerge from their undergraduate experiences with a coherent sense of the world, a useful set of values and goals, commitment to *any* discipline, or confidence that they have had a good education? I think most of them survive their college experience feeling somewhat damaged and tired—thankful to have endured it but disillusioned with education and disappointed because they didn't get anything close to what they expected and for which their families paid enough to ransom the king, the queen, and half the court. If they applied themselves, they learned some useful skills perhaps. They learned a certain form of nit-picking analysis and how to manipulate abstractions—what passes these days for "thinking." They learned how to become functional bureaucrats and technocrats and businesspersons and "professionals." They endured; they learned how to be bored for an hour or an hour and a half at a stretch, and still not lose their sanity or good humor—an important job skill in itself—though some, of course, could not learn it well enough. They learned some useful social skills. Far too many learned that one way to endure the meaninglessness and tedium of adulthood is to throw off the veneer of seriousness and *rationality* at regular intervals with cathartic binges of partying, overeating, or drunkenness.

One cause for this sorry state of affairs is that most university-level disciplines address a more and more specialized audience in a more and more abstract form, and they scarcely ever try to address undergraduates at all. As Maynard Mack has written: "We are narrowing, not enlarging our horizons. We are shucking, not assuming our responsibilities. And we communicate with fewer and fewer because it is easier to jabber in a jargon than to explain a complicated matter in the real language of men [and women]."

Creative writing, on the other hand, does attempt to address a general audience, using concrete language and conventions that all can understand. Thus, creative writing—to use an example from one of the arts that might speak for all of them—flies in the face of currently accepted practices and tendencies within the university, though its goal of addressing the broad general audience is discounted by a comfortable majority of scholars as pedestrian or boorish, as evidence of its lack of sophistication or rigor. The difficulties of addressing the general audience are not appreciated by those who have given up the desire to do so or never considered the possibility worthy of their attention. The fact that creative writers can speak in a common tongue, however, gives them a decided advantage when addressing undergraduates, or the world at large, most of whom have no inherent need, wish, or penchant to venture into the airy realms inhabited by most of their scholarly mentors.

In fact, this is true of what creative writers *do* as well as of what they *say* about what they do. As Scott Russell Sanders has noted: "The making of a poem or novel is an act of inclusion, a drawing in of readers to share an experience." Too often, "the making of literary theory is an act of exclusion, shutting out all but the cognoscenti."

The university at large is too given over to purely abstract and so-called rational modes of discourse and behavior. This is one reason that so many universities are boring students nearly to death. The arts and humanities are the natural corrective for this problem; and, in many cases, it is the absence of the arts or of a humanistic orientation in the humanities that has aggravated this difficulty. The influence of the natural and social sciences on the American university and on the arts and humanities, which has been so pervasive in our time, has often been to replace the arts and humanities with questions and procedures, with modes and methodologies, more natural to the sciences. We have seen the wholesale takeover of the curriculum by the abstract thinkers, the empiricists, and the political and social scientists. Often professors in the arts and humanities are behaving as if they were, in fact, scientists or social scientists.

Our primary curricular obsession these days, which we owe chiefly to the social sciences, is the insistence on viewing every subject through the filters of race, class, and gender. Certainly race, class, and gender are important issues—greatly in need of attention—but they are not the only issues. We also need to consider aesthetic, literary, and artistic issues again within universities. Analysis is an important mode for students to understand and use as well, but it is not the only mode worth studying, the only skill worth acquiring.

One difficulty with race, class, and gender—as rallying points or as avenues of inquiry—is that we are all born into these categories with very little opportunity to escape them. Thus, some are destined, it seems, to be victims, and others, victimizers from birth. Too often, rather than encouraging us to be more tolerant of those who were born into a different niche than ourselves, the new education encourages just the opposite—hatred, resentment, and feelings of entrapment. The old humanistic virtues—tolerance, communication, respect for the other—too often seem to be of little interest to those of the oppressed who are bent on defining their victimhood.

There are other ways of seeing and thinking that go beyond politics. Politics should not be at the intellectual center of our university culture because political thinking is endlessly contentious, finite, and adversarial—an excuse for everyone to pursue a purely personal or self-centered agenda, to attempt to climb one more mile up the slippery mountain of status and position. Too often the outcome of political thinking is that people end up yelling, "Me, me, me." I am more attracted to almost any metaphysics that moves further beyond the self and the limitations and cloying egotism of the self—which used to be one of the goals of the so-called liberal arts.

This, for me, is one of the many attractions of the arts. The arts teach empathy, and empathy is a powerful basis for moral action as well as a viable mode for understanding the world. The prophets had it right: life is suffering. I'm convinced that life is suffering for just about everyone, regardless of race, class, or gender—and that suffering *can* be redeeming, though sometimes it is only suffering. The arts open a window to help us understand others' misery, and, in this way, our hostility is blunted and we have a chance of finding peace ourselves. As Bob Dylan used to sing, "If I could stand inside your shoes, I would know what a drag it is to be you."

The natural and social sciences are not "the enemy," of course. We owe them a great deal, and we need to cultivate them and the perceptions they make possible. But these disciplines should *not* constitute the entirety of the curriculum. Some of those in the arts and humanities go about the business of perceiving the world and reflecting upon it in a somewhat different way than their counterparts in the sciences, and this is exactly why we need them.

Another way of thinking about these essential differences— between "philosophy" and "poetry"—may go beyond Plato's historic dichotomy, or offer a contemporary explanation for it. I owe this idea to some reading I have been doing in reader-response theory, an as-yet-unpublished series of interviews with writers and critics concerning their subjective responses as readers entitled "Seeing Their Way through the Text," by Ellen Esrock. I must say that I was surprised to learn that some readers, some very intelligent people, apparently do not visualize when reading, and some do not participate in any reading experience "kinesthetically," in the ways that I always have automatically. I had always assumed that such experiences were fairly common and similar for all readers of a certain level of intelligence and education.

Esrock set out to discover if "creative" writers and critics share the same perceptions *as* they read. If one reads, for instance, about a "locomotive in a jungle," what perceptions follow? Does everyone tend to visualize an actual engine sitting there, its wheels sinking into the quicksand, moss, and muck, ants exploring its crevices, snakes and giant termites crawling over its surfaces, moisture beading up along its hard surfaces, collecting in its gearbox and drivetrain, rust setting in everywhere, indignant monkeys squawking?

The novelist John Hawkes's description of his experience of reading about the locomotive was very close to what mine would be, what I previously took to be "normal." That is, all the visualizing and sensory experiences that Hawkes describes seem familiar and obvious to me; yet Hawkes must have felt as if he were trying to explain something nearly equivalent to the experience of being "on key" to someone who is tone-deaf, or who is pretending to be for the sake of the interview.

In contrast, when respondents such as philosopher William Gass and critic Geoffrey Hartman attempt to describe their experience of reading literary texts, their subjective responses to the "locomotive in the jungle" for instance, it sounds to me like the subjective description of a type of mental retardation. It is all abstraction to them, just words on a page. (But poems, one is reminded, should be "wordless as the flight of birds," and so should novels!) They don't see and feel the locomotive! Their discussions of the event are so abstract as to be stunningly tedious and mind-numbing. . . . Yet I know, of course, that Hartman, like Gass, is quite a brilliant fellow in his own way.

I conclude that, as humans, we must differ remarkably in some ways that I had previously thought we were mostly the same—in the ways we respond along the concreteness/abstractness spectrum, for instance; and, therefore, we must differ equally remarkably in our abilities to find significance both in literature and in life. Whether through training or inclination, these may be essential brain differences that determine us. If so, it would help to explain why we value different experiences and modes of discourse, why we may have trouble agreeing with one another about the ideal curriculum, and why certain abstract thinkers do not value art. *They've never tried it!* In any case, if these insights are real, we certainly need to account for such differences within education.

I remember the first time I attended a meeting of the Modern Language Association (MLA) as a young man. In the splendid corridors of the convention hotel I took note of the many bright-looking persons milling about, the corduroys and tweeds, and started to feel a sense of community and identity. I thought, "Yes, this is it—I've finally found it—this must be where I belong"—until I discovered what most of these same people were saying to one another when they got down to the business of the meeting. The goal there seemed to be to speak in more and more esoteric languages, often to trivialize, and to exclude, through what seemed to me to be the worst kind of intellectual arrogance.

We learn from the anthropologists that primates are creatures bent on establishing status hierarchies. We cannot really blame them for this, I suppose—since it is so entrenched in their natures. It is my theory that this is what the smartest people at the MLA were doing primarily—not laboring to explain the universe in ever more useful and intellectually challenging ways; laboring, rather, to establish better and better status hierarchies. It was a clever game of "we chosen few." We chosen few with IQs over 150 (or who wish our IQs were over 150) will now address one another in our own newly coined theoretical jargon and thereby distinguish ourselves from the rabble—from all those who are too stupid or ignorant to know what we are talking about—just as the social scientists do so well. Like the social scientists, our goal should be to attempt to make the obvious unreadable or, possibly, unknowable.

But I am not really opposed to these disciplines, to theory, or to abstract thought per se. I am only opposed to these methodologies so greedily, often inadvertently, pushing out all other avenues of thought and inquiry. Now, their triumph is so complete, their hold so great, that it is possible to say, with some poignancy: "Where are the *arts* in the liberal arts? Where are the *arts* in the arts and sciences? Where are the *arts* in the arts and humanities? Where is the *humanity* in the arts and humanities? I understand that it has become fashionable in certain critical circles to consider *humanistic* as a pejorative term for an outdated community of discourse. If so, I refuse to accept such usage and will work to rehabilitate the concept—because I believe that we badly need humanistic thought (and action). We badly need the humanities and the arts and all that they can tell us about the world and our own lives. Without them, we would be quite a different species.

All right. I think it is time to get down to the business of trying to describe my *theory of creative writing*. Since this is "new" and provisional, what I say here is not in the nature of an empirical proof. Let's just say it is, demonstrably, every bit as true as all the other theoretical rubrics we have seen circulating in English departments over the last several decades.

Creative writing can be, especially at the undergraduate level, one of the great undiscovered crossroads areas of the modern liberal arts curriculum, providing access to the study of literature—our treasury of style and language and our best ideas about human life—and an entrée to all sorts of vistas and mysteries, to the scaffoldings and underpinnings of the human imagination in all its forms.

Students are immersed in the process of imagination and synthesis and in the experience of relying on their own emotional, aesthetic, and visionary resources in ways too rarely explored in our curricula. Through participation as "creators," students come to understand, with greater immediacy, the motivations and accomplishments of the great writers of the past (or present), and their appetites are whetted to explore all literature (philosophy, history, theology, autobiography, criticism, even theory) in greater depth.

"A subject becomes liberal," according to Charles Frankel in his defense of the liberal arts, when it considers "ubiquitous and recurrent characteristics of the human scene and human destiny . . . [and] liberate[s] the individual from the parochialisms and the egotisms of time and place and self." According to that description, and others, the subject of creative writing, properly taught, is surely liberal, ameliorative, humanizing, civilizing, and capable of being used for the organization and illumination of ideas across the spectrum of human knowledge.

At the minimum, instruction in creative writing should cause students to become better writers and more discerning readers—and beyond that, more sensitive, knowledgeable, and articulate beings. My ongoing ambition as a teacher is to live up to these possibilities, to understand and articulate the most catholic dimensions of the subject area, to appreciate its mysteries, to seek serendipitous connections to other modes of thought and inquiry; to carry on, at the undergraduate level, in the best liberal arts tradition; to hold forth, at the graduate level, as a mentor, sympathetic critic, and fellow voyager who offers help on the way to professional development.

The "workshop method," sometimes maligned by those who know very little about it, is quite suitable for these purposes, so long as it includes close reading of manuscripts and clear and abundant feedback, allows room for potentially edifying digressions on craft, theory, terminology, and formal concepts, and includes some reading of outside examples as models or landmarks.

George Garrett points out in his essay "The Future of Creative Writing Programs" that the methodology of the writing workshop did not, in fact, originate at Iowa in the thirties but goes back to at least the sixteenth century.

> In the days of standard classical education, education in and about the classics, the composition of original Latin poetry and prose was one of the key elements. This practice continued for as long as the classics were the heart and guts of education. Thoreau, for instance, came out of exactly this kind of system, as did so many of the American nineteenth-century writers. . . . When we talk about the beginning and growth of creative writing in our time, . . . we are really talking about a *renewal, a revival*, the return, in somewhat different form and circumstances, of an old-fashioned, centuries-old form of teaching and learning rhetoric. The aims were different, but the ways and means are surprisingly alike.

Using this method, then, the main distinction I make between beginning undergraduates and more advanced students is that beginners need more guidance and more raw information, and therefore they usually benefit from a more prescriptive and structured approach. They also need, I think, to be impressed with the larger issues more frequently than their more knowledgeable peers, to be shown, for example, that creative writing is far more than mere technical mastery, far more than the effort merely to concoct a more elegant mousetrap, but is at the center of a number of crucial questions often posed by the liberal arts tradition: What is art and what is it good for? Is it good for anything? I argue that it is. What is the status of the imagination as a faculty of perception? Is the imagination educable? I argue that it is both educable and practical. What is human nature? Is it understandable? What is the nature of poetic truth? Even—what is life? And so on.

I try to avoid posing such questions in a purely abstract way, as a philosopher might, but try to make them implicit and concrete, to surround them with metaphor, fable, anecdote, and literary allusion. In my experience, undergraduates are desperate for answers to such questions—their faces show it—and they are desperate to hear the questions because, most of the time, no one has ever posed such questions to them before.

Creative writing is one of the few formal opportunities in American higher education for "self-discovery and self-creation," as Dave Smith has pointed out, and for an exploration of the imaginative faculty, perhaps our most underrated quality as human beings.

Undergraduates, in particular, can benefit enormously from their activities in these areas, whether or not they will ever prove to be gifted writers who may wish to consider working toward professional status.

The problem with the idea of teaching creative writing as a form of technical mastery is the fallacy that the art of writing may be taught using the principles of science. But the presumption that writing is the same intricate kind of purely formal or technical achievement as science and that it can only be performed by someone who has had years of study of the rational, analytical, and theoretical sort in order to understand the *principles* of writing is a bad idea. Students may be made to feel that unless they understand all these higher principles, which are at least as difficult as nuclear physics and which only someone like their professor has already mastered, they can't possibly even begin to perform the difficult feat of writing. The opposite problem sometimes occurs as well—when students are made to feel that the realm of art is so mystical and intangible that it is always just out of grasp, and that no standards or rules or conventions are there to guide them. Students may be caused to feel inadequate to the task of writing for several different reasons because a certain type of professor wants to feel indispensable.

I believe that there is useful technical information that can be transferred in the classroom, and that, through a steady diet of good reading and careful teaching, students can begin to get a grasp of the conventions. But more important than acquiring this "knowledge," even from the beginning, is pointing out what the student brings to the classroom, the quality of the imagination he or she already possesses and how that valuable attribute can be expanded. We are not primarily rational creatures. We can exercise rational thought, though it takes some considerable effort, discipline, and training. But we are, much more essentially, imaginative creatures. We use our imaginations without trying or thinking or even being aware that we are using them. We enjoy doing it.

The first issue of the creative writing class might be what sort of discipline and useful training can we bring to this very powerful attribute that students already possess and have quite a lot of unexamined experience exercising. Whatever else happens, they must be given permission to use it, since most of their previous teachers seem to have conspired to shut it off.

What's wrong with teaching only interpretation, analysis, history, and theory in English departments? I have to say: Because of what it leaves out, namely, the energy of art! the vision! the beauty! the suffering! It would be as if, in a music symposium, the "experts" spent all their time arguing about the rules of grammar and syntax of song lyrics and failed altogether to mention melody or rhythm or what the lyrics *mean* or the capacity of the whole beautiful, throbbing ensemble of attributes to make you feel goose bumps on a particular morning in June. My trouble with many of the theorists and abstractionists is that they don't seem to be able to hear the music at all. They are like the man John Cheever describes who "had lost the gift of evoking the perfumes of life: seawater, the smoke of burning hemlock, and the breasts of women. He had damaged, you might say, the ear's innermost chamber." Or perhaps he never had it to lose. But, to put the best face on it, let us simply say that when the room grows still, in the privacy of their minds, these people simply hear different music than I do. These are, perhaps, basic perceptual differences over preferred ways of seeing and essential habits of knowing.

My point is that all would benefit by recognizing that critics and creative writers have certain goals and pedagogical practices in common and much to gain by cooperation with one another—though they do inhabit different discourse communities and therefore have a difficult time communicating. Also, in some major respects, critics and writers are trying to accomplish very different ends and using different modes and styles of knowing to achieve their ends. But these differences are perfectly all right so long as they do not lead to internecine hostility, for, ultimately, writers and critics must sink or swim—together.

THE THEORY OF
CREATIVE WRITING II

The Uses of the Imagination and
the Revenge of the Pink Typewriter

Literature, like all the arts, is primarily *about* imagination, empathy, emotion, and aesthetic and poetic truths—not *about* analysis or intellect primarily, though it may, of course, represent a challenge to the intellect. Therefore, if we wish to experience the arts and to know them, why spend all our time engaged in purely analytical and theoretical approaches? Pure reason and abstraction are fine—necessary—in the sciences, but they are often useless in the arts and humanities, as should be evident from the present predicament of those disciplines. The rationalistic mentality is responsible for every sort of mischief, for reducing great art—that which gives us a reason to live—to nihilism, absurdity, and futility.

What the creative writer brings to the classroom is a healthy contrast to the usual sorts of analytical and theoretical practices. Although the writer may engage in practical criticism, when the writer asks students to write a poem or a story, he or she asks them to pay attention to the imaginative, the emotional, and the aesthetic aspects of writing and to explore and use these resources within themselves. The students must approach the work from the point of view of the artist or creator, and that experience is . . . playful, . . . infuriating, . . . exciting, . . . challenging—potentially all the things that art is, at its best. This process, this creative effort, is an attempt to synthesize the world, to see it as a whole, rather than to tear the world apart or to systematize it in order to understand it; and in many ways it is a more demanding activity than the purely cerebral processes of analysis or theorizing.

I believe strongly that the mental processes exercised in creative-writing classes need much more attention in our culture—the attempt to integrate instead of, always, to analyze or to make abstract;

not to take feeling out of our mental processes, but to put it back in. Everyone engaged in teaching in *every* subject area ought to teach imaginative inquiry. Some of our so-called well-educated college students are not so well educated without such experience.

Perhaps it is not surprising that former president Bush, who had such trouble with the "vision thing" and who copped out so completely in his responsibility for defending the National Endowment for the Arts, would neglect to put the arts in any form in his educational recommendations for the future as described in his America 2000 plan. But he did not act alone. He had help!

What the best art has to offer us is vision, and we need it! The worst of popular culture oversimplifies the world and teaches citizens to leap to foolish conclusions about character, motive, loyalties of every sort, and the nature of the world. It creates a world of black-and-white choices where human character is easily, instantaneously readable. Art says not so fast—life is not that simple. Art teaches empathy, a higher and wiser form of knowing.

The longer I think about it, the more I am amazed at the small place given in the curricula of American colleges and universities to the education of the imagination—our most important mental faculty. I believe the imagination is the great underrated domain of human perception, far more natural to us, and therefore far more practical, than analytical and other abstract modes of perception. Yet analytical and abstract modes have so dominated the college curriculum that there is hardly any place left for education of the imagination—except in the arts and, occasionally, in the humanities.

The imagination is like a muscle—it can be strengthened through use. It is educable. Conversely, without use, the imagination can wither and atrophy, or never develop properly. If we do not expose our citizens to an education of the imagination, we may have a high price to pay; for failure of the imagination is certain to have serious consequences—not only an absence of innovative technologies and competitive businesses, but also imperfect and inaccurate perceptions, a lack of ability to understand and cope, and even violent crime. We may be breeding a nation of sheep, citizens unable to discriminate between the truth and the lie, citizens easily swayed by spurious appeals, citizens incapable of imagining the consequences of their actions or alternatives to violence.

At present we have a substantial and growing segment of the population in the United States made up of moral and imaginative

idiots. Such citizens go through their lives committing moral out-
rages. Most normal people play out their violent impulses through
fantasies and thus have no need to act them out in the real world. It
is, in a sense, through the suppleness of their imaginations that they
navigate the choppy waters of life, which, I'm convinced, represent
a struggle for nearly everyone.

Jerome L. Singer has written of the link between lack of imagination and aggression in several studies of delinquents and criminals.

> The risks of an undeveloped fantasy life may include delinquency, vio-
> lence, overeating, and the use of dangerous drugs. . . . Children of equal
> intelligence but unequal imaginations also differ in their sensitivity to
> reality. We often assume that children with active fantasy lives have a
> weaker grasp on hard facts than their pedestrian brothers and sisters. But
> the truth may be just the opposite. Research indicates that children whose
> games are poor in make-believe and fantasy are likely to have trouble
> recalling and integrating the details of events they hear about. . . . A well-
> developed fantasy life seems to be partly responsible for independence,
> tranquility, and realism.

We have Freud to blame for the view that the imagination is
escapist. Freud recognized that children's play is succeeded by adult
fantasy but tended to treat both activities as evasions of reality. (Freud
considered science and art evasions as well.) But Erikson, Jung, and
other major thinkers since Freud have regarded fantasy much more
positively and have been interested in its implications. According to
Erikson, play "provides the infantile form of the human propensity
to create model situations in which aspects of the past are relived,
the present re-presented and renewed, and the future anticipated."
Erikson also felt that humans should "vie with each other for the
right vision."

Another persuasive commentator on this subject was the noted
child therapist Bruno Bettelheim. In *The Uses of Enchantment,* Bettelheim set out to show "how fairy tales represent in imaginative
form what the process of healthy human development consists of,
and how the tales make such development attractive for the child to
engage in." Bettelheim insists that his work made obvious to him the
realization that if children were reared "so that life was meaningful to
them, they would not need special help." He was confronted, he says,

> with the problem of deducing what experiences in a child's life are most
> suited to promote this ability to find meaning in his life; to endow life in

general with more meaning. . . . [S]econd in importance [after the impact of parents] is our cultural heritage, when transmitted to the child in the right manner. When children are young, it is literature that carries such information best.

In child or adult, the unconscious is a powerful determinant of behavior. When the unconscious is repressed and its content denied entrance into awareness, then eventually the person's conscious mind will be partially overwhelmed by derivations of these unconscious elements, or else he is forced to keep such rigid, compulsive control over them that his personality may become severely crippled. But when unconscious material is to some degree permitted to come to awareness and worked through in imagination, its potential for causing harm—to ourselves and others—is much reduced; some of its forces can then be made to serve positive purposes.

Freud's prescription is that only by struggling courageously against what seem like overwhelming odds can man succeed in wringing meaning out of his existence. . . . This is exactly the message that fairy tales get across to the child in manifold form: that a struggle against severe difficulties in life is unavoidable, is an intrinsic part of human existence— but that if one does not shy away, but steadfastly meets unexpected and often unjust hardships, one masters all obstacles and at the end emerges victorious. . . . Morality is not the issue in these tales, but rather, assurance that one can succeed.

Morality may not be the point of fairy tales, or the primary purpose of grown-up art either, but I would argue that the empathetic awareness fostered by fairy tales and other childhood excursions into the imagination that begin to teach us to see the world from someone else's point of view is a strong incentive to moral behavior.

Art helps create a readiness to experience that strange process where you actually move outside your own body and for a while you feel what it feels like to be someone else. Surely this feeling is a basis for kindness, for forbearance, for communication, for moral response. Without empathetic awareness, we are hopeless, I think, as a species. Art teaches empathy, and many students need experience in this area, some students in particular. If they don't get it somewhere along the way, they've wasted their educations, I think.

I have said that the imagination, which is sometimes thought of as a purely escapist faculty, is, in fact, practical. How can this be? Whether we are reading about characters in a novel or simply trying to understand the people in our own lives, we must use our imaginations minute by minute to get through our lives. We must imagine one another—and ourselves. We do, in fact, use our imaginations to understand one another; and, if we are normal, we do *not* imagine without any basis in fact. We imagine *given* the facts. Most of us know that simply making things up to please ourselves—without regard for the facts—is a strategy that does not work for anyone for very long. If we are intelligent, we adjust our visions of one another each time we receive new information. An important aspect of intelligence is the ability to use your imagination, given the facts, to understand someone else, simply to be better able to predict that person's behavior and to be able to understand your relationship to them. This is, of course, one of the essential concerns and *processes* of fiction and drama, exercising this particular human capacity and pushing it, in the best work, to very high levels of discrimination.

As humans, we are forever engaged by the mystery of human character and behavior, by the potential revealed in a human face. It is said that dogs, who mark their territories by urinating, can detect one part of urine in fifty thousand parts of water. This is why dogs behave as they do, constantly sniffing and making fine distinctions that we know very little about. Humans have, I think, a similar peculiar obsession with face reading, and we go about it with equally stupendous powers of differentiation. All of us look essentially the same, after all: two eyes, a nose, and a mouth in approximately the same locations; yet we are able to detect differences that must be nearly microscopic. We are so adept at this that we can tell one another apart! Further still, we seem to think that we can read character, motive, and intention in the human face. We do not accomplish this through reason or logic but through the imagination. We seem to think we know when virtue may be found there, and it pleases us. We seem to think we can recognize beauty, and we worship it without reason. Most probably, this natural face-reading talent that we have, as in canines, has powerful survival value, especially in such a highly social species as ours and one with such inferior noses. The dogs have their mighty proboscises to get them through their lives, and we have our good eyesight and our luminous imaginations to do the important work.

Another aspect of getting through life moment to moment—which undoubtedly makes use of the imaginative faculty—is in figuring out what you want for yourself, what and who you want to *be,* and then setting out to live your life, to do things in such a way that you will end up at that point, if possible. It seems to me that this process is almost entirely practical and almost entirely imaginative in basis. And one's ability to perform it shrewdly or not has enormous consequences. A French wit of the nineteenth century who was apparently in awe of the writer Victor Hugo is said to have remarked: "Victor Hugo is a madman who believes he is Victor Hugo." One could say the same in our own time, I suppose, of Madonna. Each of us is a creative or not-so-creative imaginer who believes that we are who we say we are. Each of us creates an identity, a self, through imaginative means and our best understanding of the facts of the case, and we can choose to enjoy a relatively generous interpretation or conception of ourselves, as Hugo did, or a relatively more conservative one; and then, as new facts come in, we make adjustments.

Often these adjustments are based on further imaginative constructions. We live constantly on the basis of imaginings that we revise from day to day. We are essentially mind-creatures, and our essential mental activity is to use our imaginations in a purely practical way to live our lives.

Yet another illustration of how literature and the imaginative faculty have a practical benefit is their ability to help us navigate in *time.* One of the original pleasures of the novel as a form was that the novel permitted the reader to imagine the *whole* of a life. We have the unfortunate problem that we never get to *see* our whole lives. We live our lives minute by minute, in a fragmented sort of way. We try to cast ahead and imagine the shape of what will come, as best we can. We try to remember in some detail what life has been, as best we can, and to use that information, if possible. But we never really know what it will be, until we live it; and we never really know entirely what it has been, until we get to the end of it. But when we get to the end of it, it's over. The value of the novel in this regard is that by seeing others' lives, as a whole, we are better able to imagine our own lives, as a whole, and thus better able to compose our own lives, better able to choose how to live them.

Also, of course, literature gives us the incredible opportunity to "live" lives we could never even imagine on our own, trapped as we are within the confines of our own lives. So literature offers the priceless additional benefit, not only of revealing the whole of lives, but also of providing a wide range of totally different lives for us to contemplate, so that we can compare the content of other lives, minute by minute—the aspirations, the mistakes, the victories, the things said and done and the things not said and done—to our own.

In trying to navigate in *time,* we constantly replay the past and we constantly project alternative futures; and these memories and projections are functions of the imagination as well. If there is anything in particular that distinguishes us from what we call the lower creatures, I think it is this capacity to range through time within ourselves, to escape the eternal present of the animal world. Quite possibly, this process is the first step in a new stage of evolution.

In any case, memory is a peculiar thing. We think of memory as having an exact factual relationship to the events we recall, but in many instances it does not. Memory is rather elusive, in fact. Every time you remember the past, a little bit of the place, time, and mood of the present rubs off onto the past. By the time you remember the same experience twenty years later, the memory will have evolved and you may have changed considerably as well, and the original event might seem very different both from the original event itself and from your earliest memories of it. So I would argue that even memory is a product of imagination.

It is probably of some importance to make every effort to remain accurate as we remember our lives, to keep the imagination in line with what actually happened. Otherwise, we take the chance of losing our sense of everything, of losing our sense of ourselves.

One thing that creative writers want, and one luxury that writing allows them to have, is a better, clearer relationship to their pasts—a better sense of memory and a clearer relationship to the present. Writing allows them to slow down the rapid-fire progression of events and examine them, evaluate them, and store them— otherwise, life escapes. Otherwise, the merry-go-round of events overwhelms memory. How *can* one hold it still long enough to get any sense of it? Life is fleeting. How else *can* one preserve it? Writing fiction is one way. Reading fiction is another.

Creative writers, like other artists, are people who are perhaps more frequently overwhelmed by their own feelings and imaginings than ordinary citizens. Writers have the habit of writing their feelings down in order to try to understand them and to try to relieve the pressure of excessive emotion. Some writers are more able than others to translate their efforts to achieve clarity—through groping with bewilderment and anguish—into useful social documents.

Once the writing is finished, however, if the writer has done the job well enough, the experience is trapped right there on the page, permanently and indelibly, for anyone to use. This seems quite obvious, but it is, in fact, quite miraculous. To see the world *through* the mind, through the memory, through the imagination, through the language, of a great writer is potentially a consciousness-expanding experience in the best sense. Potentially, it is as powerful as a brain transplant, without half the difficulty. It changes you. It changes your imagination and your capacity to imagine, so that you may never be the same again. If it works, it makes you smarter, more empathetic, and more eloquent. If you cause it to work often enough, you finally have a chance to experience what we might wish to call, without any irony whatsoever, "a good education."

In 1963 I lived in an old house in Yellow Springs, Ohio, that had been split into apartments. Upstairs from me lived a student-artist who spent most of his time out in our backyard banging on, prying at, and unscrewing a truckload of dilapidated school desks. While I would be sipping my coffee and trying to write a new story, I would stare at him out my kitchen window and wonder what in God's name he was doing out there. What he was doing was this: He made a huge pile of these disassembled desk parts, and then he laboriously reassembled them into absurd sculptural shapes and painted them pink, so that, soon, we had a backyard full of odd pink objects that had never before been seen on the planet. You might say that he was an early sixties deconstructionist, working in an uncharacteristic medium, somewhat ahead of his time.

Another of his creations had been mounted prominently on a wall at the art building on campus. It was a typewriter that he had jumped up and down on several times and then smashed with a sledgehammer and painted that unmistakable pink. The keys were bent around in a truly heartbreaking sort of way. I imagined that he was seeking revenge for too many painful years spent in classrooms that bored him, which I could understand, but I found his pink-typewriter piece especially haunting and upsetting. It seemed to me a potent symbol for the hatred and distrust that some feel toward the written word and the world of literacy and, perhaps, for civilization itself.

I had shared some of this same suspicion, frustration, and anger—who hasn't who's been to school?—but I had not given in to it so completely as my friend with the pink typewriter. My own response to the pressures of undergraduate angst, unfulfilled potential, too many deadlines, and too many papers to write had been to give in in a different way, to perform what was asked of me, to meet the deadlines, to *use* the typewriter and to value what it produced.

Many nonliterary artists, of course, rightfully distrust the verbal as a manifestation of the conscious mind, something they associate with tyranny and stereotypical responses and bad art. Many artists, in their art, are busily trying to escape the strictures of the conscious mind; and this is, perhaps, why they represent such a worry to Plato and to the left-brain-abstraction-and-reason addicts within the university and beyond. But the pink typewriter had in it a level of despair and misunderstanding that troubled me as well.

I suppose you could say that the pink typewriter was a subversive piece of art, and Plato and William Bennett and George Will might wish to banish my former apartment mate—and *me* for living in the same house—for the shocking overtness of his creation, or what they might imagine to be its foolishness. (For all I know the young man who created the art may have gone on to become an insurance salesman, and, unless he received some encouragement, he probably did.) But I, for one, have come to value the example of the pink typewriter because it reminds me in a vivid way—as a writer and a teacher of writing—of what I am up against, of what we are all up against, if we value civilization.

THE IOWA MYSTIQUE AND THOSE WHO LOATHE IT

Here is the argument, usually made by writers, critics, or professors of writing who earned undergraduate degrees at elite colleges but who have never acquired an M.F.A. themselves, who feel threatened by what they imagine to be a proliferation of competitors, or who don't believe that people with SAT scores lower than their own deserve to participate in the cultural enterprise:

> *There is some considerable evidence that American writing has become too academic, claustrophobic, and mediocre. The cause of this problem is directly traceable to the fact that our writers have been spending far too much time studying for M.F.A.s and then teaching at places such as Iowa, stifled unto extreme perplexity and boredom in the ivory tower, absorbed in trivial matters. Thus, they fail to grasp the larger issues and passions of our time. They have become creators and victims of a system that rewards careerist mediocrity, mere "workshop" literature, which is the literary equivalent of hamburgers from McDonald's. No one wants to read this rubbish except other careerist creative writers, who are multiplying at an alarming rate; and the fact that there is no serious audience for this work proves that it is essentially worthless. If we wish to revitalize American writing and clean up this pitiful situation, the real writers should go back to their garrets and barstools where they belong, and the hoards of mediocre students with no legitimate talent for writing anyway should be forced to study other subjects and to try to become productive members of society.*

I have heard this stupid argument repeated in various forms so often that I think it is about time to say something about it. The main thing I would like to say is: Shut up and go away! You don't know what you're talking about.

Iowa takes it on the chin so often because the Iowa program is the oldest of its kind and because it is the prototype for the graduate degree in creative writing, the M.F.A. degree, and because it is still the most prestigious writing program in the country. But anyone criticizing Iowa in the usual ways is criticizing, by extension, all the other programs in creative writing, which are its offspring, and, often, the idea that creative writing or imaginative inquiry can be, or ought to be, taught at all.

The conditions of American society and of the American university are such that anyone wishing to search for a more spiritual life and at least a temporary escape from materialistic values—the sort of life represented, for instance, by a devotion to truth and truth-seeking, by a commitment to examining one's own life (in the manner of Socrates or of James, of Faulkner, of Whitman or of Jane Austen)—is ridiculed and stifled! I think we should stop doing it! Is it really so important whether or not this line of spiritual inquiry or method of education leads, in every case, to the production of great works? The traditional pursuit of scholarship does not always lead to the production of great works either. What is so terrible about helping to educate a certain number of literate and articulate citizens (with master's degrees in writing) who complete their college educations and who still like to read and write?

Where else should writers go? Where should students of writing go? The English departments have not always greeted them with open arms—that's for certain. Some arts colleges have taken them in on the theory that creative writing belongs, pedagogically, with the other art forms. But many of the other art forms still feel threatened by "the word," so this practice has not become the norm. Unfortunately, it seems that the rest of American culture wants writers even less than English departments or arts schools do. The rest of American culture does not often understand or value what writers produce—unless it *sells* and therefore is given the imprimatur of anything in America that sells. But what sells readily is often the most conventional or escapist, the most plot-ridden and derivative, and the least demanding work. Where should *serious* writers go? Literary achievement does not often spring full-blown from the head of Zeus. It has to be cultivated—somewhere.

Like it or not, there really is no place else for writers to go other than the university in American culture. Whether they like it or not, or whether their colleagues like it or not, writers are intellectuals and are part of our intellectual subculture. It makes no sense to ask them to spend their lives working as janitors, bartenders, farmhands, or delivering boxes door to door for UPS. There is nothing inherently edifying in any of that. "Some are drawn to the university," according to Scott Russell Sanders,

> as the last sanctuary for books in a marginally literate culture. . . . For all students, regardless of talent, and for faculty members as well, the university can serve as a substitute for the cafe, the salon, the literary circle. . . . What the workshop ideally provides is a community of people who read widely and well, who savor words, who enjoy using their minds, who take seriously what young writers wish to take seriously. Such a community is all the more vital in a society where books in general and literature in particular have been shoved to the margin, where language has been debased, where the making of art seems foolish beside the making of money.

Also, "[C]reative writing programs have provided a refuge," according to David Fenza, "from the babble of literary specialists. Writing workshops and seminars have been places where one could talk about books in a public tongue, and talk about them as if they were extensions of one's life—books as talismans and friendly accomplices. In writing workshops and seminars, stories and poems are spoken of as works with meanings, rather than as texts with endless indeterminacies."

Dave Smith has pointed out that critics who complain about the spread of creative-writing instruction and who argue that it dilutes the quality of our writing have their facts seriously out of perspective: "One of their complaints is the size, the cost of a writing program. It is worth remembering that one Air Force bomber costs more than the entire budget for the National Endowment for the Arts; that no school in this country provides the salaries, support, or attention to creative writing that it does for computers, music, engineering, biology, or ROTC; that in every state university . . . the athletic budget for laundry alone exceeds the budget for creative writing."

Critics who complain that there are too many creative-writing programs often quote inflated numbers. In fact, there are about sixty or so M.F.A. programs, or, on average, slightly over one per state. Is this number really going to lead our nation down the primrose path toward intellectual bankruptcy? I doubt it. It's a big country, Jim. Out of three thousand colleges and universities, there are approximately thirty programs wherein it is possible to earn a Ph.D. with "creative dissertation," and there are also about one hundred and forty schools that offer creative writing as part of an M.A. program (though only a handful of these are truly programs *in* creative writing). Then there are a few hundred undergraduate programs that offer introductory courses in creative writing as part of an undergraduate major. All things considered, these figures seem rather modest to me.

Yet, to hear some critics complain, one would think we were near the brink of a literary Armageddon. In *Talents and Technicians*, for instance, John W. Aldridge blames the M.F.A. programs for all manner of crimes and malfeasance. They are responsible, according to Aldridge, for producing what he calls "the new assembly-line fiction," as practiced by writers such as Ann Beattie, Frederick Barthelme, Bobbie Ann Mason, and Raymond Carver, whose work he finds "like Type O blood" and "instantly forgettable." (One begins to wonder whose memory should be at issue here.) Writers of this sort, Aldridge continues,

> learned in the MFA writing programs that very often when such underdone fiction was presented during a workshop session, the students assumed that a profound meaning was contained somewhere within it but that they were too stupid to perceive it. They therefore were inclined to praise the work without in the least understanding it rather than take the risk of exposing themselves as stupid. Thus, failure to achieve meaning becomes widely and enthusiastically recognized by the timid as extreme subtlety of meaning.

Aldridge goes on to claim that *"because of the homogenizing influence of their training in the creative writing schools* [italics mine], writers like Beattie, Frederick Barthelme, Mason, and Carver seem virtually interchangeable, and any one of their novels and stories might conceivably have been written by almost any one of them." This is ridiculous! Even if one could agree that these four highly original and accomplished writers were similar (which I cannot), and that they deserve to be singled out as examples to be deplored (which I certainly do not)—what about their educational backgrounds? Apparently Aldridge was so possessed by his delusions about M.F.A. programs that he didn't even bother to check! In fact, only Carver, among the four, even attended an M.F.A. program. Mason has a Ph.D. from the University of Connecticut; Beattie studied for a Ph.D. but left before finishing; and Barthelme has an M.A. Ironically, the two younger writers who Aldridge seems willing to single out for praise—Lorrie Moore and T. Coraghessan Boyle—both *did* pursue study within M.F.A. programs (though Boyle finished a Ph.D. as well).

Despite the glib generalities and outright errors one encounters in the criticism of M.F.A. programs, the ongoing blather has created two enduring interrelated myths that are especially inaccurate (both of which John W. Aldridge subscribes to): one, that graduates from workshops all write in the same homogeneous, "workshop" style, in part because they are isolated from real life; and two, that workshops are so lacking in rigor that they coddle and overpraise young writers, to the point that they end up suffering from illusions of grandeur or illusions about future employment.

Maybe somewhere among the sixty or so graduate creative-writing programs these sins may be found occasionally. But, in my experience, the real problems and challenges for graduate students in creative writing are exactly the reverse of these.

More often, being a member of a workshop is "like being one of 60 cats locked in a closet," as Larry Levis has aptly observed; and there is seldom any agreement about aesthetic matters or even about individual manuscripts. Unadulterated praise is a commodity in extremely short supply, while moderately restrained contempt and even derision are more often the staples of the day. Keeping one's ego intact, and one's talent on line, in the face of tough criticism is the hardest job; but even getting the writing done may not be easy, because usually grad students have to work at *something else* in order to stave off poverty. "People in workshops also work in restaurants, on farms, in factories, and in offices; they have children and affairs; they miss the work, people, and places they have left behind," in the words of David Fenza. They *do* have real lives, in other words, as real as any, and why shouldn't they? The valuable part of being in a workshop is that a writer may find a helpful mix of instruction, suffering, rivalry, resistance, and congeniality.

When a young man switches from premed to English and announces that he wants to be a writer, as I did, his elders are likely to recommend a trip to the psychiatrist, and his girlfriend's mother is likely to advise her daughter to hurry up and find someone with better prospects. So for me, the most important feature of the Iowa Writers Workshop was that in Iowa City a world existed where writing was considered both important and honorable work and where real writers lived and struggled, writers who had made it, and other hopefuls like me, who hadn't yet and maybe never would. The assembled novices had many of the same interests and ambitions as I did, although they had as many theories of how to get where they were going as there were heads in the room; many of them had the talent to know they weren't fooling themselves, and if they didn't yet know, they were there to find out. Most regarded writing as a desirable, achievable, and even a noble calling.

I hasten to point out that the record of Iowa speaks for itself; and anyone who knows the record would be worse than foolish to put forward the sort of criticism described earlier. Iowa graduates have won every major literary prize we have to bestow, from the Pulitzer and the Yale to the Bollingen and the National Book Award. To remove the Iowa names from the pantheon of American letters would leave a gigantic abyss. Iowa students have included: Flannery O'Connor, Tennessee Williams, Wallace Stegner, John Gardner, Margaret Walker, Raymond Carver, Gail Godwin, John Irving, Jayne Anne Phillips, T. Coraghessan Boyle, Robley Wilson, Jane Smiley, James Alan McPherson, Bharati Mukherjee, Clark Blaise, John Casey, W. P. Kinsella, Richard Bausch, Bob Shacochis, Laurie Alberts, Allan Gurganus, Ron Hansen, Joy Williams, Andre Dubus, Mark Costello, Al Young, Ted Weesner, Jonathan Penner, Gish Jen, John Edgar Wideman, James McConkey, William Kittredge, Denis Johnson, C. E. Poverman, Asa Baber, James Crumley, Sandra Cisneros, Robert Olen Butler, Robie Macauley, Colin Harrison, Kathryn Harrison, W. D. Snodgrass, William Stafford, Robert Bly, Marvin Bell, Michael S. Harper, Donald Justice, Albert Goldbarth, Tess Gallagher, James Tate, Joy Harjo, Mark Strand, Mona Van Duyn, Rita Dove, Anthony Hecht, Robert Dana, Jane Cooper, Constance Urdang, Knute Skinner, William Dickey, Larry Levis, Peter Klappert, Jerry Bumpus, Roger Weingarten, Philip Levine, Charles Wright, James Whitehead, Jorie Graham, James Galvin, Susan Power, and Deborah Digges, just to name a small number.

Iowa professors have included: John Cheever, Philip Roth, Kurt Vonnegut, Janet Burroway, Robert Penn Warren, Vance Bourjaily, Doris Grumbach, Paul Engle, Wallace Stegner, Walter Van Tilberg Clark, Malcolm Cowley, Marguerite Young, Robert Coover, Hilma Wolitzer, James Alan McPherson, Frederick Exley, Richard Yates, C. D. B. Bryan, Robert Lowell, John Berryman, John Crowe Ransom, Anthony Burgess, Nelson Algren, Mary Lee Settle, John Hawkes, Madison Smartt Bell, Paule Marshall, R. V. Cassill, John Leggett, T. Coraghessan Boyle, Dianne Benedict, Bette Pesetsky, Angus Wilson, Sandra McPherson, Frank Conroy, Richard Hugo, Marvin Bell, Louise Glück, Mark Strand, Galway Kinnell, Jose Donoso,

Carol Muske, Leonard Michaels, Carolyn Kizer, William Matthews, Stanley Plumly, Barry Hannah, Edward Hoagland, Ian McEwan, Larry Levis, Hortense Calisher, Dan Wakefield, George Starbuck, Rosalyn Drexler, Lynne Sharon Schwartz, James Salter, Gerald Stern, James Galvin, and Jorie Graham. The closest American letters has yet advanced toward an American equivalent of Periclean Greece is at Iowa. All those who think they are helping American culture by berating Iowa and the M.F.A. degree should hang their heads in shame and self-loathing.

In a midcareer appraisal of the Iowa empire that he helped to create, Paul Engle wrote: "Of course, there are risks. The mild frost of a university air may kill the tender plant. Excess of self-consciousness can slow down a talent which has little momentum. . . . V. S. Pritchett laments," Engle continued, "that the American university may induce 'an unnatural hostility to vulgarity' in the writer. I have seen twenty-five years of American writers at a university. Have no fear. They will not lose their vulgarity."

FINDING ONE'S TRUE VOICE

Everyone knows the story about the manager of the paint factory in Elyria, Ohio, a man approaching forty who longed to be a writer and who suddenly one day discovered his voice and arose from his desk and walked out of the factory, never to return, believing he was Sherwood Anderson. Such stories involving references to "the voice" are part of writers' lore and are presumably instructive.

If a writer starts out thinking that what he or she most needs to learn is technique, his or her progress, in fact, may be poor, slow, or never realized. To pursue "technique" is to resort to the rationalistic methods of a technological culture and to the idea that all problems should have technical or intellectual solutions. Writing fiction according to this principle may become equivalent to the solving of complicated crossword puzzles. Although fiction writing sometimes calls for such solutions, most of the time it calls for the use of another sort of mind-set altogether. Compared to this orientation, technique is nothing but trickery or lying or showing off.

Far better to try to grow in your art by searching for "your voice" or learning how to listen to "voices," in the manner of Sherwood Anderson. But what is the voice and how does one go about finding it?

First of all, in one regard you have no choice. You were born into a certain family in a certain region of a certain country that used language in a certain way. Most likely, at the deepest level of your unconscious, or at the floor of your mind, that inheritance is a kind of bedrock or coral reef. Through education and travel, through exposure to other dialects or other languages and the ripples of current changes in usage that we all absorb, layers of influence have been laid down upon this essential topography, like the masses of rock, sand, gravel, and clay carried along and deposited by glacial ice.

Writers lucky enough to have been born in the American South or in some obscure bailiwick where the language is rich and exotic may not feel compelled to seek, as some writers do, to escape or to repudiate this mother tongue. But wherever one is born and however flat, dull, crude, or inexpressive you may believe your linguistic legacy to be, and however determinedly you might struggle to elude it, you do so at your own peril. A first step in locating voice is in coming to realize what you have inherited and in coming to terms with it. Every language, no matter how apparently gauche, has the potential for transformation as a literary idiom. Consider the example of Mark Twain.

A quality of voice that may emerge from the process of returning to one's linguistic roots is something we might call honesty or integrity or clarity. Art is primarily "about" emotion, imagination, empathy, and energy. It is also "about" truth and lying and about the human effort to separate the truth from the lie. Start out by finding the truth of one's own tongue.

THE LEARNED VOICE

Conventional Ph.D. education in English is a process of inculcating, and of the students' absorbing, a certain voice, the "learned" voice—pompous, slightly patronizing, critical, presumably objective. Most signs of feeling, of the personal, are removed. Even after they have become immersed in the ebb and flow of life within their departments and no longer have to, graduates of this system who have become instructors of English often delight in "talking graduate school" to one another, in parading their "learned" mannerisms, in attacking and parrying to see if their fellows can still answer back in the accepted, the certified, lingo.

And then they try to teach this same voice and attitude to their undergraduates. The more closely the student imitates the "learned" voice, the more he or she is rewarded. This approach and this voice do sometimes help teach analysis and orderliness and fit in nicely with the technocratic requirements of postindustrial society, preparing students to become functionaries within the technocracy. But their dominance within English departments often works contrary to liberalizing or humanizing values presumably espoused by the faculties of such departments—because of what they leave out and because of the attitude they engender: that analysis and "objectivity" are the only approaches worth cultivating, either in reading or in writing . . . and such teaching is often puzzling and destructive for students who wish to do any other sort of writing, to cultivate any other sort of voice.

THE ANALOGY TO SINGING

In thinking about the use of voice in fiction, it is helpful to consider the use of voice by famous singers or rock stars—not just any singers, but the few, the greatest, vocalists. For most people in our civilization, singers do a better job of communicating emotion than writers do, and singers are, in fact, more widely admired and loved. What is it about the most inspired vocalists that draws us to them?

For one thing, the singer enables us to feel his or her emotions without embarrassment or contempt. To accomplish this, the singer is involved in a kind of emotional trance, lost in the song, buoyed up by the expression of actual passion—something we all seek but rarely find—and swept along by it to a point beyond self-consciousness. There is a kind of elegant detachment, an ecstatic commitment to rhythmic, to organic, truths.

One of the reasons that voice-sync singing is sometimes so painful to watch is that it deprives us of this firsthand emotional experience of the song and reduces the emotion to a lie or, at best, to the memory of an emotion.

When the writer of fiction finds his or her true voice, the writing takes on the same purity or integrity as the haunting song sung by a great singer, and for many of the same reasons. Listening to that voice takes very little effort, because real emotion is irresistible.

Seeking one's voice is a matter of trying to make oneself the perfect instrument for the song. It is an abandonment to the one authentic voice or the many surprising voices within. If this sounds suspiciously like "listening to the muse," it should. The idea of the muse has been the predominant idea about artistic inspiration since the beginning of time, and one reason it has been so persuasive is that it is, indeed, very close to the truth.

LITERARY
SATIRISTS

T. CORAGHESSAN BOYLE
AND THE RENAISSANCE
OF THE SHORT STORY

At the fiftieth-anniversary celebration of the Iowa Writers Workshop in 1986, Raymond Carver and T. Coraghessan Boyle were members of a panel called "Renaissance of the Short Story." Carver stood up and explained why he thought realism was the dominant mode in the short story, always had been and always would be. Coming from the man who had helped to turn the American story back toward realism, it was quite a plausible and convincing statement, presented very much in the manner of a Carver story—direct, spare, authoritative.

Boyle stood up to respond. He was wearing red Converse All-Stars, a black T-shirt, and a boiled-linen jacket. He was as loose-jointed as a spider monkey, and his electric hair would have made an inviting roosting place for several species of birds. In short, he resembled a character from a story by T. Coraghessan Boyle. Boyle said, essentially, "Ray is absolutely right about his kind of fiction, but that's only half the story. Some of us can't write that way and shouldn't have to, and there ought to be a place for us in the world of literature too; and in fact, there is."

Perhaps the best argument for the accuracy of Boyle's statement that day in Iowa City is the success of his own work. Over the last decade and a half, he has given us ten books, six novels (including *World's End*, a winner of the PEN/Faulkner Award), and four collections of stories (his fourth collection of stories, *Without A Hero*, appeared in 1994; and his sixth novel, *The Tortilla Curtain*, in 1995).

In his story collection, *If the River Was Whiskey*, which I would like to discuss as a case in point, we are faced once more with a sensibility keen about comedy, playfulness, protean horror, madcap imaginative leaps, and the dazzling excesses that have become Boyle's trademarks.

Boyle has, in fact, become the most credible inheritor of the mantle of those postmodernist writers of the sixties and early seventies—

Barth, Donald Barthelme, Coover, Hawkes, Pynchon, Vonnegut—whose excesses, subterfuges, formidable cerebral indulgences, and rampant experimentalism sometimes seem to have driven a generation of American writers back toward realism, if only to locate a different venue (but most probably for several other reasons as well).

But unlike some of the most demanding of the postmodernists (or superfictionists), Boyle is a writer who never forgets his audience. He is less an experimentalist than his immediate brilliant postmodern predecessors and more of a showman. Boyle's main connection to the superfictionists is in his baroque imagination. Most of the time, Boyle is simply not interested in prosaic reality, but rather in the magical, the visionary, the unexpected, the horrific, and the comically bizarre.

Yet there is good evidence in his latest work that Boyle does not wish to become simply the Gary Larson of our literature. *If the River Was Whiskey* shows a wider range than his previous collections, *Descent of Man* and *Greasy Lake*. The funny stories are as funny or funnier, but often more probing than some of the earlier work, braced with a more mature satirical intention that goes beyond the joke to something very much like social criticism.

As a satirist, Boyle is sometimes lighthearted, but he is often crueler and angrier than mellow Vonnegut, though less political and practical (less realistic) than John Irving or Tom Wolfe. Yet Boyle is certainly as capable of writing for the mass audience (while still pleasing the elite or intellectual audiences) as any of these big three.

In *If the River Was Whiskey*, Boyle seems more interested, in general, in taking a look (and in taking potshots) at suburban Americana, rather than dealing exclusively in exotic locales as was often the case in his previous stories, though even in suburbia Boyle finds traces of the primitive, the jungle, or hell itself.

In "The Devil and Irv Cherniske," for example: "Just outside the sleepy little commuter village of Irvington, New York, there stands a subdivision of half-million-dollar homes, each riding its own sculpted acre like a ship at sea and separated from its neighbors by patches of scrub and the forlorn-looking beeches that lend a certain pricy and vestigial air to the place." Irv Cherniske is a cynical stock trader who resides in this Eden, but one evening when an errant chip shot takes him deeper than usual into the woodsy gloom near his backyard, he meets a dark stranger (a very persuasive guy), and the reader gets a comic but harrowing contemporary rendition of what it might mean to sell one's soul to the Devil. This is magical realism, where the Devil actually enters the fiction as a credible character, though with real devilish (supernatural) powers. But the vision seems based as heavily on a contempt for materialistic values, that is, on a satirical intention, as on any desire simply to tell a whimsical or magical tale.

In "Sinking House," an elderly woman whose husband has just died has an unusual response to death and loneliness—she turns on all the water faucets in her house. Next door are the Terwilligers, a nice conventional couple: Meg, who spends her life doing stretching exercises, listening to CDs, and running errands, and her husband, Sonny, who "was shocked anew each time the crisply surveyed, neatly kept world he so cherished rose up to confront him with all its essential sloppiness, irrationality, and bad business sense." When the widow's water begins to inundate the Terwilliger's house and yard, what is there to do but call the police and eventually have the old woman carted off to the loony bin? But a smidgin of the old woman's anguish seems to take root, before the end, with consciousness-raising potential, in the mind of Meg, the young matron; and no one, including Boyle, is exactly laughing at the implicit heartlessness of these featureless suburban landscapes, where people are far more worried about the appearance of their yards than the catastrophes in their neighbors' lives.

"Peace of Mind" is another story about the insanity and paranoia of modern suburban life, where even the reputed tranquillity of safe streets and shops is no longer dependable. The protagonist is a yuppie alarm-systems saleswoman who goes around telling true-to-life horror stories of rape, murder, and senseless torture to the nice families who are her potential customers, causing one worried hubby to brood: "He'd been a fool, he saw that now. How could he have thought, even for a minute, that they'd be safe out here in the suburbs? The world was violent, rotten, corrupt, seething with hatred and perversion, and there was no escaping it. Everything you worked for, everything you loved, had to be locked up as if you were in a castle under siege." All this is a preliminary to his laying out more than five thousand dollars for a security system. But, ironically, because of the "Armed Response" signs in his front yard, a maniac picks out his house for special treatment and murders the man and his family with uncommon viciousness.

Even the more comical and magical stories often feature at least a dollop of moral ire or provide a platform for outraged rectitude.

In "The Miracle of Ballinspittle," Boyle dispenses with the laws of nature as we know them to poke some irreverent fun at Catholicism and at human vanity and sin. A forty-year-old Irish American named Davey McGahee, on a pilgrimage to Ireland to visit a "snotgreen likeness of the Virgin," has the time of his life: a celestial visitation. All of his sins are enumerated and dramatized before the crowd of petitioners: huge kegs of liquor fall from the sky, bales of marijuana. The Virgin screams "Gluttony!" and McGahee is "surrounded by forlornly mooing herds of cattle, sad-eyed pigs and sheep, funereal geese and clucking ducks, . . . even the odd dog or two he'd inadvertently wolfed down in Tijuana burritos and Cantonese stir-fry." McGahee's "Sins of the Flesh" include visions not only of every woman he has ever made love to, starting in the twelfth grade, but of everyone he has ever lusted after, including Linda Lovelace, Lot's wife, and the "outrageous little shaven-haired vixen from Domino's Pizza. . . . The mist lifts and there they are, in teddies and negligees, in garter belts and sweat socks, naked and wet and kneading their breasts like dough." McGahee is even accused in the "False Idols" category of having an autographed picture of Mickey Mantle.

Of course Boyle seems to be kidding when he goes into one of these fire-and-brimstone tirades, and he is, but not entirely. It is easy enough to laugh at Davey McGahee's anguish, but Boyle's ending to "The Miracle of Ballinspittle" brings the onus of sin back into the reader's own living room: "For who hasn't lusted after woman or man or drunk his booze and laid to rest whole herds to feed his greedy gullet? . . . Ask not for whom the bell tolls—unless perhaps you take the flight to Cork City, and the bus or rented Nissan out to Ballinspittle by the Sea."

In "The Human Fly," a down-at-the-heels Hollywood agent receives a strange visitor, a weirdo who wants to be famous. First the new client, on his own initiative, hangs in a bag from a skyscraper for two weeks and creates a sensation. Then he goes on to greater fame and glory by dangling from the wing of a DC-10 in flight and, later, from the axle of a Peterbilt truck from Maine to Pasadena. The story is a comical and satirical meditation on the American ideal of success and how it can drive people to destruction—and how there are always those ready to capitalize, commercialize, and mythologize such behavior.

In a few of the stories collected here, we also see a new, more mournful Boyle, capable of depths of feeling, regret, pathos, a writer willing to pass up the temptation for an easy joke in order to try breaking your heart. The title story is the most impressive instance of this sort of departure. It is a sensitive realistic piece of work, an initiation story that poignantly describes the relationship between a young man and his well-meaning alcoholic father. Whether this story represents a new phase for Boyle or is simply his way of proving that he can "do" realism too, if he really wants to—he can—is yet to be seen. (Updike wished to prove, at one point, that he could write like Donald Barthelme, and, sure enough, he could. But the effort didn't seem to do any permanent damage to either writer.)

There are also several charming love stories here to be relished. In "Modern Love," a comic fable about the trials of contemporary courtship, the narrator is in love with a beautiful girl who places a high premium on sanitation. The story begins: "There was no exchange of body fluids on the first date," a line that epitomizes an age and an attitude. His love smells, romantically, of Noxzema and pHisoHex. But when the involvement leads inevitably to passion, she asks him to wear a full-body condom.

"I'm clean," he says. "Trust me."

"Do it for me," she says, in her smallest voice, "if you really love me." What choice does he have?

In "Thawing Out," a young teacher overcomes his fear of commitment and the glib advice of a friend—"Before you know it you got six slobbering kids, a little pink house, and you're married to her mother"—to finally claim his lovely Naina. But not before he nearly loses everything he most wants and needs.

In "The Ape Lady in Retirement," Boyle shows his skill at point-of-view narration by returning to the ape-and-human interaction that he mocked so hilariously in the title story of his first collection, *Descent of Man.*

Throughout this collection, Boyle's strengths are in plot, in dramatic instinct, in sheer imaginative vitality, in his knack for spotting cultural shibboleths in need of a pasting. He is a master of the pregnant transition, the loopy departure, and the infallible punch line. The average Boyle story can skewer as many pretensions as a shish kebab and turn from the fantastic to the vulgar, from the sweet to the almost unthinkable, within a page. If there is a renaissance in the American short story, then Boyle is certainly a part of it—riding onward, carrying his own peculiar kind of banner—and American fiction is the richer for his outlandish contributions.

TOM WOLFE AS
VISITING MARTIAN

In the introduction to his first book, *The Kandy-Kolored Tangerine-Flake Streamline Baby*, Tom Wolfe explains how "the whole thing started" accidentally one afternoon in the early sixties when he was sent to do a newspaper story on the Hot Rod & Custom Car Show at the Coliseum in New York and how this led to his eventual interest in stock-car racing and free-form, Las Vegas neon-sign sculpture and "all these . . . *weird* . . . nutty-looking, crazy baroque custom cars, sitting in little nests of pink angora angel's hair for the purpose of 'glamorous' display." While he was trying to understand why the conventional newspaper story he wrote failed to capture some essential truth of the experience, Wolfe was struck by the animating insight that "the proles, peasants, and petty burghers" of America were "creating new styles . . . and changing the life of the whole country in ways that nobody even seems to bother to record, much less analyze." He was onto something.

Wolfe goes on to relate how *Esquire* became interested in the custom-car phenomenon, how they sent him to California, and how he ended up staying up all night, "typing along like a madman," in order to meet the *Esquire* deadline, elaborating the perception that suddenly "classes of people whose styles of life had been practically invisible had the money to build monuments to their own styles." Among teenagers this meant custom cars, rock 'n' roll, stretch pants, and decal eyes. In the South, he was to discover, it took the form of stock-car racing, which in fifteen years had replaced baseball as the number-one spectator sport. All over the country, at every suburb, supermarket, and hamburger stand, Las Vegas–style neon sculpture was transforming the American skyline. "The incredible postwar American electro-pastel surge into the suburbs," Wolfe would later call it. It was "sweeping the Valley, with superhighways, dreamboat cars, shopping centers, soaring thirty-foot Federal Sign & Signal Company electric supersculptures—Eight New Plexiglas

Display Features!—a surge of freedom and mobility."[1] The *Esquire* story Wolfe finished that morning long ago was eventually called "The Kandy-Kolored Tangerine-Flake Streamline Baby," and thus the New Journalism was born.

Tom Wolfe's ascendancy as spokesperson for this era in American life developed through the medium that came to be called the New Journalism—but by reason of his own special gifts. The novelists, those erstwhile cultural chroniclers, failed to fulfill this role, according to Wolfe, because they were "all crowded into one phone booth . . . doing these poor, frantic little exercises in form."[2] Therefore, the new journalists "had the whole crazed obscene uproarious Mammon-faced drug-soaked mau-mau lust-oozing Sixties in America all to themselves,"[3] and the seventies too, for that matter, "the Me Decade," as Wolfe described it.

But Wolfe's success is based upon realities that go beyond the theory that the novelists weren't paying attention and the fact that Wolfe himself came to be the most accomplished and notorious practitioner of the New Journalism, and its chief architect and advocate. Wolfe's banner of the New Journalism was flown, in large part, to gain acceptance for a whole new set of literary conventions, conventions that, not accidentally, allowed full expression of his particular virtuosity. Encompassing the aesthetics and methodology of the nineteenth-century realist novel and the modus operandi of the big-city, streetwise police-beat reporter, it was a form, Wolfe noted, that consumed "devices that happen to have originated with the novel and mixed them with every other device known to prose. And all the while, quite beyond matters of technique, it enjoyed an advantage so obvious, so built-in, one almost forgets what a power it has: the simple fact that the reader knows *all this actually happened.*"[4]

Probably, the New Journalism was also part of the same evolution in consciousness that led, in different ways, to the new fiction, the new poetry, and the old psychology: an idea about the importance of focusing attention on subjective emotional experience, dramatized

1. Tom Wolfe, *The Electric Kool-Aid Acid Test* (New York: Farrar, Straus and Giroux, 1968), 39.
2. Joe David Bellamy, *The New Fiction: Interviews with Innovative American Writers* (Urbana, Chicago, London: University of Illinois Press, 1974), 80.
3. Tom Wolfe, *The New Journalism* (New York: Harper and Row, 1973), 31.
4. Ibid., 34.

point of view, and unique sensibility and of delving beneath appearances for deeper meanings. In formulating new conventions and then serving as a propagandist for his own kind of art, Tom Wolfe, like Fielding, like Zola or Joyce, was following in a time-honored tradition, the formal innovator modifying received forms and methods to suit his own historically exceptional circumstances. "Every great and original writer," wrote William Wordsworth, "in proportion as he is great and original, must create the taste by which he is to be relished."

Among the trickiest of the conventions Wolfe entertained was his inventive application of the principles of point of view. Wolfe describes in *The New Journalism* how and why he aspired to treat point of view in nonfiction writing "in the Jamesian sense in which fiction writers understand it, entering directly into the mind of a character, experiencing the world through his central nervous system throughout a given scene." The idea, he says, "was to give the full objective description, plus something that readers had always had to go to novels and short stories for: namely, the subjective or emotional life of the characters."[5]

How can a nonfiction writer pretend to know exactly what a person is thinking or feeling at any given moment? He asks them. If a reporter bases his reconstruction of the subjective life of the character on the most scrupulous reporting, Wolfe would contend, he can get close to the truth of the inner life. Wolfe's ideal of saturation reporting is far more ambitious than anything the old journalists had thought to try. His approach is to cultivate the habit of staying with potential subjects for days, weeks, or months at a time, taking notes, interviewing, watching, and waiting for something dramatic and revealing to happen. Only through the most persistent and searching methods of reporting, Wolfe would emphasize, can the journalist's entrée into point of view, the subjective life, inner voices, the creation of scenes and dialogue, and so on, be justified.

Another aspect of Wolfe's treatment of point of view is his playful use of the downstage voice, the devil's-advocate voice, and other voices in his work. Here is a writer with a marvelous ear for dialogue, an easily galvanized, chameleonlike faculty for empathy, and a ventriloquist's delight in speaking other people's lines. From the start of his career, he was bored silly by the "pale beige tone" of

5. Ibid., 19, 21.

conventional nonfiction writing, which seemed to him "like the standard announcer's voice . . . a drag, a droning," a signal to the reader "that a well-known bore was here again, 'the journalist,' a pedestrian mind, a phlegmatic spirit, a faded personality."[6] So, early on, he began experimenting with outlandish voices and with the principle of skipping rapidly from one voice or viewpoint to the next, sometimes unexpectedly in the middle of a sentence, and often enough without identifying *whose* voice or viewpoint except through context. Anything to avoid the stupefying monotony of the pale beige tone.

Even in expository sections, he often adopts the tone or characteristic lingo, point of view, or pretense of a character he is writing about: the "good old boy" voice he assumes, for example, in the narration of "The Last American Hero," the slangy L.A. vernacular of the Mac Meda Destruction Company in "The Pump House Gang," the freaked-out lingo of the Merry Pranksters in *The Electric Kool-Aid Acid Test*, the ghetto jive of *Mau-Mauing the Flak Catchers*, or the sugary, gossipy persona of *Radical Chic*. Any voice he wishes to take on, he assumes with incredible smoothness and fidelity. Frequently, however, the voice produced turns out to be a put-on voice that reveals and dramatizes personality as it revels in the flaws, prejudices, and affectations of the character. The voice, that is, is both part of the character and, at the same time, above or outside it, interpreting and passing judgment.

Literal-minded critics have sometimes leaped to the assumption that Wolfe's put-on voice was expressing his actual opinions on a subject. Thomas R. Edwards does this, for instance, in discussing a passage about the Watts riots in "The Pump House Gang":

> Watts was a blast. . . . Artie and John had a tape-recorder and decided they were going to make a record called "Random Sounds from the Watts Riots." They drove right into Watts . . . and there was blood on the streets and roofs blowing off the stores and all these apricot flames and drunk Negroes falling through the busted plate glass of the liquor stores. Artie got a nice recording of a lot of Negroes chanting "Burn, baby, burn."

Edwards claims that Wolfe's "general view of 'serious' social concern makes the passage a virtual endorsement of the attitudes it mimics,"[7] when, obviously, the passage is expressing the lack of

6. Ibid., 17.
7. Thomas R. Edwards, "The Electric Indian," *Partisan Review* 3 (1969): 540.

social concern of the Pump House Gang. The mercilessness of their attitude toward the Negroes serves to document the insularity of their tribal bond. The put-on voice here is Wolfe's way of dramatizing the group's attitude toward other groups, a trait he also illustrates in showing the kids' outrageous prejudices against anyone over the "horror age of 25."

Now, in any case, the New Journalism is a fait accompli. Whatever quibbling one might still occasionally hear about the dubiousness of its procedures, it is practiced every day across the land, from *Rolling Stone* to *The New Yorker*, from *The Atlantic Monthly* and *Esquire* to the sports pages of the *New York Times*, the *Fresno Bee*, and the *Bangor Daily News*, in some cases by writers who don't even know what to call it, who might be surprised to learn they are committing it. Although Wolfe has always remained loyal to the journalistic calling and has expropriated its methods in all earnestness for his own purposes and has thus permanently changed the definition and the shape of journalism, he clearly is, and always has been, more than a journalist.

Temperamentally Tom Wolfe is, from first to last, with every word and deed, a *comic* writer with an exuberant sense of humor, a baroque sensibility, and an irresistible inclination toward hyperbole. His antecedents are primarily literary—not journalistic, and not political, except in the largest sense. All these years, even before *The Bonfire of the Vanities*, Tom Wolfe has been writing Comedy with a capital C, Comedy like that of Henry Fielding and Jane Austen and Joseph Addison, like that of Thackeray and Shaw and Mark Twain. Like these writers, Tom Wolfe might be described as a brooding humanistic presence. There is a decided moral edge to his humor. Wolfe never tells us what to believe exactly; rather, he shows us examples of good and (most often) bad form. He has always proffered these humanistic and moral perspectives on his subjects.

Which is not to say that beneath the cool surface of the hyped-up prose we should expect to find either a fire-and-brimstone preacher or a Juvenalian sort of satirist seething with indignation about the corruption of his fellow men. Neither will we discover, in Wolfe's work, any sign at all of a political or social activist who might argue on behalf of a particular party, issue, system, creed, or cause.

The satirical element in Wolfe's sort of comedic writing is most often sunny, urbane, and smiling. Like all Horatian comedy, it aims to reform through laughter that is never vindictive or merely personal, but broadly sympathetic:

> Comedy may be considered to deal with man in his human state, restrained and often made ridiculous by his limitations, his faults, his bodily functions, and his animal nature. . . . Comedy has always viewed man more realistically than tragedy, and drawn its laughter or its satire from the spectacle of human weakness or failure. Hence its tendency to juxtapose appearance and reality, to deflate pretense, and to mock excess.[8]

Classical comedy outlives causes and headlines because of its freedom from parochial ideology. It is a human response based upon the conviction that human nature is so prone to folly and vanity that it cannot be helped or changed, except possibly through self-awareness, through admission of its innate silliness. Whatever side of whatever issue we are on, the comedian believes, we are likely to end up making fools of ourselves. Yet there is always a forgiving or good-natured quality to Horatian (and Wolfean) comedy, since it assumes that this peculiar, flawed human condition is universal and any one of us (including the writer poking fun) may be guilty of demonstrating it at any moment.

A close connection between laughter and reproof is evident throughout Wolfe's oeuvre. In works such as *The Electric Kool-Aid Acid Test* and "The Me Decade and the Third Great Awakening," for example, Wolfe mocks the idea that "letting it all hang out" is likely to offer a road to salvation or improvement. In *The Electric Kool-Aid Acid Test*, Wolfe shows again and again how destructive the sixties' phony wisdom about the "joys" of abandonment to chemical cornucopias, in particular, could be. Similarly, by parodying facile aspects of the human-potential movement in "The Me Decade and the Third Great Awakening" ("Esalen's specialty was lube jobs for the personality"[9]), Wolfe demonstrates his concern about the exploitation and misdirection of human energies in what he sees as a foolish, limited, and petty cause. In "The Intelligent Coed's Guide to America," Wolfe exposes the preposterous ironies of a certain brand of fashionable intellectual bellyaching in the seventies and shows

8. C. Hugh Holman, William Flint Thrall, and Addison Hibbard, *A Handbook to Literature* (Indianapolis: Bobbs-Merrill, 1972), 108.

9. Tom Wolfe, *Mauve Gloves & Madmen, Clutter & Vine* (New York: Farrar, Straus and Giroux, 1976), 145.

how the pronouncements of certain American intellectuals may have had more to do with their own status and identity needs than with any authentic repression or doom worth taking seriously. In *From Bauhaus to Our House*, Wolfe shows how a status-related infatuation with things European in the 1930s and 1940s led to a redirection of American music, art, psychology, and especially architecture that was ultimately reductive, excessive, and nonsensical.

Or in *Radical Chic*, as Wolfe observes the socially elite of Manhattan indulging the fad of inviting members of the Black Panthers to their opulent parties, he poses the theory that the ostensible desire for social justice and the display of generosity involved had somewhat less to do with the proceedings than with the secret motive, which was the longing of the aristocrats to feel in its fullest degree the heady sensation of "How chic we are." Switching his angle of vision diametrically in *Mau-Mauing the Flak Catchers*, Wolfe shows hilariously how enterprising blacks gleefully intimidated, outwitted, and hoodwinked social-agency do-gooders during the heydays of the Poverty Program.

All of these perspectives arise out of a sense of the moral insufficiency of the participants and reveal Tom Wolfe pointing a finger and laughing wholeheartedly at what people do when they fly in the face of the hard facts about their own natures or their unconscious or concealed motives or aspirations. The merriment is intense; the laughter is real. But there is little cause for feeling vastly superior to the miserable fools, tarnished folk heroes, rebels, fanatics, and hustlers from Wolfe's rogue's gallery of humanity. For lurking just beneath the swirling surface of his prose is the sobering realization that the potential for vanity of similar proportion is common to us all.

One indirect moral service that great comedic writers perform is to promote self-awareness, and Wolfe's major contribution here has been in his emphasis upon the hidden and sometimes peculiar manifestations of status-seeking in American life. In the manner of a conscientious Martian anthropologist, he has tried rigorously to apply the principle that all primates, including humans, organize their societies according to status hierarchies and struggles for dominance. The importance of status behavior as the source of society's most mysterious subtleties has, of course, been recognized and studied by the social scientists for years. The proof of the existence of such behavior is not original to Tom Wolfe, but the wholesale exploration of its features in American culture and its exploitation for comical purposes are certainly important aspects of Wolfe's novelty and uniqueness.

The tool of status analysis, and other gleanings from the social sciences, has led Wolfe, over the last three decades, to these basic assumptions about American life: (1) That the fragmentation and diversity of American culture resulted in the emergence of subcultures or enclaves that have evolved their own bizarre art forms, lifestyles, and status rituals independent from the "elite" culture of the past, the "high" culture of the American Northeast via Europe ("the big amoeba-God of Anglo-European sophistication"[10]), or other common references. (2) That these enclaves, generally ignored by serious social observers, deserve the closest scrutiny, both because they are the truest, most authentic, examples of "the way we live now," and because they illustrate comically that human nature follows the same quaint, barbaric patterns regardless of class, region, or circumstance. (3) That fragmentation of American society has sometimes caused rampant status confusion (as in *Radical Chic*); emphasis upon enunciating weird new tribal identities (as in "The Pump House Gang," *The Electric Kool-Aid Acid Test*, or *The Right Stuff*); the evolution of status dropouts who discover they can compete more favorably with some new set of rules in lifestyle (as in "The Mid-Atlantic Man"); and a remarkable array of bewildering or ridiculous behavior (as in "The Voices of Village Square" or "The Girl of the Year")—all ripe for Wolfean analysis—including the widespread frantic search for spurious forms of salvation (as in "The Me Decade and the Third Great Awakening" or *The Electric Kool-Aid Acid Test*).

Thus, Junior Johnson's stock cars of "The Last American Hero," as seen through Wolfe's eyes, are like the totems of the Easter Islanders or the formal architecture of the Regency period, critically important cultural artifacts that are the focus of both veneration and status competition for their creators. Or, as in *The Right Stuff*, among the test pilots, the fraternity of "the right stuff" is the basis for the display of almost incredible forms of heroism, which Wolfe clearly admires. But even here it is the fierce status competition within the group that serves to motivate the men, a desire for the "sinfully

10. Tom Wolfe, *The Kandy-Kolored Tangerine-Flake Streamline Baby* (New York: Farrar, Straus and Giroux, 1966), 82.

inconfessable . . . feeling of superiority, appropriate to him and his kind, lone bearers of the right stuff."

Grounding his insights about human nature firmly on his belief in the potent force of status in human affairs, and its expression through fashion, Wolfe claims—in *The Painted Word* and in *From Bauhaus to Our House,* for instance—that styles in contemporary painting and architecture can be understood more plainly by examining the ambitions and status games of influential artists, architects, critics, and patrons than by trying to comprehend their creations as personal miracles, a position that has been somewhat less than stupendously popular in the art world.

As his career has matured, Wolfe's aspirations as a cultural chronicler have been greatly enhanced by his ability to grasp, to digest, and to stimulate human interest in large, sometimes esoteric subject areas usually thought to be the domain of art historians, sociobiologists, or other specialists. Few would have dared, as Wolfe does in *The Painted Word,* for example, to take on the whole bloody history of modern art and to offer a waggish, but devilishly shrewd, critique of how modern art came to serve fashion and theory instead of humankind; or, as in the scorching sequel *From Bauhaus to Our House,* to deal with "what went wrong" during the past fifty years of American architecture.

Wolfe's unfailing wit and his faculty for selecting the truly memorable example are undoubtedly a part of this ability to assimilate, transform, and humanize his subject matter. "Yale had completed a building program of vast proportions," he explains in *From Bauhaus to Our House,* "that had turned the campus into as close an approximation of Oxford and Cambridge as the mind of man could devise on short notice in southern Connecticut. . . . For better or worse, Yale became the business barons' vision of a luxurious collegium for the sons of the upper classes who would run the new American empire." But when an addition was built for the Yale art gallery after the Second World War, "the building could scarcely have been distinguished from a Woolco discount store in a shopping center" and the interior "had the look of an underground parking garage." And all this in the name of "unconcealed structure"—another instance for Wolfe of how mindless fashion and buzzword aesthetic theory were allowed to undermine good sense and consistency of design—but also an instance of how Wolfe is able to concretize and persuade by skillful elaboration of the perfect example.

Typically, as Wolfe unspools yard after yard of theory, he forces us to test it against our own understanding of the nature of things. And he compels us to ask questions: Why in the name of God should painting and architecture in our time have become so trivialized, so specialized, so uniform? Why would an accomplished, clever man want to give up his work and french-fry his brains and invest his earthly time tooling around the countryside in a psychedelic school bus? Why in the world would a normal, sane, and healthy person want to risk his life on a day-to-day basis as a test pilot or an astronaut? Why do people *behave* as they do? How do we live? How should we live?

Clearly, as Wolfe has grown in stature, he has become more interested in reform and more concerned about what he sees as "the wrong stuff" and "the right stuff." At the heart of *From Bauhaus to Our House* and *The Painted Word* is a straightforward wish to humanize art and architecture by showing how "the freight train of history"[11] got off on the wrong track by the most ludicrous sort of historical coincidence. All of Wolfe's recent books, and many of his earlier essays, are also parables offered as intellectual history. They show how political power and orthodoxy and fashion-mongering have often run roughshod over originality, virtue, fair play, exuberance, and panache. The moral would seem to be that those who succumb to the temptation to aspire to the merely fashionable, who thus sacrifice the noble impulse toward individual vision, may end up "succeeding" and thereby mucking up whole centuries. This failing, he seems to warn us, is so common that all of us should be on guard against it, lest we too be tempted to repeat it. Substance over surface, he proclaims, should be our guide—be alert to the frailties of human nature and pay attention to values that truly matter. Yet there is nothing self-righteous in Tom Wolfe's moral stance, and it is so well disguised that the average reader often may be unaware that an implicit moral position is being assumed.

After roughly thirty-five years of development—by combining the methodology of the journalist with his own special sense and sensibility—the young writer whose life was forever changed by one amazed afternoon at the Coliseum at the Hot Rod & Custom Car Show has gone on to become the most astute and popular

11. Tom Wolfe, *Radical Chic & Mau-Mauing the Flak Catchers* (New York: Farrar, Straus and Giroux, 1970), 17.

social observer and cultural chronicler of his generation. If Tom Wolfe sometimes interprets the American scene with the apparent detachment and freedom from constraints of a visiting Martian, he remains a Martian with an enviable sense of humor, energy, and playfulness. If he is often the maverick skeptic among us, the ultimate "king-has-no-clothes-on" man of principle, he is a skeptic with the power of empathy. If, at times, he seems to be viewing his own culture like an anthropologist studying the strange habits of the Trobriand Islanders, he is an anthropologist with an ear for every kind of idiomatic speech, for loaded language and the multiple meanings it contains, and with a conviction about the value of skewering pretentiousness wherever it may be found. No other writer of our time has aspired to capture the fabled Spirit of the Age so fully and has succeeded so well.

KURT VONNEGUT
FOR PRESIDENT

The Making of a Literary Reputation

Iowa City. The spacious faculty lounge in the new ultra-modern English-Philosophy building (EPB) at the University of Iowa. We are waiting in this glittering room for the appearance of Kurt Vonnegut Jr., who taught here a few years back, before he won a Guggenheim and signed a three-book contract with Seymour Lawrence and became famous. From my spot in this sea of legs and Arrid Extra-Dry and sprawling book bags, I have a terrific view of the big chartreuse chair where Vonnegut will be sitting down. Perfect.

Some people in the back are still milling around by the coffee urn. That bearded man there, just raising the cup to his lips, is Robert Scholes, the critic. The door swings open and in walks Vance Bourjaily and someone, and with them is, yes, there he is— unmistakable—there's Vonnegut.

The audience rolls back like the Red Sea before Moses, and Vonnegut meanders purposively to the chair with his bowlegged, unpretentious gait. It is the sort of "diffident bloodhound lope"[1] that could allow a man to stumble gracefully or even fall down flat, then get up and walk away as if nothing had happened. He makes it. He sits, facing us. He is a huge, slouching, loose-jointed man with a really impressive mustache. Seated here, he resembles exactly—as C. D. B. Bryan, also present, will later write in the *New York Times Book Review*—"a corduroy-covered batwing chair that has been dropped 2,000 feet from a passing airplane."[2]

"I know you'll ask it."

"Are you a Black Humorist?" someone quips.

1. Wilfrid Sheed, "The New Generation Knew Him When," *Life,* September 12, 1969, 66.
2. C. D. B. Bryan, "Kurt Vonnegut, Head Bokononist," *New York Times Book Review,* April 6, 1969, 2.

"You asked it," Vonnegut booms.

He talks easily, this great wounded bear of a man; and when he laughs, he booms. He has a presence, like a politician, without being portly. He fills a room. He is moody, truculent one instant, laughing contagiously the next. The audience follows on cue.

He begins to talk about his latest book: "I was present in the greatest massacre in European history, which was the destruction of Dresden by firebombing. . . . We got through it, the American prisoners there, because we were quartered in the stockyards where it was wide and open and there was a meat locker three stories beneath the surface, the only decent shelter in the city. So we went down into the meat locker, and when we came up again, the city was gone and everybody was dead—a terrible thing for the son of an architect to see. . . ." Vonnegut's eyes avert—those eyes have seen God in a burning bush. He has come down from the mountain with eyes like Charlton Heston's in *The Ten Commandments* by Cecil B. De Mille. His beard would be white now if he had one. This man should be president, someone is thinking. Now it is time for a joke.

This is the first time I have ever seen Kurt Vonnegut Jr. in person, in action.

I JOIN THE KARASS

The first time I ever *read* Kurt Vonnegut was two years before when I heard he was going to be one of my instructors that fall at the Iowa Writers Workshop. I bought *Cat's Cradle* and put it on a shelf in my abysmal, gray apartment, and one day when I was trying to write and the Hamm's (Land of Skyblue Waters) wasn't working and my eyes were straying around the room, I lit on *Cat's Cradle* again and picked it out and started to read. "Call me Jonah," I read. . . . I turned off my study light and spent the afternoon reading.

Shortly after that well-spent afternoon, I found out that Vonnegut had just won a Guggenheim and wasn't going to be one of my instructors that fall after all. So it goes. So it didn't go. Later that year Robert Scholes's *The Fabulators* came out in Iowa City, and seeing that it was a critical consideration of Kurt Vonnegut (and some other writers I liked), I actually laid down my five bucks and carried home a copy. Although it seemed perfectly clear to me that Vonnegut's growing critical and academic respectability had wrenched him right out of his karass[3] with me, I had almost no inkling at that time that through another series of accidents I would end up writing about it here.

THE FUTURE CLOSE UP

The extent of the pilgrimage he was to make (not to mention the no doubt quixotic adventures he would be having along the way) could hardly have been guessed then by anyone, especially those hardened realists around Iowa City who know better than most that writers don't usually get what they deserve. But, in fact, as we have now seen, Vonnegut was to move from his Guggenheim to the publication of his "big book," and then on to Harvard and Broadway. He was to parlay his move from the revolving drugstore book racks into the college bookstores—which began with the republication of his books in 1966—into faculty offices, and with increasing momentum, into classrooms, anthologies, movie contracts, television appearances, and even critical respectability. Following a lengthy retrospective review by C. D. B. Bryan in *The New Republic,* Scholes's assessment in *The Fabulators,* and the appearance of *Slaughterhouse-Five* (with its attendant reviews), Vonnegut was to be treated seriously and in rapid succession by other such venerable tastemakers as Wilfrid Sheed, Leslie Fiedler, and Benjamin DeMott—and, surprisingly enough, *in* the mass circulation magazines, though a few scholarly journals were sizing him up as well, with others not far behind. Just then Vonnegut seemed poised on the verge of becoming the subject of a cover story for *Time* and a simultaneous deluge of dissertations. Yet perhaps the most astonishing element of all in this Vonnegut's odyssey is why the all-encompassing cultural embrace took so long to develop in the first place.

YOU'RE HOTTER'N A
TWO-DOLLAR PISTOL, POP

Like Professor Barnhouse, a protagonist in one of Vonnegut's earliest published stories who becomes "the most powerful weapon on earth" by cultivating his psychic powers after accidentally throwing ten sevens in a row in a crap game, Vonnegut is "self- taught." In a

---

3. In Vonnegutian (Bokononist) metaphysics, a karass is defined as one of the "teams that do God's Will without ever discovering what they are doing."

sense, of course, most writers are self-taught, but one gathers that Vonnegut, a chemistry major with a spotty education and an unusual apprenticeship, is more self-taught than most. This factor, along with the possibly related accidents of publication and classification, are the most obvious explanations for the slow emergence of Vonnegut's serious reputation.

"You are writing for strangers," he used to scrawl on the blackboard at the beginning of each writing class at Iowa. "Face the audience of strangers." What he meant by this seemed to be, according to some of his ex-students: Don't expect to be automatically understood or loved or even appreciated. A writer must be a "skilled seducer . . . to persuade people to share his dreams."[4] Surely this lesson was the fruit of his bitter professional experience as a freelancer, when, as a junior public-relations hack for a good company, he gave up his job and his future and staked his life on the silly notion that an unpublished, unknown writer from Indianapolis, who wasn't even an English major, should be able to support his family and himself in the United States of America by writing fiction for a living. "It was damned unpleasant for a number of years," he said later, an "hysterical effort."[5]

Not only was the dewy-eyed amateur prematurely pigeonholed as a "sci-fi" writer but as a second-rate one at that, as his first novel, *Player Piano*, was written off by many as crudely written and largely derivative, a rehashing of Orwell and Huxley. The volume of hack work he *did do* in the fifties, to keep himself afloat, tended to confirm this judgment; and even if all of these early stories were not science-fiction stories, many were, at best, skillful, and, at worst, slick, gimmicky, and "popular," just a notch or two above the pulps.

Some, such as "Miss Temptation" or "A Long Walk to Forever" treated straightforward boy-meets-girl, boy-gets-girl themes. There were tearjerkers written for the women's magazines ("D.P.") and others ("The Foster Portfolio," "More Stately Mansions," "The Kid Nobody Could Handle") from the most-unforgettable-character-I've-ever-met genre with period decorations, settings, and costuming and heartwarming surprise endings where characters either

4. Roger Henke, "Wrestling (American Style) with Proteus: Symposium Highlights," *Novel* 3 (spring 1970): 205.

5. Loretta McCabe, "An Exclusive Interview with Kurt Vonnegut," *Writer's Yearbook '70*, no. 41 (1970): 100.

get what they want or get what's good for them. By and large these stories do make interesting enough reading—even in those days Vonnegut knew how to tell a good story—but it is hardly any wonder that the stories frequently made use of stock themes, were stylistically run-of-the-mill, and failed therefore to generate lavish praise.

A writer-critic I know, in fact, who shall remain unnamed, turned down an invitation to review the story collection *Welcome to the Monkey House,* which repeated much of the early work, for the *New York Review of Books* because it seemed to him, he said, "just old-fashioned slick stories." Vonnegut "didn't intend it seriously, I didn't think; he seemed to be doing it for the money, which he says himself in the preface; so I just thought I would take him at his word."

This frank toleration for Vonnegut's economic motivations seems to have been fairly rare, however. Typically, Vonnegut's toil in the lists, seen by himself as one reasonably honorable way to turn an honest buck in the fifties, has been given short shrift by those writers and critics more at home in a university setting, who are more apt to take the cultivation of a reputation as a serious matter and to have the leisure and economic security to do so.

Following *Player Piano* and the years of story writing, the publication in paperback of *The Sirens of Titan* and *Mother Night* (headier stuff) and *Canary in a Cathouse* did little to revitalize Vonnegut's reputation. The books went without benefit of reviews, and the latter, of course, was simply the best of his hack work, dressed up between two covers, interesting enough now to buffs but far from vintage Vonnegut.

Why the eventual hardcover publication of *Cat's Cradle* and *God Bless You, Mr. Rosewater* went relatively unheralded is a tougher mystery to unravel. If, like *Catch-22,* the books had to depend on a snowballing word-of-mouth reputation, it may very likely have been the result of a lag in sensibility. Vonnegut's "mistake" here was in being out of joint with the times, or, in this case, slightly ahead of the times—for exactly as long as it took the increasingly socially aware reading public, its conscience grated by the atrocities of Vietnam, to catch on to the game of shattered time sequences and the applicability of Vonnegut's brand of gallows humor to their experience of the present.

The Black Humor label, which Vonnegut credits Bruce Jay Friedman with affixing to him (in Friedman's foreword to his *Black*

Humor anthology, edited for Bantam Books in 1965) became part of this process of recognition and indicated the beginning of a more hospitable attitude toward Vonnegut's work. But even here Vonnegut was thrown in with a decidedly mixed bag of writers, which tended to obscure rather than to clarify his unique vision of things. Critics tended to reject the Black Humor label because of its lack of precision, and a number of the writers classified as Black Humorists (including Vonnegut and Barth, among others) jumped at the chance to disassociate themselves, either because they didn't like the company or feared being associated with yet another ephemeral "school" as it quietly disappeared into oblivion. "The label is useless except for the merchandisers," Vonnegut was saying at Iowa. "I don't think anybody is very happy about the category or depressed about being excluded from it—Vance Bourjaily was, and took it very well, I thought."[6]

While it is true, to a great extent, that the times have finally caught up with Vonnegut, part of his emergence as a major figure, as should now be clear, must be credited simply to his growth and improvement as a writer. Although heresy to admit, it is nonetheless accurate, I think, to observe that the benign neglect of Vonnegut's first decade as a writer was partially justified. Here was a marvelously original but erratic writer. He was a "skilled seducer" in the making but a long way from fulfilling his potential, tempering steadily in the hard-nosed slick magazine and exploding mass-circulation–paperback trade, a uniquely modern professional initiation. *Welcome to the Monkey House* gives perhaps the clearest perspective on this growth, for in almost *every* case the more recent stories are the all-around better stories; the title story, the best in the collection, is the most recent of all.

During his faculty-lounge performance in Iowa City, Vonnegut himself admitted frankly that much of the early work had been either crude or potboiling stuff, though one suspects he may only have appreciated this retrospectively. Half-seriously, he credited his success as a writer to the fact that he was not trained in the humanities—so that he never "learned to dislike" anything he wrote.

6. See John Casey's partial tape transcript-interview of Vonnegut's Iowa City appearance: *Confluence* 2, no. 1 (spring 1969): 4–5, or as reprinted in *Apocalypse: Dominant Contemporary Forms*, ed. Joe David Bellamy (Philadelphia, New York, Toronto: J. B. Lippincott, 1972), 381–87.

"I loved every word I wrote," he said, "which is important for a writer—I mean, even though a lot of it was miserable crap."

How *could* a writer who had just written "Tom Edison's Shaggy Dog" write *The Sirens of Titan* or a writer who had just written "The Long Walk to Forever"—"a sickeningly slick love story"—write *Cat's Cradle*? Possibly the same way another self-taught writer who had just written *Soldiers' Pay* and *Mosquitoes* could write *The Sound and the Fury* and *As I Lay Dying*—and in both cases, editorial resurrection was necessary through republication. Vonnegut's republication is a factor that should by no means be underestimated in an assessment of his emergence as a dominant figure by the early seventies.

VONNEGUT'S RISE TO RESPECTABILITY

A number of other factors important to Vonnegut's rise are, I think, worth pondering. In the first place, Vonnegut himself was smart enough to figure out that his categorization as a science-fiction writer was not working to his advantage; and he took an active part in sloughing off the stigma of the sci-fi label and, as part of the same process, in suggesting that some so-called science-fiction writing was in fact worthy of serious consideration. His 1965 essay "Science Fiction" for the *New York Times Book Review* is the most readily accessible and most public example of this. In the essay Vonnegut says that after publishing *Player Piano* he "learned from the reviewers" that he was a science-fiction writer. "I supposed," he went on, "that I was writing a novel about life, about things I could not avoid seeing and hearing in Schenectady, a very real town, awkwardly set in the gruesome now. I have been a sore-headed occupant of a file drawer labeled 'science-fiction' ever since, and I would like out, particularly since so many serious critics regularly mistake the drawer for a tall white fixture in a comfort station."[7] In the most direct possible way, Vonnegut was indicating that he wanted to be taken seriously, and by "serious critics." And surely, by that time, with five of his novels behind him, such attention was overdue, as he accurately perceived. Similarly, he was ready to admit that his earliest work had been, as he would later call it disparagingly in his preface to *Welcome to the Monkey House*, "the fruits of Free Enterprise."

7. Kurt Vonnegut Jr., "Science Fiction," *New York Times Book Review*, September 5, 1965, 2.

Vonnegut was saying this sort of thing to everyone he met no doubt. He was saying it on the college-lecture circuit—"I speak a lot at universities now"[8]—and at writers' conferences, which, like conventions for the science-fiction crowd, he seems to have become cynical, if knowledgeable, about through attending too many.[9] He was still saying it, in fact, in the EPB faculty lounge that day in Iowa City.

A related sort of minor strategy, which Vonnegut confided about to us budding writers in the lounge that day, has been the accomplishment of his aspirations as a virtuoso blurb writer. Write a lot of original blurbs for books you like, he recommended, and then you get to be in great demand as a blurb writer and your name will be plastered all over other people's book jackets and advertising copy and this doesn't cost you a cent and is great for public relations. This approach would be especially recommended for a writer, he said, who might have a real zinger of a name in any way resembling a name such as, say, Vonnegut.

But the maturing of Vonnegut's comic-satiric vision, his feeling for, or just plain synchrony with, the Zeitgeist, and his improving technical finesse must be considered as dominant factors in the upswing of his fortunes. At a time when critics such as Susan Sontag and Richard Poirier were learning to appreciate the Beatles and the Supremes *as well as* Bach, and comic strips as well as Shakespeare— without shame—and were providing sophisticated justifications for such tastes, Vonnegut could begin to assume something of a position merely as a pop writer. The age of "pop" was at hand. But Vonnegut was more than just a pop writer; he was the *thinking* reader's pop writer. He was an American writer who was actually writing about ideas and incorporating contemporary experience in his work; and his basic assumptions, his attitudes and prejudices, were, as Benjamin DeMott has pointed out, "perfectly tuned to the mind of the emergent generation."[10] To the surging youth culture, the proper conduct of life, man's inhumanity to man, and the possibility of the end of the world, were and are viable issues. And Vonnegut

8. Bryan, "Head Bokononist."

9. Kurt Vonnegut Jr., "Teaching the Unteachable," *New York Times Book Review*, August 6, 1967, 1, 20.

10. Benjamin DeMott, "Vonnegut's Otherworldly Laughter," *Saturday Review*, May 1, 1971, 30.

as fatalistic moralist, cynical pacifist, holy atheist, anti-intellectual philosopher, apocalyptic futurist, and grim humorist complexly encompassed all the right paradoxes.

And not only that, but also, more important, I think, than anyone has yet to emphasize, Vonnegut had latched on to a truly original contemporary idiom, as American as television or napalm or napalm-abhorrers, as fragmented and discontinuous as contemporary experience. A consideration of Vonnegut's idiom, I would say, should take into account everything from his great ear, his sense of the way Americans talk, his sense of timing (as active and keen as Paul McCartney's—a compliment one does not bestow lightly), to his formal idiosyncrasies, beginning with *Mother Night* in 1961: the short chapter form, the sharp image, the short, quick scene, the fragmented time sequence, the speed of narration generated by these formal characteristics. If one were to play Marshall McLuhan here, one might point out that Vonnegut's fiction is a clever, formal approximation of, or at least shares many elements of the experience of, . . . watching television. This might offer another explanation for Vonnegut's appeal to the television generation, those who have *always* had television, not to mention those of us, more or less aged, who, according to McLuhan, have also had our sense ratios hopelessly rearranged by it.

TASTE THAT BEATS THE OTHERS COLD

One might just as well go on to hypothesize simply enough that, aside from other factors such as his discovery of a style and a pace attuned to the television age, Vonnegut may owe his rise to his achievement, to his art. Is such a thing possible?

Starting in 1966, Vonnegut finally began to receive the sort of critical attention from "serious critics" that he had been asking for previously. Robert Scholes's "Mithridates, He Died Old: Black Humor and Kurt Vonnegut Jr." in *The Hollins Critic* (later included in Scholes's seminal book *The Fabulators* in substantially the same form) and "Kurt Vonnegut on Target" by C. D. B. Bryan in *The New Republic* were the essential groundbreaking efforts. Both pieces mentioned pertinent biographical details, the fact that Vonnegut had "not received the acceptance due him from the reading public,"[11]

11. C. D. B. Bryan, "Kurt Vonnegut on Target," *New Republic*, October 8, 1966, 21.

and went on to treat several of the novels and to place Vonnegut in historical perspective by assigning him a pedigreed niche (Scholes, at *length*) in a distinguished tradition (Voltaire and Swift, according to Scholes, seemed appropriate antecedents). Vonnegut's recognition "as an important American writer is all but accomplished already," Scholes rhapsodized, predicting "a literary success of the best sort." For Bryan, Vonnegut was "the most readable and amusing of the new humorists."[12] Clearly, Vonnegut's reputation was winging beyond the drugstore and barbershop stage, from which it was about to soar.

This same duo of Scholes and Bryan attended the 1969 labor and delivery of *Slaughterhouse-Five* to the reading public in the *New York Times Book Review*; and if any skeptics were looking for more proof of Vonnegut's legitimacy, they now had it, in the form of both a splendid novel and an enthusiastic reception of it. In his front-page review, Scholes called Vonnegut "a true artist" and placed him "among the best writers of his generation." Bryan's piece, combining an interview and a summary of the career to that date, mentioned a star-studded list of Vonnegut's "earliest fans" and "the fact that Vonnegut's novels are now being taught at universities" and were accruing a "cultish attention . . . [among] the under-30's."[13]

Later that year Wilfrid Sheed did an appealing personality piece on Vonnegut for *Life. Writer's Yearbook, 1970* carried a lengthy interview, and by the fall of '70 Vonnegut was being treated by that honorable and honorific bell cow of American letters himself, Leslie Fiedler, and in the pages of *Esquire*, long since past its days as an aspiring titmagazine and coming on strong with some heavy critical-intellectual fare. "Understandably enough," Fiedler said, "many survivors of the old critical regime find it difficult to persuade themselves that if, recently, they have come to esteem Vonnegut, it is not because they have been converted to the side of Pop, but because—though they did not at first realize it—he has all along belonged to the other side of High Art." But this "other side" of High Art, Fiedler maintained, is in fact not High Art but "the mainstream of myth and entertainment: a stream which was forced to flow underground over the past several 'decades' because of the influence of critics such as T. S. Eliot and

12. Robert Scholes, "Mithridates, He Died Old: Black Humor and Kurt Vonnegut Jr.," *Hollins Critic* 3, no. 4 (October 1966): 8; Bryan, "Vonnegut on Target."
13. Bryan, "Head Bokononist."

Cleanth Brooks." And it is to *this* mainstream of myth and entertainment, "to what we know again to be the mainstream of fiction,"[14] that Vonnegut *does* belong. In his way, then, Fiedler paid Vonnegut the ultimate compliment in his frame of reference by promoting him beyond High Art, which he sees as part of a dead tradition as far as the novel is concerned, and into his special category of mythic and still vital alternatives, the *real* mainstream of fictional art.

In a more traditionalist vein, Benjamin DeMott—in his cover story for *Saturday Review* in May 1971—saw Vonnegut's best work as transcending dogma and sermonizing and the simplicity of the themes that the youth cult grooved to. But here Vonnegut is seen as a tried-and-true classicist. Vonnegut's highest comedy is produced, according to DeMott, "when the subject in view is that of classical satire, namely self-delusion." In this context, Vonnegut is a "potent satirist," DeMott believes, "and an undeservedly good break for the age." This is because, DeMott sums up, with an obvious reference to Scholes's formulations, as "a *fabulist* [italics mine] in love with images of goodness, generosity, [and] hope," he has still managed to articulate "the blackest suspicions of a skeptical, cynical generation without running on into orgies of hate or ironical partisanship of evil."[15]

It is easy enough to see, I think, one might even say *aside* from its merits, why Vonnegut's work has finally become so attractive to the critics. Although the spade work has started, much more presumably will be necessary; for the texture of Vonnegut's work invites, if not literally *cries out* for, critical analysis and interpretation. The jolting connections, the recurrent imagery, the extractable meat of seductive thematic material, the elusive simplicity of technical virtuosity, the cross-references from book to book (and within each book) are intriguing to even the casual reader. As Jerome Klinkowitz has aptly pointed out, Vonnegut "teases us" with a whole "Mod Yoknapatawpha County."[16]

A case in point, which leads nicely into the last major point I wish to make about Vonnegut's rise, is that matter of "Call me Jonah"

14. Leslie Fiedler, "The Divine Stupidity of Kurt Vonnegut," *Esquire*, September 1970, 196.

15. DeMott, "Otherworldly Laughter," 38.

16. Jerome Klinkowitz, "Kurt Vonnegut, Jr., & the Crime of His Times," *Critique* 12, no. 3 (1971): 38.

at the beginning of *Cat's Cradle*. Those were the first three words of Vonnegut's I ever read, and with those three words Vonnegut hit me with an avalanche of implications that I have *yet* to get out from under. Even if "Call me Jonah" is nothing more than a "gratuitous though delightful"[17] parody of the opening of *Moby-Dick* together with an invocation of the biblical story of Jonah and *his* whale, it succeeds, as Robert Scholes has mentioned, in "preparing us for a story on the Job theme" with its "anti-Joblike conclusion." Yet it does more than that. It leaves you with the suspicion, doesn't it, that *Cat's Cradle* may very likely be *full* of hidden whale imagery or other references to *Moby-Dick* or Jonah? One of these days I'm going to take the time to find out—if somebody doesn't do a dissertation on it first.

KURT VONNEGUT FOR PRESIDENT

The further implication for me of Vonnegut's metaphor in the first three words of *Cat's Cradle*, suggesting a number of stories wherein heroes are put through trials and labors to test their virtues, is that the author himself is just such a figure. In a way he is Job, Jonah, Ahab, Christ, and Lot's wife all rolled into one. Prominent in nearly every published critical evaluation or review of his work, every glib summary or interview or portrait, especially since the appearance of *Slaughterhouse-Five*, has been the reiteration of the details of Vonnegut's now-famous trial by fire in Dresden and comment, always highly sympathetic, about Vonnegut's burden, about how the magnitude of the event devastated his psyche and nearly struck him dumb, and how he has spent the last twenty-five years of his life struggling to come to terms with this single overwhelming event. This biographical detail has captured the imaginations of the public and the publishing world, of the youth culture and the critics, as few others have since the days of Ernest Hemingway. What's more, Vonnegut looks the part and acts the part. He is perfectly cast.

The photograph that accompanied Robert Scholes's laudatory front-page review of *Slaughterhouse-Five* in the *New York Times Book Review*, for example, consciously or unconsciously, was a stroke of public-relations genius. Vonnegut is pictured before the bust of a very white lady atop a pillar, presumably Lot's wife, and, facing us, he has a perfectly remarkable expression on his face, the look

17. Scholes, "Fabulation and Satire," *The Fabulators*, 51.

of a man who has seen the end of the world and come back to tell the story. His eyes are closed. He is suffering cryptically. And he is suffering, we readily imagine, not merely from what he has *seen* but from his labors, from his years of service to an ideal of artistry, stifled so long not merely because of the difficulty of the artistic task he had set for himself but because of the uncooperativeness of the world, the demands it made of him to prostitute himself for its ignoble commercial purposes. Clearly, this man pictured before us has *earned* whatever small reward the world may be able to offer him.

In short, I believe that one explanation for Vonnegut's rise to fame is his role as a throwback to the good old days when life may or may not have made sense, but when artists, at least, *suffered*. Artists don't suffer much anymore, but Vonnegut is one who does. Artists aren't eyewitnesses to anything anymore, but Vonnegut was. He was there; he suffered. And significantly, I think, while he has managed to evade the "boring norms of realism"[18] in his work, he has done this without forfeiting the historically connected mystique of the existential hero-author.

Back in Iowa City, Vonnegut is telling a cocktail party joke. "So I wrote my first book, *Player Piano*, about Schenectady and it was published. But I would run into people who would downgrade me. I ran into Jason Epstein, a terribly powerful cultural commissar, at a cocktail party. When we were introduced, he thought a minute, then said, 'science fiction,' turned and walked off. He just had to place me, that's all." Vonnegut laughs. He is creating an atmosphere of tremendous sympathy for himself. This is one thing he is very good at.

"But I continued to include machinery in my books and, may I say in *confidence*, in my life. . . . Machinery is important. We must write about it. . . . But I don't care if you don't; I'm not urging you, am I? To hell with machinery." Tremendous. A living legend. Kurt Vonnegut for president!

Is it an accident, I wonder in looking back, that Robert Scholes, C. D. B. Bryan, and, later, Leslie Fiedler (not then present in Iowa City but a participant with Vonnegut during a symposium at Brown in 1969) had all met Vonnegut and knew him personally, were subject then to this tremendous personal appeal at about the time or just before each of them became interested enough in him to

18. DeMott, "Otherworldly Laughter," 30.

commit themselves to print on the subject of his work? Fortunate for Vonnegut and for us, I think, and suspicious possibly in a lesser writer, but in this case simply good luck for all concerned.

After Iowa City, the next time I saw Kurt Vonnegut he was sitting around with some CBS newsmen on television, giving his advice on a moon-landing. And after that I saw him again on *60 Minutes*, being interviewed in the orchestra pit of a darkened theater by Harry Reasoner. The media had undoubtedly caught on to his animal magnetism and sheer physical potential. He had passed his screen test. He filled the screen, as he filled a room, with the right kind of cool-image electricity, the right sense of subdued violence and heroic promise. Yes, indeed. Watching those brooding eyes on my screen, the "eyes of a sacrificial altar-bound virgin,"[19] Vonnegut seemed to me at that moment, as he must have for many others, a highly credible embodiment of the possibly fallacious idea that suffering ennobles.

19. Bryan, "Head Bokononist."

LITERARY
VICES

THE AUTOBIOGRAPHICAL TRAP

The first rule, if you have a choice, is that you should not write your first novel about the tragic and unfair events that occurred in your own life at age eighteen—even if they involve, as my novel did, the romance between a premed student and a Cincinnati striptease dancer.

If you are still young, write about an old folks' home, as John Updike did in *The Poorhouse Fair*. If you are a male, write from the point of view of a woman, as Reynolds Price did in *A Long and Happy Life*. In other words, show that you can escape the bounds of ego, that you have some essential capacity for imagining a life outside your own narrow and circumscribed world. The subject you choose to write about is far more important in determining your eventual success, or lack thereof, than you might at first imagine.

Having said that, I must admit that I am qualified to hold such an opinion because I did just the opposite. I knew it was a bad idea from the beginning, but I couldn't help myself. The events and characters of my own life at age eighteen dominated my imagination for years afterwards to such an extent that, simply in order to get on to the next chapter in my life, I felt I had to consider, to figure out, to capture, those elusive sensations, memories, and people—in order to be free of them.

Writing such a book eventually raised all the usual questions. Not just: How do you write a novel? (which is hard enough in itself). But: How do you get past the clichés of coming-of-age novels? How do you make an eighteen-year-old protagonist interesting enough to an audience of adults to make them care about his problems? I was not, after all, trying to write a book only for teens. Most adults have already encountered and solved eighteen-year-old problems— at eighteen—and are looking for some help with, or some news about, grown-up problems. Of course, my protagonist's problems were grown-up problems, and once I began to realize that, I was finally able to see the way.

By going through this agonizing process, I've learned some hard facts about the perils of autobiography that have taught me to be on guard for what I have privately come to call "the autobiographical trap." The autobiographical trap may cripple potentially good fiction in several ways: When one writes from life and from memory, there is always a tendency to become so involved emotionally with the material that the work becomes "too thin" or anorexic. The least suggestion (the slimmest outline or reminder) of the traumatic events you wish to write about causes the floodgates of emotion to open up for you. You are amazed at this latent power. So it is not difficult at all to persuade yourself that the floodgates will open for the reader as well. Of course, the disadvantage that readers have is that they have not lived your life and do not know the characters and have not had the benefit of the emotional attachment to these memories that are so easy for you. So they may have considerable trouble figuring out what is expected of them. They may have considerable trouble figuring out what is going on at all.

In other words, this natural emotional attachment to the subject matter leads the writer to unearned emotions. The emotions may have been earned in real life—of course—but they have to be earned in fiction all over again. This means a careful and full rendering of the action, the motivations, and the expository details that are so familiar to the writer that they are easy to overlook.

Another tooth of the autobiographical trap is the tendency to include irrelevant details in place of convincing (and much more potentially exciting) story development *simply because those details were part of the original memory or event.* Most often, this tendency mucks up endings, but it can do damage every step of the way.

It is a sorry fact that life does not often work out in perfect story or novel form. That is, if you adhere stubbornly to the actual details of some chain of events from your own life, most often you will end up with a flawed and self-centered piece of drivel. At best, you will end up with interesting autobiography. But fiction is not autobiography—it is something more than that—and hardly anyone's life is interesting enough, minute by minute, to sustain autobiography that will have anything more than local appeal.

The trick is to find those elements in the material that help to universalize it and, based on those realities, invent the best story you can imagine. Imagination must enter the process. Writers must be willing to change the details of actually lived events in order to make a better story—and that is the most difficult lesson to accept. They must do this because they have an obligation to reach out beyond their own narrow boundaries if they ever wish to reach a wide audience. Too often, writers are counseled to "write about what you know" without any qualifications. My advice would be: "Only write about what you know if what you know is worth something to someone else." Also: "Only write about what you know as long as what you know is interesting."

Two other crucial processes deserve more attention—equal billing with "write about what you know" (autobiography). They are: "Make up what you can't know" (imagination) and "Find out what you need to know" (research). To summarize: Three important processes are usually involved in writing good fiction, and these are (1) writing from memory, (2) writing from invention, and (3) writing from research. The judicious writer eventually learns when each process must be set in motion and when each must be brought under control.

STILL ARGUING ABOUT
MORAL FICTION

In 1972 John Gardner published a seminal essay, "The Way We Write Now," in which he expounded upon some of the same ideas that he would later consider, more lengthily and carefully, in *On Moral Fiction*. Gardner's polemic, in both cases, interests me because the effort to understand and constantly redefine "the way we write now" is important. But I still find it difficult to reconcile Gardner's ideas with the facts, then and now, and with the opinions of several of the writers I had spoken to in preparation for my book *The New Fiction*, many of the same, including Donald Barthelme, William H. Gass, and Joyce Carol Oates, who were given individual treatment in "The Way We Write Now" and *On Moral Fiction*. I believe the premises of Gardner's arguments were aesthetically retrograde and the ideas, in some cases, downright silly and wrong—which is harmless perhaps in itself—but he *did* seem to be trying to make his analysis into a prescription for us all.

Gardner's diagnosis included these two major complaints: One, the work of then-contemporary novelists was "doomed by indifference to novelistic form"; and two, contemporary writers were too apt to sacrifice "thought-out values" in favor of pure style or simple (rather than complex) affirmation.

It is obvious, we are told, that American novelists "can never get rid of the qualifying effect of American literary and cultural tradition—that is, the American character—as long as they write to or about Americans." Since Gardner's definition of "the American character" was limited to "the American hunger for . . . affirmation" and "American innocence" as embodied in such characters as Huck Finn, Yankee Doodle, and Holden Caulfield, it is little wonder perhaps that he found those attributes exemplified in some form in every American writer worth mentioning—whatever else he felt they might be lacking—and Huck Finn under every rain barrel.

All living American writers have their problems, he seemed to be saying, mainly due to sloth or lack of skill or intelligence (neglect of form) and failure of moral fiber or moral perception (absence of thought-out values); but . . . *are they ever* Americans from first to last! Here you have these poor, stupid, heroic, aging writers, all struggling along, all thinking they are onto something new or vital, when actually, blindly, they are simply repeating Mark Twain or Melville, responding to the monstrous, unseen forces of the American landscape that require that they forever mysteriously affirm "American innocence" and "cautious optimism" and other lit-crit clichés. Also mysteriously, even though working independently, each writer in his own way—from Barth to Updike—ends up falling prey to exactly the same foolishness. A remarkable state of affairs.

Gardner's analysis still sounds to me like a well-intentioned but wrongheaded effort to reduce (and therefore comprehend?) the genuine diversity, the manifold variety of American fiction by means of a pet "system" of dubious principles, faulty premises, graduate-school drivel about American innocence and "the American character," and stodgy Jamesian prejudices. Why must critics forever attempt to reduce such multiformity to a single spurious unifying principle? This does not enhance understanding but is rather an example, it seems to me, of the very simplemindedness Gardner urged writers to attack.

Is it true that most American fictional efforts (over, say, the last thirty years) are "doomed by indifference to novelistic form," as Gardner argues? If he means that current writers are not concerned enough with form, I think he is demonstrably wrong. In fact, most of the writers he mentions—certainly Barth, Barthelme, Coover, Gass, Kosinski, Oates, and Vonnegut—seem especially notable for their attention to form and for a great variety of formal experimentation. Among the writers interviewed for *The New Fiction*—including all of the above—and others such as John Hawkes, Ishmael Reed, Susan Sontag, and Ronald Sukenick, none, in fact, mentioned "indifference to novelistic form" as a symptom of decrepitude in the prose fiction of their contemporaries. Tom Wolfe, clearly a black sheep in this company, though then working on his novel *Bonfire of the Vanities*, argued plausibly enough that "the novelists are [in fact] strangling themselves on what is now a very orthodox . . . aesthetics *based* on the manipulation of form" [italics mine].

Even Susan Sontag, whose famous complaint Gardner echoed— that "the sense of what might be done with form in fiction . . . written by Americans . . . is . . . rudimentary, uninspired, and stagnant"

("Against Interpretation," 1964)—no longer agrees with this assessment. She believes, as I do, that "a kind of explosion in prose fiction" has taken place in this country since 1964 due (among other things) to the influence and the competition of other forms and that "more sophistication, more awareness of form" is characteristic of this change.

If, on the other hand, Gardner meant also that most current fictional efforts are "doomed by indifference to novelistic form" because writers are indifferent to the conventional forms of the novel—Victorian, realistic, or Jamesian à la Percy Lubbock—which, I fear, is one thing he did mean, then I can hardly agree that such a state should be cause for their doom.

Is it true that our fiction needs more emphasis on "thought-out values—the solid foundations of character that Henry James or Jane Austen fictionally develop and *recommend* to the reader"? [italics mine]. *Is* it in "the careful scrutiny of cleanly apprehended characters, their conflicts and ultimate escape from immaturity, that the novel makes up its solid truths"? *Is* it true that "what great novelists always do" is "to build tight form out of single-minded psychological and moral analysis"?

The achievement of Henry James (or Jane Austen) will always, of course, survive shifts in literary taste and changing political and cultural conditions, and will always in a sense remain unequaled. But, as Wayne Booth has pointed out, James, for one, was far less dogmatic than his followers (Lubbock and others). James's wide-ranging and flexible critical explorations quickly became schematized, reduced, and misconstrued. I am not at all sure that James himself would agree with Gardner's reformulation of his principles, or that John Gardner's own novels, some of which are very good indeed, exemplify such principles.

For that matter, even though James's technical constructs were right for him, and helpful to many of us, we can't go on forever relying on James's aesthetics, can we? Every new writer, it seems to me, must become his own aesthetician.

Personally, I think I would object if any current novelist tried to "recommend" any "thought-out values" to me, and I'm happy that most of them have the common decency and good sense not to. True: "The assertion that style is life's only value—that style redeems life—is false both to life and to the novel." I agree. But nobody is saying this—not even Genet (to use an amoral example), and certainly not

Barth or Coover, both keenly aware of "novelistic form" and of "thought-out values."

And what does Gardner mean by "solid foundations of character"? One might describe American fiction of the last few decades as particularly marvelous for its unexplicit acceptance, or discovery, of new ideas about character. Maybe eighteenth- or nineteenth-century ideas about character simply do not apply accurately to "life lived" or "life formed and identified" in our time. And maybe characters should not always be "cleanly apprehended"—as real people aren't—even by American writers steeped in the Protestant-and-Proctor-and-Gamble ethic. I'm sure ideas about character will continue to change.

Neither do I believe that a character's "ultimate escape from immaturity" necessarily provides a basis for some "solid truth" in the novel. Does Gardner's own Grendel ultimately "escape from immaturity"? Start naming great characters who are immature to the bitter end. As William H. Gass has said, "I distrust people, including artists, who make pretentious claims for literature as a source of knowledge."

I submit that the chief fault of John Gardner's argument is his adherence to the historically discredited idea that art should provide moral exhortation. He wants a sermon, or, at best, a Victorian novel with a message, characters as moral exemplars, and a coherent system of universals. What he gives us, in the end, are some highly conservative ideas couched in authoritative-sounding, more-hip-than-thou rhetoric, placing himself, as a critic, squarely in the same camp with Plato and William Bennett.

All right, what can be said about the state of fictional art in America? I do not believe the American literary and cultural tradition—especially the cutting edge of its movement through the present moment—can be accurately characterized in a few pat phrases such as "American innocence" or "hunger for affirmation," even if these were apt phrases.

Where Gardner finds in the work of Donald Barthelme, for example, the "childishness and befuddled innocence of Yankee Doodle," I find perhaps the sophistication and the jaded sensibility of the metropolitan libertine. I find it difficult to imagine Yankee Doodle as the author of *Unspeakable Practices, Unnatural Acts*. What this difference means exactly or where it gets us is hard to say, except perhaps to the conclusion that one of us is wrong, or that sophistication may be expressed as innocence, or that beyond a certain level of complexity almost anything may seem plausible that one wishes to imagine as such. I think one must at least acknowledge the complexity of the problem of defining, or even speaking intelligently about, such difficult concepts as traditions or sensibilities.

In any case, imagination—that highly underrated but absolutely essential faculty of perception—is very much a part of the issue. What other, more convincing justification is there for art now—to lay my premises on the table—than its radical usefulness in remaking our models of ourselves and what we find around us? Imagination is a most powerful form of perception—this bears repeating. I do not think we turn to a great novelist necessarily because she or he is a great thinker, a great psychologist, or a person of great virtue or moral perception (whatever that is exactly)—but almost always because she or he is at least a great imaginer.

If one is looking for moral exemplars, however, I think they are available too. Joyce Carol Oates's novel *Wonderland*, for instance, was widely reviewed and too frequently dismissed as yet another gothic horror novel. Certainly some horrible events do occur in *Wonderland*. The protagonist's deranged father attempts to murder his entire family and nearly succeeds!—except for the young protagonist, Jesse Vogel. The novel poses the question: How can such a person go on? *Wonderland*, I believe, can and should be read at one level as the story of how this one fragile man, Jesse Vogel, followed into adulthood, survives against incredible odds. It is above all a desentimentalized and brilliantly unobtrusive story of human triumph—not such an easy subject to write about these days. Jesse's triumph may be described as limited in comparative terms. He may not live a happy life; he may be frequently on the verge of some madness. But he always does manage to stop just short of chaos, to draw on some resource, some native capacity for goodness or equilibrium—a person who has every right to end up absolutely balmy, a man who has every right to become a complete failure.

Yet it is not the moral perfection or the "thought-out values" of her work or life for which one most values Joyce Carol Oates, in this or in any of her other creative work, but the evocative power of her imagination, which makes all else possible.

In the decades since the deaths of Hemingway and Faulkner, much has been written about the future, gloomy or bright, of American prose fiction. Entrants in the ongoing fiction sweepstakes have continued to proliferate in spite of dire predictions, and the jockeying for position to fill vacancies in the pantheon has been a tacit, if not always clearly acknowledged, preoccupation of numbers of writers, critics, reviewers, and readers. Writers were seen to be struggling against a "whole way of using language," as Louis D. Rubin Jr. pointed out in his mid-sixties essay "The Curious Death of the Novel," "a whole way of giving order to reality," which had been imposed on the sensibility of the times by the great writers of the immediate past. Rubin went on to comment, "What we are likely to have . . . is a period lasting as long as a full generation or more in which our better writers are more or less engaged, however unintentionally, primarily with learning to see things in their own right again so that what they produce is no longer importantly compromised by the version of reality afforded them by their great immediate predecessors."

Since that prediction was made, a surprisingly short time ago, massive, bewildering changes in the literary climate have taken place in precisely the way that Rubin described—except that change itself has come about with greater swiftness than anyone might have guessed. Fiction, that most arrière-garde of contemporary forms, was suddenly involved in the process of catching up with painting, music, and film, and was suddenly in the process of catching up with the age.

This movement has been characterized by amazing transformations of sensibility and language, and by a great variety of formal and technical innovation. Generalizations about it are dangerous because it is by no means monolithic or the result of any conspiracy, and it is a process still in motion. But suddenly writers have emerged who face us with compelling new versions of reality—more sophisticated though no less stylized than "realism," highly contemporaneous, and in decidedly idiosyncratic, imaginative, and personal idioms.

If, indeed, language is in some way constitutive of our reality and if imagination is as important a mode of perception as rational-analytical or other modes of perception, then, it seems to me, several current American fiction writers—and I would list most of those Gardner was interested in and complained about, and several others who have begun writing since "The Way We Write Now" first appeared—are especially responsive to the vibrations of a culture hardly resembling that of their predecessors. And they are busily transforming us all. We should be grateful.

In one respect, of course, John Gardner was perfectly accurate. We don't write like Henry James anymore. But rather than bemoaning that development, I see it as a sign that we are already, after all, better than ninety years into the twentieth century, nearly to the twenty-first, and about to set forth into a new millennium.

FIVE SEX ACTS
AND WILD THING

John Frohnmayer's Last
Days at the NEA, and Mine

The first indication that the literature program might be in for trouble was a Freedom of Information Act (FOIA) request from a neoconservative watchdog organization about a grant to a magazine called the *Portable Lower East Side*. The issue the watchdogs wanted to know about had just hit the newsstands, and it had the sort of memorable title that certain prudes and zealots of the religious right prayed for every day but seldom experienced firsthand. It was called "Live Sex Acts."

We had not yet seen that issue of the magazine, and we quickly determined that we had not approved any such grant for any such issue, though we had supported some previous issues of the *Portable Lower East Side,* and we knew from past experience that it was a magazine with an urban sensibility that would not ordinarily be applauded by the folks in, say, Tupelo, Mississippi.

When we did finally locate a copy of "Live Sex Acts," the then-current issue of the *Portable Lower East Side,* it turned out to be a thematic issue that made an effort to document the environment of sex clubs and sex-for-hire that was very much a part of the street life of the city. The editor thanked the NEA for its support, though he may have been referring to past support. One feature of the issue was a series of black-and-white photos by a photographer who liked to take pictures of partially nude women in public places.

The women were not posed seductively, and the style had a kind of gritty realism about it that made it altogether different from something one might see in *Penthouse*. If one wanted to defend the photos, one could always fall back, I suppose, on talk about the tradition of the nude in the history of art. I certainly didn't find them offensive, or in need of defending, but then I am one of those people who admires women, with or without clothes, and who actually admires female anatomy above almost any other form, whether in art or in real life. In my opinion, men who are frightened or offended by women who have their clothes off or women who have chocolate syrup on their breasts have a problem that no amount of censorship is going to cure.[1]

But I realized that to some people the photos would simply look like a bunch of dirty pictures; and I could already imagine some of the headlines and angry letters to the editor from outraged citizens who felt that their sixty-eight-cent donation to the arts that year gave them the right to decide what was art and what wasn't.

Up until that point the literature program had maintained a kind of immunity from the attacks of the right-wingers, primarily, I believed, because the watchdogs did not have the patience to read everything we were supporting. Literature is less accessible than the visual and performing arts and film. One has to be able to exercise a certain patience and a certain intelligence to read something, after all—and ascertaining the meaning is not as easy as reading a sign and is somewhat less than instantaneous. Ascertaining meaning in the other arts is often less-than-instantaneous as well, but finding deeper meanings is not something the detractors of the NEA are very interested in. So having a bunch of photographs was more of a problem for us than usual, even though, as I say, *we had not funded the project and there was nothing wrong with the pictures.* We had the luxury of deniability, but that hardly mattered. Any number of other projects that the agency had not, in fact, supported—from Annie Sprinkle's flashlight show to the New York Shakespeare Festival's semi-nude production of *A Midsummer Night's Dream*—had been hung around our necks like albatrosses. Whatever was the opposite of the Teflon phenomenon, we were it.

In pointing out the differences between works of art and signs in *The Shock of the New*, critic Robert Hughes has suggested an explanation for some of the difficulties the NEA has been having from popular audiences unaccustomed to exercising the patience necessary to understand works of art. According to Hughes, "Mass production strips every image of its singularity, rendering it schematic and quickly identifiable, so that it resembles a sign. A sign is a command. Its message comes all at once. It means only one thing—nuance and

1. Here I am referring to the work of performance artist Karen Finley.

ambiguity are not important properties of signs." On the other hand, Hughes continues, "Works of art speak in a more complicated way of relationships, hints, uncertainties, and contradictions. They do not force meanings on their audience; meaning emerges, adds up, unfolds from their imagined centres." In addition, film, television, and photography tend to exacerbate the tendency to read all images as signs, according to Hughes. Because of the barrage of images we receive in our culture, we tend to skim. There "is no way of paying equal attention to all that surplus. . . . The image we remember is the one that most resembles a sign: simple, clear, repetitious."

Another ongoing problem for the NEA that is seldom taken into account—at least in terms of potential to create controversy—is the fact that grants are based on an applicant's past work. But once a grant is made, the NEA has no idea what the artist will produce; and what's more, unless Congress is willing to allocate many more millions to increase the staff and oversight capabilities of the agency, it is unreasonable to hold the NEA responsible for what the artist eventually produces, though that is what the critics of the NEA seem to expect. In fact, the NEA, at present, takes very little interest in what the artist produces after the fact of the grant, since by then all resources are going into evaluating applications for the next round. When you bet on talent, you don't always win the first round. You don't always win any round—as in any other research and development arena, from biological research to minor league baseball. You support the best work, the best talent you can find; years go by; and you take it as a matter of faith that, eventually, something of passing greatness will turn up that wouldn't have turned up otherwise.

Our research indicated that the literature program had a laudable record of supporting talent. Not that winners of prizes are the only ones in possession of great talent—certainly not. But using that criterion as *some sort* of yardstick: During the decade of the eighties, 60 percent of writers who later won major national awards, such as the Pulitzer, the National Book Award, and the National Book Critics Circle prizes, had previously been encouraged early in their careers by grants from the literature program. Some 70 percent of the Pulitzer Prize winners in poetry had been supported early on by the NEA, as had 66.7 percent of the winners of the PEN/Faulkner Award for Fiction. And 57 percent of the creative writers awarded MacArthur "genius" fellowships up to 1988 had previously been supported by the literature program of the NEA. Considering the fact that NEA individual fellowships are judged anonymously by a different panel each year, this record shows a remarkable ability to target and support some of America's most promising emerging writers.

In any case, we watched the clips, and there was a certain amount of noise about "Live Sex Acts." Someone in the conservative press then apparently misread it as "Five Sex Acts," which must have sounded even more ghastly to them. So we watched a second small ripple of complaint make the rounds of several other publications, who referred to "Five Sex Acts" attributed to the NEA (though never indicating which five). But, all in all, the controversy seemed to be blowing over without much effect.

Then the bombshell exploded. Another issue of the *Portable Lower East Side* had just hit the streets, and the Reverend Wildmon had somehow gotten hold of an issue before almost anyone else in the country and discovered a poem there called "Wild Thing" that he found extremely offensive. The poem went on for six pages, but Reverend Wildmon just Xeroxed the part that he found particularly contemptible:

> Christ sucked my dick
> behind the pulpit
> I was 6 years old
> he made me promise
> not to tell no one.

And he sent the Xeroxed copy of his excerpt to every member of Congress and to every member of the White House staff and to the president. We received a copy of Wildmon's memo and Xerox before we received the magazine itself, and we heard that the phone lines in the Congressional Liaison Office were burning up. A lot of yelling was going on.

My first impression was that if your goal was to juxtapose sex, religion, and child abuse in the shortest possible space with the maximum of gross-out potential, it would be hard to beat these five lines of "Wild Thing."

We ran around trying to get our hands on a copy of the issue, and in the meantime we checked our files. What we found was that this issue *had* been supported by a grant from the literature program, though its potentially provocative street title, "Queer City," had not been part of the initial application. The application had asked for support for an anthology that would contain "the best writing" by gay and lesbian writers in New York, and the grants committee had supported it, the national council had approved it, and John Frohnmayer had signed off on it.

Randy McAusland, the deputy chairman for programs, my immediate boss, showed up that afternoon with a copy of "Queer City" under his arm, which he handed to me as if it were literally about to detonate right there in the Nancy Hanks Center of the Old Post Office. He said: "Joe David, you're our literary expert. Take a look at this magazine and give me your honest opinion. We're especially interested in what you think of the poem, 'Wild Thing,' but we'd like to hear your expert opinion on the whole publication. Then we'd like your recommendation about what you think we should do about this." I said I would give it a shot.

I took the magazine home that night and read it from cover to cover. What "Queer City" turned out to be was mostly okay-if-not-great writing by a number of gay and lesbian writers in New York, some of whom had never been heard from before, some of whom had. But it was certainly close enough to the original description that there was no arguing with the source or intent of the support, even if we had wanted to, which I certainly didn't but I suspected others might. It contained another series of black-and-white photos, some of which were unusual though not blatantly explicit, and it had some fairly good writing in it. Like any other issue of a literary magazine, it reflected the culture from which it had sprung; and some of the material was raw, just like life on the Lower East Side.

The poem "Wild Thing" turned out to be a persona poem by a black woman poet named Sapphire. In the poem, Sapphire tries to imagine what was going on *inside the head* of one of the assailants in the Central Park jogger attack. As you can imagine, what she found there was not pretty. She hypothesizes that the young man had been abused as a child (hence the passage quoted earlier) and that his mind is full of racism, sexism, and murderous rage. The poem uses strong language, exactly the kind of language that might actually occur inside the mind of a violent rapist. I found it to be an upsetting poem—because the act was upsetting—but the imaginative reach of the poet was impressive and credible. I remembered that when I had first read about the case, I had wondered, "What could those young men possibly have been *thinking?*" The crime seemed so utterly random and brutal. "Why would anyone *do* such a thing?" I couldn't imagine a plausible reason, but after reading "Wild Thing" I understood the crime, and the motivation for it, quite a bit more clearly. I was grateful to the poet for having committed herself to such a harrowing task and for accomplishing it so convincingly. I thought "Wild Thing" was the best piece of writing in the magazine.

The average citizen, who perhaps expects poetry to be a harmless evocation of hearts and flowers, would not be likely to appreciate the poem, however. Reverend Wildmon, quite obviously, had not understood the poem—according to several press sources he believed the poem *advocated* child abuse—and it seemed quite likely that several members of Congress would not understand or appreciate the poem either, no matter what anyone might say to them. But what was the National Endowment for the Arts supposed to do? Repudiate a grant because one poem, arguably the best piece of writing in a particular issue of a magazine, used "bad" words? Repudiate a grant because powerful political forces were lining up against it? Repudiate a grant because too many people were too stupid or badly educated to see what the poem was really about?

Of course, the White House was running scared and wanted the NEA to go away as a political issue. Pat Buchanan had been doing too well in the primaries. He had captured 31 percent of the vote in New Hampshire, and he was marching through Georgia describing the Arts Endowment as the "upholstered playpen of the eastern liberal establishment." One of his campaign ads excerpted scenes from the award-winning film *Tongues Untied*—which the Arts Endowment had subsidized during the Reagan administration (of which Buchanan himself was a part)—and attacked Bush by claiming the Bush-supported Endowment was nothing but a purveyor of pornography, which glorified homosexuals, exploited children, and perverted the image of Jesus Christ, all at the taxpayers' expense. And he was getting away with it.

The next day I gave Deputy Chairman McAusland my opinion about "Wild Thing," and I recommended that we stand strongly behind the poem and the grant and take the consequences, whatever they might be, because I didn't see any other possible course of action.

I have no way of knowing what sorts of deliberations went on in the chairman's office that day, but I do know that John Frohnmayer was under pressure from all sides to close down the grant; and there were even forces at work within the agency to close down the grant behind his back. To his great credit, he put a stop to them and he came out in support of the grant and the poem. He issued a press release and sent a memo to members of Congress and to the White House staff that included a copy of the complete poem and that defended "Wild Thing" as "a serious work of art conveying a serious message about a serious problem," and explained further that the excerpt had been "taken out of context and sensationalized. The poem, in its entirety, is emotional, intense and serious. It uses a traditional literary format in which the author writes from the point of view of the character, which in this case is a hostile and violent young man. The poem . . . must be read in its entirety in order to receive a fair appraisal."

But the forces marshaled against him had lost all patience. Ask members of Congress and the White House staff to *actually read six pages of dirty poetry!—during an election year!* Within a few days, he was ordered to report to the White House, and Sam Skinner, the president's chief of staff, fired him.

John Frohnmayer called together all 278 members of the staff of the National Endowment for the Arts to tell us he would be leaving. He said:

> I believe that art is essential to our lives. . . . I believe that our government, in promoting the general welfare of its people, must support the arts—at a substantial level and without content restrictions. Only by so doing does our government encourage us to dare, to create, to grow. . . . I believe that human decency does not come at the call of any political body, group, or individual, but rather from a willingness to share, to think, to attempt to put ourselves in the mind and position of others. . . . And I leave with . . . a fundamental belief in the goodness of the American people and the ability of our society to right itself. I leave with the belief that this eclipse of the soul will soon pass and with it the lunacy that sees artists as enemies and ideas as demons.

Then, in a ghostly voice, he sang us a verse from the Shaker hymn called "Simple Gifts" to illustrate the idea that leadership means service, and, at the end, he recited a poem by William Stafford and then waded into the crowd, up and down the rows, shaking hands and hugging people.

I knew after that meeting that I didn't want to hang around the place much longer myself. My two-year term was almost over and I could see that, temporarily at least—certainly until after the election—the agency's primary goal would be to try to put a lid on any controversial grants. Without Frohnmayer there to stand up for artistic freedom and negotiate in behalf of the arts with the herd of philistines and gibbering idiots who oversee the budget and the legislation for the Endowments (which Frohnmayer, incidentally, was very good at doing), we could be in for a long night of the soul. I know the writers and artists of America mostly believe otherwise, but, whether they know it or not, they owe a big debt to John Frohnmayer, Esq. He made some gaffs early on and put his foot in his mouth more than once, but he is a true lover of the arts and he managed to achieve reauthorization of the NEA without content restrictions at a time of savage hostility to the arts in America, when the danger of losing the agency altogether was more than likely. That was a major achievement. He was often blamed for holding positions or attitudes that he, in fact, opposed strenuously, including Jesse Helms's "decency" language, which, if enacted into law, would have outlawed 90 percent of the American novels written in the twentieth century as too indecent for support from the federal government. Frohnmayer withstood incredible abuse from all sides, including those he was most trying to help.

As I watched him bowing out on that final day, I remembered one of my first impressions of John Frohnmayer: I had just arrived in Washington and I happened to pass him hurrying down the hall. He called out, "Hi, there, Joe David. I just checked your novel, *Suzi Sinzinnati*, out of the Endowment library and I'm reading it!" "Fine," I said. "Let me know what you think of it." *Oh, God,* I thought, if he actually does read it, this may be one of the shortest terms of office in NEA history. I was surprised that I had managed to proceed that far without anyone at the Arts Endowment apparently finding out what was *actually in* my novel. What they might have found, if anyone had read it, was a love story that, strictly speaking, involves hot lust, striptease, and quite enough frank and explicit sex to make Reverend Wildmon blush, not to mention a lengthy satire of fundamentalist religious bigotry—though I, of course, think it offers a bit more than that—all played out against a backdrop of nostalgic tunes of the late fifties and early sixties. But, amazingly enough, the next time I saw the chairman, he came up and shook my hand and said: "Joe David, I absolutely loved *Suzi*! My wife is reading it too and cracking up on every page. So far her only complaint is that she thinks you didn't put enough 'na-nas' in 'Sha-na-na.' She made me sing 'Sha-na-na' to her several times so that she could count the 'na-nas.' *I think you got them all.*"

As soon as my resignation became public, I was barraged by calls from reporters. The *New York Times*, the *Washington Post*, the *Los Angeles Times*, the *Boston Globe*, and *Variety* were especially determined to talk to me and get my version of why I was leaving and why so many directors seemed to be leaving simultaneously. Was it a purge by the new regime? No, it wasn't. I talked to about half a dozen reporters, and when I stopped taking calls at the office, they called me at home at night. Most of them seemed to hope I would say something provocative or incriminating and come out swinging, and they were highly skillful at manipulating the conversation in such a way as to increase that possibility.

Of course, it would be bigger news if I was resigning to protest the decisions of new Acting Chairman Anne Radice or if I was being forced out. But I resisted the temptation to rise to that bait. My sense of it, at that moment, was that yet another inflammatory news story was not going to do the agency any good and that, while I certainly had my differences with Anne Radice's decisions and modus operandi—and didn't want to be identified with her regime—it was simply not in the best interests of the agency, and the writers and other artists it was created to support, to say so publicly, especially while the 1993 budget for the NEA was still kicking around in Congress.

One of Anne Radice's first acts as acting chairman had been to veto two grants in support of exhibits that included images of the human body, including genitalia. Arts supporters cried foul. Anne Radice's "reforms" went down very well with Congress and the executive branch, however. At least five senators who had been NEA supporters actually calculated that they were about to lose their jobs because of the NEA controversy all by itself. Word out of the Congressional Liaison Office was that these particular senators were greatly relieved after Radice's vetoes and that, following Radice's tough public stance against sexually explicit art, the mail to members of Congress was overwhelmingly positive regarding the NEA, for the first time in years.

One incident I still remember most vividly about Anne Radice took place during a meeting of a national council working group in my office at the Arts Endowment. Somehow the subject of support for gay or lesbian writers came up, and I said I believed, unequivocally, that homosexuals "ought to be entitled, like anyone else, to write about their own lives," which seemed to me such a fundamental right that it was simply unarguable. Before I had finished the end of the sentence, Anne stood up abruptly and said, "Well, now we're getting into the area of policy," and hustled them all out of the room as fast as she could.

Late in my tenure at the NEA, board members of one of the major service organizations in the literary field, Associated Writing Programs (AWP), began talking with me about the possibility of my joining them as executive director once I had completed my term with the NEA. Previous to my employment at the NEA, I had served as a board member for AWP, and so to avoid any appearance of a conflict of interest I had resigned from the AWP board upon my hiring by the NEA and I had recused myself from all panel meetings when AWP grants were under consideration. In any case, at the time that talks regarding my future employment with AWP were beginning, I had been working for months on developing a new series of special projects grants—involving summer seminars for high school teachers—that would bring new money into the literature program, and I had persuaded the powers-that-be within the agency to support this ambitious new million-dollar program, which was even then wending its way toward final approval. One of the chief beneficiaries of this new money was to be AWP, the very organization that wanted to hire me on as executive director.

As anyone knows who has worked in the field, one of the cardinal rules of such an office is that the appearance of a conflict of interest, even if none exists, is considered the same thing as a conflict of interest. Public perception of the fairness of the processes of grant-giving is extremely important. So, sensing that I might be heading for an "appearance of conflict" situation, though I was satisfied that I had acted all along in good faith, I broached the subject and discussed it at length with my immediate supervisor, the deputy chairman for programs. I explained the lengths I had gone to to avoid any conflicts of interest involving AWP, both in their annual professional development grants and in this new round of special projects grants. I then offered to withdraw from any further consideration as an officer for AWP if he felt it would jeopardize the special projects funding or create any sort of problem for the literature program, the NEA, or AWP. As an additional safeguard, I explained that I had arranged for a buffer zone between the end of my term at the NEA and the beginning of any sort of future employment for AWP—a six-month sabbatical after leaving the NEA and a delay on any announcement of my new affiliation until well after I had departed.

His response was clear and immediate—essentially, it was that he did not see any problem, "not at all." He agreed, in considering all the details, that I had acted appropriately, and he agreed, further, that I had every right to proceed with post-NEA-employment talks, since, "everyone who joins the NEA comes from the field, and one expects that most people departing the NEA will return to whatever field they have represented." Otherwise, no one would be willing to serve.

Thus reassured that I was on a firm footing, I held further talks with representatives of AWP and moved closer to a commitment to join them, stressing that I could consider it only if they would agree to the six-month buffer zone and complete confidentiality about the possibility of my appointment—since failure to do so might jeopardize their future grants or my ability to follow through.

However, on Anne Radice's first trip to New York as the new acting chairman, firm in her resolve to control all potential controversy, someone put a bug in her ear about my plans, which she had not known about previously. A member of the AWP board—either from naïveté, stupidity, or because they were opposed to my candidacy—had leaked information about the possibility of my joining AWP—an action, as it turned out, that came close to killing the organization. The executive director for a competing literary organization, who perhaps feared that his own funding might suffer if I were to join AWP, told Radice of his deep concern about this potentially explosive and shocking subject.

When Radice returned to D.C., she moved swiftly and decisively to prevent any controversy: She put a hold on the progress of the special projects grants from the literature program and she declared that the regular AWP organizational grant would have to be repaneled, though it had already been approved by a panel from which I had recused myself. Although we had been on cordial terms previously, she refused to talk to me. So I was left with no choice but to plead my case in behalf of the AWP grants via memo. I felt the repaneling of the organizational grant was particularly unfair, since without it, AWP was dead; and I had done everything by the book. (Fortunately for all concerned, the new panel eventually felt the same way that the first one had, and the AWP organizational grant was eventually approved.)

But soon it became clear to me that AWP was going to be held hostage on all future grants if I joined as executive director. Radice simply did not want some fool to be able to claim that Bellamy had secured so many hundreds of thousands for AWP, then he jumped aboard the ship himself and sailed out of town, however wrongheaded that claim would have been. To join the organization would have been to do irreparable harm to it, short-circuiting its NEA funding for the unknowable future. And so I ended up withdrawing and disappointing a lot of people at AWP, some of whom decided on the spot that I was a shit and had always been a shit, even though they had no idea of the whole story behind my withdrawal or refused to believe the facts. Not incidentally, my decision cost me roughly half a year's salary, which I could not really afford to lose. But neither could I afford to be executive director of an organization with its major source of funding cut off forever and the guilt of having helped to cause such a demise. By November 1992 all of this would have been moot, but who could have predicted at that point that the Democrats would win the election? It seemed like a long shot.

Down the road, after my departure from the NEA, AWP did receive some of the special projects funding, and I am pleased to be able to report that under its new executive director it now has the biggest annual budget in its history and is prospering as never before. If there is a moral to this story, it is that the personal costs of public service may be high; that when election politics and millions of dollars are involved, people can be ruthless and unreasonable; and that sometimes those who take the biggest risks on behalf of others are the last to be thanked, if they are ever thanked at all. But sometimes, in spite of the confusion, betrayal, resentment, and bad behavior, good things happen anyway.

Noontimes, I used to go for a long, slow jog down the Mall and around the Tidal Basin beneath the Japanese cherry trees and along the concrete esplanade beside the Jefferson Memorial. On a good day you could see the planes trailing down the Potomac toward National Airport in the distance or the sudden noisy beating of helicopters blasting by overhead on their way to the White House or the Pentagon. Halfway around the loop I would usually rest on a park bench near where the resident homeless person was deeply and blissfully sleeping and, like him, try to forget about my problems and stare at the ripples for a few minutes and the marvelous edifice of the Jefferson Memorial across the water—and sometimes think about Jefferson's words on the circular frieze inside before returning to the agony of the literature program office: "I have sworn upon the altar of God eternal hostility against every form of tyranny over the mind of man."

In responding to the brouhaha after my resignation was announced, I said to the press: "Whatever the future for the NEA, I'm hoping that freedom of expression will prevail. If the public knew the truth, I think they would support the NEA. The truth is that it is extraordinarily difficult for serious talented writers and artists to find encouragement in the United States; and most of them are enormously grateful for any support they receive and they work hard to earn it. The truth is that we would look like baboons to the rest of the civilized world if we abandoned Federal support for the arts and thus became the only Western nation to do so. I am not attempting to make a statement by my resignation about anything, except that this is a hard job and I did it for as long as I could and I hope I helped while I was here."

CONTEMPORARIES

MAX APPLE

The spirit that made America what it is today is still operative, according to Max Apple in his remarkable debut, *The Oranging of America*. That peculiar combination of resourcefulness, fanaticism, greed, and dumb luck is all around us, just waiting to launch another multibillion-dollar franchise. This spirit is embodied for Apple during a fill-up at the world's largest gas station, in a real-estate woman's yen to transform the Astrodome into a climate-controlled subdivision for middle-income bungalows, or in an elderly scientist's obsession with the health-giving properties of yogurt that leads him to hypothesize a yogurt-based theory of history.

Most appealingly, it turns up in the fictionalized figure of Howard Johnson, the restaurant magnate of ice-cream-in-twenty-eight-flavors fame, who is spending his last years still traveling the byways of the nation with his longtime assistant, Millie (in a 1964 Cadillac), shrewdly plying his unique gift for sniffing out the perfect location for yet another orange-roofed eatery or rest stop. There is something almost biblical in Howard Johnson's quest: "HJ raised his right arm and its shadow spread across the continent like a prophecy." Of course, Apple is putting us on, but only part of the time and with our best interests in mind. Behind Apple's accomplished stories, behind every satirist, is a disillusioned moralist pointing a guilty finger.

Apple is at his grimmest in the story "Noon," a macabre satire of daytime television that unfolds as a game-show emcee is assassinated by one of his contestants, and the fever pitch of avarice is running so high they don't even bother to stop the program to cart away the body. In a droller mood, as in "Inside Norman Mailer," Apple pokes some fun at his own ambition as well as at a slew of lit-crit shibboleths. The intense narrator, a "campy lightweight," swaggers into the ring with an aging, fictional Mailer, bent upon dethroning the champ. He imagines actually frightening Mailer with his crispness; and Mailer seems, in fact, to be reeling. But as the callow beginner throws his knockout punch he is suddenly "absorbed" by his opponent like some sort of microscopic slime, and from somewhere above him Mailer's rumbling voice intones: "I am the Twentieth Century."

But what is most special about *The Oranging of America* is its mellowness, the unusual quality of affection and a charming nostalgia that Apple generates for these characters and their times, even as they are butts of ridicule. It is a quality that makes this collection far more than just another cute barrage of potshots at the ravaged American Dream. In a word, Apple exudes what Faulkner sometimes called "compasshun," one of those forgotten essentials that is nowadays at an absolute premium. Howard Johnson's faithful elderly sidekick, Millie, for example, develops an ulcer in the title story and has reason to be glum when her medical condition seems to dictate that she leave the road and remain cooped up in her lonely apartment at the Lawrence Welk Building in L.A.—because of its proximity to the Cryonic Society, for freezing her remains "was the closest image she could conjure of eternal life." (All of Apple's best characters are fanatics, each with one eye open a thirty-second of an inch too far.) But HJ's genius saves the day, allowing the two old friends to resume their pilgrimage, to drive off into the sunset toward Disney World: "The man who hosted a nation and already kept one freezer in his car [for ice cream] merely ordered another, this one designed according to cryonic specifications and presented to Mildred housed in a twelve-foot orange U-Haul trailer connected to the rear bumper of the limousine." Thus, surprisingly, the buoyant, unashamed fondness between the characters carries the story as surely as the sarcasm and wit.

In addition to an eye for cultural clichés, an ear tuned to the self-satirizing vagaries of American business jargon, and a lot of heart, is the scrupulous and generally unpretentious elegance and balance of the Apple prose style, and the throaty gratification the reader feels at his sense of a patient intelligence at work along the way. Occasionally in danger of succumbing to that old *Saturday Evening Post* kind of sweetness, as in a Norman Rockwell–like portrait of a fictional Gerry Ford as a donut-lover, Apple is most of the time infallible.

In the world's largest gas station, for instance, a traveler headed west longs for the good old days at Ted Johnson's Standard station: "They don't clean my windshield and my hood is tinkered with less than a fat girl's skirt." The traveler's fantasy is to start an old-time three-pump gas station complete with rubber machines, ten-cent Cokes, recaps, and firecrackers. "I'll lend out tools too," he whines, "and give a dollar's worth to anyone who's broke. . . . At night, Ted, they won't even make change and in the best of times you have to beg for the rest-room key."

Max Apple creates fabulous fantasies within which few of the laws of nature are suspended except the laws of probability, and for the utterly improbable he makes us grateful. How probable is it that a nice Jewish boy from Detroit like Ira Goldstein should rise from the junkyard of his youth to manage a Marxist, Puerto Rican middleweight named Jesus, and that the fate of the free world in the mid-sixties should depend upon the outcome of a mythical prizefight, with J. Edgar Hoover—suspended above the ring in a hanging basket like a topless dancer—as the spoils? Just as in his well-received collection of shorter fiction, *The Oranging of America*, such novelty of vision as we find in Apple's first novel, *Zip*, is made to seem somehow strangely plausible and without pretension because it contains the germ of some larger truths about us.

From the moment that Jesus saves Ira from an irate scrap-iron dealer and the two form a friendship and hatch that improbable version of the American Dream—making it in the fight racket—they are creatures with essentially different ambitions. Jesus is seeking political power; he will eventually betray his friend to further his political ends. Meanwhile, Ira is conducting imaginary conversations with Howard Cosell about getting Ira's mother and grandmother a small condominium in Florida and contributing to Jewish charities. Ira Goldstein is a hero who believes that people are more important than ideology, but who is trapped in a world of ideologues and grudge-holders.

Ira's friends and relatives too, particularly the influential females in his life, are often heartbreakingly principled in their wrong-headedness, stalwart in their dogmatisms, or unwittingly cruel. His beloved grandmother is a racist. His girlfriend, an activist who wants to "sit in front of the White House and fast until they stop it all," thinks they had better not get married because "the way things are in the world I don't know if I can just live my personal life as if it was all that mattered." While Ira consistently perceives the actions of the novel in a larger, more humane context than any of them, he is frequently made to feel guilty—sometimes comically so—because he believes he lacks "zip," an amalgam of chutzpah, hustle, and zeal in the service of a cause. What Ira doesn't understand, though the reader comes to, is that he possesses far rarer and more valuable qualities: simple goodness, loyalty, and forbearance—fundamental human virtues that, Apple believes, should transcend politics or blind ambition.

In following Ira's quest for happiness and the right kind of zip, Apple exhibits an enviable sense of formal economy, balance, and purposefulness of action and plot that most first novelists lack. Apple's whimsicality and imaginative bravado are hardly ever forced or merely on display. But it is ultimately his fidelity to the probabilities of human nature, and his qualities of sympathy, empathy, and compassion, and his sense of humor—all of which he shares with his narrator, Ira—that are most impressive and most characteristic.

RUSSELL BANKS

Hamilton Stark deserts or drives away, in succession, five wives. He sneers at old people on park benches and kicks dogs and dares them to bite him for it. He likes to sit on the front porch of the house he took from his own mother, guzzle Canadian whiskey, and take potshots with his 30.06 at the piles of trash heaped around the perimeter of his yard.

According to his first wife, Hamilton is a "despicable man." According to his only daughter, Rochelle, who loves him, he is "morally obnoxious." Yet according to his friend, the narrator of the heady novel *Hamilton Stark,* Stark is more than just a good barroom brawler of a hero. He is "above all else, . . . a reasonable man," even "a holy man." He possesses qualities that can, upon close examination, "be seen as both wisdom and passion." How are we to account for these mysterious discrepancies?

Hamilton Stark is a pipe fitter and job foreman who lives on 700 acres in rural New Hampshire in the home his ancestors built in the shadow of Blue Job Mountain late in the eighteenth century. His earliest ancestor in the region, one Lemuel Stark, was, in fact, murdered atop Blue Job Mountain in 1703 by an Abenooki Indian under circumstances that led his fellow settlers to believe wrongly that he was a coward and a deserter. To what extent are we to understand that Hamilton Stark's character and life, nearly 300 years later, have been affected by this pathetic and costly accident that befell his distant ancestor and by the misinterpretations, and the fictions, that surrounded it?

Another, related, mystery: Where *is* Hamilton Stark now? On the very day that the narrator/author decided to begin his novel about Hamilton Stark he dropped by the Stark place to visit his friend and discovered him absent, the doors locked, and Hamilton's green Chrysler parked outside the garage with three spidery bullet holes in the windshield. Throughout the period of the novel's composition, then, Hamilton Stark is both literally and figuratively missing, and the narrator/author is busily tracking him.

Within the narrator/author's novel are fragments of *another* novel, one presumably written by Hamilton's only daughter, Rochelle, based upon a series of interviews she has conducted over several years with her father's five ex-wives, several of his friends, and his estranged mother, sisters, and brother-in-law. Rochelle is a twenty-six-year-old, red-haired beauty who is also, we learn, having an affair with the narrator/author, a romance that was consummated on an evening that began as a literary discussion of the modern novel. So the novel *Hamilton Stark* is, among other things, an elaborate artifice by Russell Banks, presumably a collaboration between lovers, both of whom are hopelessly mired and implicated in the action.

Those already familiar with Russell Banks's work will not be surprised by the philosophical, psychological, and structural high jinks of *Hamilton Stark*. Banks is a writer who has a mind— always a dangerous combination, though in Banks's case, mostly a fortuitous one. He has a fondness for a Chinese-box kind of structure of narrative, parable, or riddle—a series of apparent digressions that come together suddenly with provocative illuminations or tantalizing implications. He wants to write fiction that readers will puzzle over, wrestle with, and be bothered by late at night. He wants to be seen grappling with huge historical, philosophical (especially moral and metaphysical), sociological, and literary issues.

The particular issues raised here cover some fairly grim hypotheses about the human condition, though not without humor: the world is what *we say* it is, and none of us sees it in quite the same way. We live by the fictions that surround us. Whether or not our fictions correspond to "reality," they are all we have and are frightfully consequential.

Character is such a complex issue that we can never get to the bottom of it. Thus, the question of who Hamilton Stark really is may never be answered. Banks's narrator suffers the continuing frustration of trying to define character, assess motive, assign blame: "I thought I *knew* this man. . . . I thought I knew how he had been perceived by the people who loved him as well as by those who hated him"; instead he finds that "The very thing one person used as evidence of the hero's madness, his illness, another person cited as evidence of his genius, his transcendent good health." "We are the only creature that does not know what it is to be itself," another character comments. "We are the only creature that must perceive itself through the use of images."

To illustrate the range of his and his narrator's efforts to understand "these deformed browbeaten mind-animals," to borrow Robert Coover's phrase, Banks tries everything, from a glib but plausible-sounding Freudian analysis of Hamilton Stark to the creation of a whole fictionalized anthropology and geology of Stark's region that takes us back to the time of glaciers covering New England and even a celebratory parody of creation itself. Banks's early Yankee traders and American Indians bear somewhat the same haunting relation to New Hampshire as the Druids do to Thomas Hardy's heaths.

All in all, *Hamilton Stark* is a stunning and original novel full of provocative symmetries, engaging theories about imagination and character, and the pleasures of complication—sustained, intricate, and impressive. It is a sign that Russell Banks wants to be the Faulkner of New England.

DONALD BARTHELME

Who *is* the Dead Father and where is he going and why? In the first place, see, he isn't really dead, just kind of paralyzed and senile. He *is* dead but, I mean, he talks, for instance. He's conceited, bombastic, and sensitive about his age; and when he gets huffy, he runs off down the road and begins slaying innocent forest creatures and groves of musicians with his huge sword. This Dead Father is thirty-two hundred cubits high (which is close to a mile, give or take a cubit or two); one of his feet is seven meters thick; and he has a mechanical leg.

This version of a male Statue of Liberty/yakking Mt. Rushmore/combination six-million-dollar man and android Jahweh is being towed across country like a circus monkey on the end of a cable. It is a pilgrimage or quest of sorts through hostile terrain for some consequential but mysterious purpose. The expedition is led by Thomas, a fortyish harlequin, two nubile females (Julie and Emma), one retarded drunkard, and nineteen cable laborers. Sometimes mutiny threatens! A strange horseman is following, following! Every so often, Thomas takes a time-out with Julie, and the two of them enthusiastically perform unnatural acts behind the shrubbery.

Within this surreal superstructure, Donald Barthelme establishes the conditions for another incredible magical circus, featuring puns, parodies, anachronisms, put-ons, artful non sequiturs, heights of metaphor, droll juxtapositions, death-defying paradoxes, kooky feats of imagination and association, and lists. In fact, as in most of Barthelme's fiction, language itself is the main subject in *The Dead Father,* and debunking tired metaphors and the sheer delight of invention are among the chief aims.

Always alert for the significant absurdity, Barthelme fences with ennui in his characteristically jaded, resourceful, ebullient, playful, frivolous manner, sometimes just a bit doggedly, feigning weariness with his design, but never flagging, only treading water between bursts of exhilarating virtuosity.

Consider this litany of tortures for "anyone who dares trifle" with the Dead Father: "On the eighth [day] the trifler is slid naked down a thousand-foot razor blade to the music of Karlheinz Stockhausen.

On the ninth day the trifler is sewn together by children. . . . On the eleventh day the trifler's stitches are removed by children wearing catcher's mitts on their right and left hands."

In spite of such boasts, however, we gradually discover that the Dead Father is all pomp and circumstance. "There was a time," Thomas tells Julie, "when his voice, his plain unamplified voice, could turn your head inside out." But now he is not only helpless and insecure, but he is also behaving like a spoiled brat; and Thomas and the other characters seem to enjoy insulting him about his age, bullying him, baiting him with flattery, and making fun of his crudely lascivious advances toward the women.

The metaphor of "fatherhood" is the butt of so much foul good humor that one begins to wonder if Barthelme hasn't rigged the whole extravaganza for the purpose of arousing our sympathy for maligned fatherhood. A detailed "Manual for Sons" shows fathers as petty, boring, and ineffectual; reveals how fathers seldom have pure or honorable motives; and charges that fathers are the insidious agents responsible for school!

Yet, in the end, the Dead Father, beguiled into believing the journey has been to attain "the Golden Fleece," a symbol of his own rejuvenation, is himself fleeced and buried with bulldozers—only to assume some truly renewed spiritual role as a monument described as working "ceaselessly night and day through all the hours for the good of all."

Barthelme delights again and again in confounding us with such metaphorical claptrap. He insists on having everything both ways, in creating art resistent to rational interpretation. In coming to terms with *The Dead Father*, one must first concede: Barthelme is primarily an absurdist, a creator of emotional complexes and imaginative structures, not a "realist," not a spiritual midwife forever recapitulating "human experience." For Barthelme, "art is not about something but *is* something," as he states in an early manifesto.

Readers looking for "meaning" in the traditional sense are treading on ideological quicksand. "There are cases which are not clear," Thomas tells the cable pullers when they beg to be informed of the "purpose" for their labors. "You must be able to tolerate the anxiety [of not knowing]."

Similarly, in his early story "The Balloon," the multitudes fail to comprehend "the meaning" of the balloon and decide "that what was admired about the balloon was finally this: that it was not

limited, or defined." For Barthelme in *The Dead Father*, this same
position takes on the grandeur of a metaphysical argument as well
as the facile grace of an habitual aesthetic ploy. Readers may quibble
with his contention, but hardly with the sustained brilliance of its
transfiguration into art.

When we look back on this period, will the work of Donald
Barthelme seem the forerunner of a whole new variety of consciousness or merely a particularly skilled and elegant example of
decadence? His collection of short fiction, *Great Days*, is another emotional and linguistic demolition derby in the characteristic manner:
whimsical, elusive, and miraculously inventive.

Barthelme's aesthetic elevates the liberation of pure imagination
above all other notions. Bringing novelties into being is his primary
objective, and he faces the task with the surefootedness of a tightrope
walker and the precision of a clock maker. He believes utterly in the
delights of mind-travel and in the healing powers of dreams. Art,
as it embodies these modes, is one of the few human activities, he
seems to be saying, to save us from despair.

Despair has become one of his favorite subjects for jest. "At dusk
medals are awarded those who have made it through the day,"
someone quips in his story "The New Music." "The New Music" is a
collage of fractured dialogues, where the characters are seen "sighing
and leaning against each other, holding their silver plates"—as if to
say, "If we're so rich, how come we ain't happy?" Another, more
consoling voice chimes in: "Luckily we have the new music now. To
give us aid and comfort." The implication is that "the new music"
will save us from despair, or "sadness," as Barthelme called it in
another of his books; and "The New Music" is, after all, not simply
music but also the title of his own literary concoction.

Characteristically, there is always *something else* going on in a
Barthelme story, something other than the apparent subject or content. Metaphorical traps and tricks proliferate in an apparent effort
to describe emotional conditions and human situations too obvious,
personal, ridiculous, difficult, embarrassing, or full of pain to confront directly. The astute reader is stimulated to speculate at length
over these hidden mountain ranges of feeling and content, or else
to supply his own filler. Snatches of eavesdropped conversations
as matter-of-fact and believable as those overheard in the local bus
station may alternate with subconscious voices answering implied

questions the reader must seek on his own. Meanwhile, on the surface of the narrative, the laws of nature are suspended, as are the laws of human probability. The improbable is commonplace, and ironies abound.

In "Cortes and Montezuma," for example, we are entertained by a wealth of bizarre customs and sights: puddles of gold, crickets in cages, gods with names such as Smoking Mirror and Blue Humming-bird. We are apparently the privileged observers of the historical meeting and "friendship" between the Spanish explorer Cortes and the Aztec emperor Montezuma (prior to Cortes's conquest) in ancient Mexico. It is a dreamlike landscape rife with ominous tensions and signs, cross-cultural misunderstandings and lurking paranoia, wherein the two leaders discuss, for instance, the relative merits of the Holy Trinity as it incorporates the pagan concept of human sacrifice. Each man, secretly suspicious, hires a detective to follow the other. "Visions are best," Montezuma remarks, "better than the best detective," as if to glorify his own powers of surveillance. But, ironically, Montezuma himself is stoned to death at the end, in a manner foreseen in a vision by Cortes's lover.

"The Abduction from the Seraglio" is an oddly affective tale of unrequited love told as a comic/surreal science-fiction yarn. The characters live in enormous I-beam-constructed buildings, and the hero spends his creative energies making "welded-steel four-thousand-pound artichokes." Constanze, the girl for whom he yearns, has run off with a Plymouth dealer who "has this mysterious power over people and events which is called ten million dollars a year, gross."

There are repeated complaints and bitter jokes throughout *Great Days* about betrayal and the impermanence and difficulty of human relationships. Barthelme's characters evidently *need* someone to love them forever, but they are of the opinion that such love is a romantic delusion.

More than ever, Barthelme begins to seem, in some ways, like a classic satirist, obsessed by the predominance and multiplicity of human vanities. Yet the typical Barthelme protagonist whistles along good-naturedly in the teeth of boredom, despair, absurdity, betrayal, moral decay, and deplorable behavior surrounding him. He has access to all the best technical information from a gamut of fields, but he is simply swamped by it. He has little sense of which bits of endless data should prove useful to him. The promise of science and technology—to make the world ultimately knowable—has backfired by overwhelming him with unclassifiable facts.

Great Days is challenging and funny—further proof, if we needed it, that Donald Barthelme deserves his reputation as a major literary phenomenon of these great days. Whatever his standing in the year 2000, I predict that other writers and anthropologists of the imagination, when searching for creative folklore, will continue to peruse his pages, like so many interior decorators combing through books of wallpaper samples.

RAYMOND CARVER

Like Tolstoy's Ivan Ilych (Russia's John Doe), Raymond Carver's characters are stuck with lives that are "most simple and most ordinary and therefore most terrible." In his impressive first collection of stories, *Will You Please Be Quiet, Please?*, Carver gives new specificity to the plight of "ordinary" people and brings it up-to-date for a certain familiar class of Americans. Beneath the surface conventionality of Carver's salesmen, waitresses, bookkeepers, or hopeless middle-class "occupants," lies a morass of unarticulated yearnings and unexamined horrors—the creeping certainty that nothing matters, perverse sexual wishes, repressed violence, the inadmissible evidence of their own inadequacy.

In one brief study of outraged decency, "The Idea," some just-plain-folks are choking with voyeuristic self-righteousness as they avidly watch a neighbor who likes to play a Peeping Tom game with his wife outside his own bedroom window. In "Bicycles, Muscles, Cigarets," some suburban fathers start a senseless brawl, rolling around foolishly on someone's dewy front lawn, struggling and grunting, all over the apparently insoluble problem of what happened to a child's bicycle.

Fate does not often cooperate to make life any easier for such people. Many of them are penniless, between jobs, on the verge of bankruptcy. But if they have money, they squander it, or, typically, as in "What Is It?": "They spend two hundred for a pedigreed terrier and find her run over in the street a week later." Or, as in "What Do You Do in San Francisco?," a young man waiting nervously for an important letter from his errant wife receives only a circular marked "occupant," an advertisement for a hospital-insurance plan.

But Carver's jaundiced eye is not content to linger among freshly minted ironies, or to blame politics or the weather. His characters, in their dazed, paralyzed exertions, are always guilty as charged. In "What's in Alaska?" Carver focuses with grim objectivity on a foursome whose idea of a good time is to smoke dope and then gorge themselves on junk food and cherry soda. Typically, even their vices are withering to their spirits. Beyond their utter failure to communicate lies the suspicion of even greater futility, of which the characters themselves seem only dimly aware. Their pitiful fantasy of escape to Alaska, their current answer to the vacuity of the present, is further undercut by the reader's growing realization that, for these people, there can be no promised land because of the voids they carry around inside themselves.

They are hopelessly superficial or emotionally retarded people doomed to playing out unrealized lives. The buildings, houses, and rooms they occupy are frighteningly empty. Sometimes, like Ralph, the protagonist of the title story of the collection, such characters feel themselves to be on the brink of some large discovery about themselves, but it never comes.

Mirroring the unrelieved simplicity of these lives, Carver's style is direct and unadorned, deceptively simple and colloquial. He is an expert at dialogue that reveals people who have nothing to say to each other desperately filling the air with words.

Carver's characteristic procedure is to sketch out a situation until it reaches a point of heightened misery and then to freeze the frame. There is little or no exposition, comment, or editorializing—simply freeze-frame after freeze-frame of grotesque portraiture, as if the ghost of Diane Arbus had been turned loose as a short story writer. Some of these stories are quite brief, hardly more than carefully assembled vignettes. But they move swiftly; they bear their burden of evidence. Raymond Carver's vision is somber and resolute, and the cumulative effect is startlingly powerful.

JOHN CASEY

Contrary to the evidence that argues otherwise—from *Pamela* to *Wuthering Heights* to *The Catcher in the Rye*—we persist in our superstitions about first novels. A first novel is something committed, like a faux pas or a burglary. Like a first date, it will probably be a little clumsy and embarrassing. Out of simple good taste, a first novel is best ignored. Let the poor kid learn the ropes, and if he makes anything of himself in ten or twenty years, there will always be his masterpiece to contend with and plenty of time for a retrospective. In John Casey's prodigiously accomplished first novel, *An American Romance*, we have yet another example to debunk these fallacies.

An American Romance is a major work, a finely detailed novel of character and sensibility that marks the debut of a mature, confident, and full-bodied talent. It contains no warming-up exercises, no pointless flexing of muscles, no wasted motions, and no sophomoric cutenesses. It is as ambitious and as unpretentious as an egg.

The romance of the title is an extended mating ritual enacted between Anya, a self-centered ex-Radcliffe smarty zinging with raw energy and ambition, and Mac, an ex-Cornell hockey jock whose virtues are always getting him in trouble. She is "a good idea he'd never thought of." He is the only person she's ever met who would "rather be ruled by virtue than by passion."

Both are making voyages of self-discovery while discovering each other. Both are seeking personal solutions to the unique problems posed by coming of age in a particular place (roughly all of North America, but especially the New York–Boston–Iowa axis), and both are seeking lives commensurate with their own problematic standards in a time—the present—when the old standards no longer seem to apply.

From their first meeting as graduate students on a rock-climbing outing, they seem mutually absorbed with the complex ways "their separate magnetisms sorted [ideas and objects] out into their separate styles." The true subject of the novel becomes the minute exploration of the consciousness and character of each of them and the ebb and flow of their relationship and their understanding of it as they slowly, inexorably merge.

They have to solve problems beyond each other, however, before their coming together can be made permanent or significant. At the outset, Anya finds that the "way she was leading her life, for all its academic and sexual variations, was not giving her . . . the full risks and satisfactions that she desired. . . . It was a question of finding some act that was as large as her energy." When Anya is invited to Iowa to serve as the director of a communal repertory theater and Mac decides to accompany her, she thinks she may have found it.

Her quest first takes the form of hectic ingenuity within the theater group, where she marshals her brains and sensibilities with admirable thoroughness: willing, coaxing, and bullying the players to carry out her visions; casing out promotional possibilities on the local scene; hustling seasonal engagements for them as far away as Chicago's North Shore. Her chutzpah reaps dividends, but her success seems small-scale. She still keeps wondering, "What next?" She has the urge "to rise on a magic carpet of cosmopolitanism" and isn't sure how this can be accomplished.

At the same time, she is "terrified . . . to think that her ambition was uncontrollable. That her ambition was not, after all, part of her intelligence, her talent, or her craft—that it was deep-rooted, childish, possibly crazy—that it might even betray her." Increasingly for Anya it seems that her ambition may end up preventing her from finding personal happiness.

For Mac, coming to terms seems to involve giving himself over to useful labor and becoming a self-effacing pillar of civilization. His role in the commune is that of set builder and handyman, but he also begins to work part-time as a farmhand to help support Anya and the group, cooks elaborate rustic meals, fishes and hunts for food, and generally knocks himself out. For him, the issue seems to boil down to the question of civilization versus barbarism. His experiences in the army and as a hockey gladiator have raised doubts in his soul about his own dangerously savage inclinations. He thinks his salvation lies in the submersion of self through exhausting physical labor and devotion to caretaking, building, and nurturing activities and in a solitary communing with nature, slowly listening to the music of his nerve endings. He turns out to have quite an aptitude for self-abnegation.

If this casting of the female as careerist and the male as domestic ballast seems like a reversal of traditional roles, it most certainly is; and *An American Romance* is one of the first novels to treat the complexities of such changing social patterns without demeaning either party. Casey is often surprisingly intelligent (we had almost forgotten how sheer intelligence in a novelist might feel, and, more than that, his *characters* are intelligent). Casey's most enviable accomplishment, however, is one that requires gift as well as guts, patience and intuitive force as well as technical mastery. He creates characters with depths; characters whose layers peel away like artichoke leaves, revealing even greater complexities within; characters who have the feel, the stamp, of individual temperament.

His intricate dissections of character and emotion cause one to think in new ways about personality and about the flux and mystery of relationships. Somehow he has managed to find new combinations of language to describe bubbles of feelings, inarticulate longings, unconscious habits of rumination, and the subtle interaction of humors. He persuades us so successfully that we are every bit as complicated as we always knew we were, that when Anya finally comes to the realization of "how their lives had merged, in an ordinary, lumpish way, from a sharp physical attraction—but no sharper than a lot of others, surely—to this weight of knowing him," we can fully understand how Mac and Anya have progressed beyond romance to something more enduring.

DON DELILLO

The author of *End Zone* has now given us a big, tedious, puzzling book that will be thoroughly enjoyed by summa cum laude graduates of Cal Tech. It is one of those giant, creaking, willfully original efforts, like *Moby-Dick* or *Tristram Shandy*, that not many people enjoy very much but feel obligated to admire.

The plot hinges on the attempts of one Billy Twillig, a fourteen-year-old Nobel laureate from the Bronx, to decode a radio message presumably sent by extraterrestrials living in the vacinity of faraway Ratner's Star. Billy is summoned to a vast, secret science complex, with its Space Brain computer and array of wiggy inhabitants (who are mostly other upstanding members of the scientific community), where few doubt his work will provide the key to every metaphysical riddle.

Early on in our magical mystery tour of the Space Brain complex, *the* center for the world's advanced technology and "the fulfillment of mankind's oldest dream," the fire-safety system develops a malfunction and the hollow walls and floors eerily begin filling up with "liquid preventative." Also, the toilet bowls flush backwards. Thus begins a sometimes comical, frequently convoluted satire of the inadequacies, delusions, and idiocy of the scientific mind run amuck.

DeLillo's habitual modus operandi is to introduce Billy to yet another new character, Armand Verbene, for instance, who is likely to say something such as, "For years I've been trying to convince the scientific power structure that red ant metaphysics is a hard science," but usually something a lot more long-winded and arcane. Then DeLillo will dwell upon several grotesque, usually distasteful mannerisms of the character and allow him to talk and talk, focusing on the stream of words issuing from his brain as if in one of Steinberg's *New Yorker* cartoons, each with his own characteristic, half-mad theoretical design like a signature. Everybody is expounding a theory that nobody else is listening to. They're all virtuosos of the soliloquy.

DeLillo is quite good, as a matter of fact, at this sort of characterization through unconsciously self-indicting babbling by the characters. He has a formidable abstract intelligence for a novelist and makes use of an impressive amount of quite technical scientific and mathematical lore. He fearlessly makes heavy demands on the reader's memory and attentiveness.

But, to my taste, there is simply too much overkill, too much jargon for its own sake, too much parading of abstract linguistic brilliance and excessive replication of characters, all of whom are seen as demented, hysterical, and burdened with tics, silly perversions, and irrational attitudes and behavior. There is little emotional involvement with any of them. They are all butts of humor, examples of certain classifiable extremes, or occasions for parody. And too many of them are introduced and then dropped, creating an irritating sense of discontinuity and unexplored potential.

There are hints that DeLillo sensed this problem in *Ratner's Star* or set out to cause it. In Billy Twillig's thinking about pure mathematics, for instance, he observes, "Beauty was mere scenery unless it was severe, adhering strictly to a set of consistent inner codes." Another character, and this one a fiction writer of sorts, says: "Reading my book will be a game with specific rules that have to be learned. I'm free to make whatever rules I want as long as there's an inner firmness and cohesion, right?" Well, maybe—if the reader is willing to be a certain kind of sleuth or if you can train him about your rules or convince him that your inner firmness and cohesion amount to more than a self-justifying aesthetic ploy.

At his best, DeLillo comes fairly close to convincing us. He is perhaps as oppressed by metaphysical riddles as any of his characters, or at least receptive to moods of metaphysical wonder. At these times his language can take on the complex imagery and grace of a lovely narrative poem, full of perceptual tenderness. My guess is that, unlike Freud, DeLillo has felt that "oceanic feeling."

He is also capable of cute strokes of humor, laughing up his sleeve at the damned human race as if from a God's-eye perspective—as, in *Ratner's Star*, at the failure of the Logicon Project, an attempt to devise a totally logical system of discourse with the idea of using it eventually as an aid in celestial communication. But what happens is that the Logicon Project and all of the Space Brain complex are eventually taken over by an international cartel interested in cornering the world's market on bat guano—"the whole operation computerized to an extent and level of complexity never before known."

Ratner's Star is prodigious, accomplished, undoubtedly brilliant. Yet one is compelled to imagine what Pynchon, Barth, or Vonnegut might have done more successfully with the same material. The greatest drawback of Ratner's Star may be that it is more a feat than an entertainment.

FREDERICK EXLEY

The character Frederick Exley is still beating himself to death with booze, gluttony, insomnia, and his voracious Rabelaisian appetite for experience. But in *Pages from a Cold Island*, author Frederick Exley creates a character (Frederick Exley) who seems to possess more self-esteem and affability and less desperate nastiness and nasty desperation than the Exley of *A Fan's Notes*.

In *Pages from a Cold Island*, Exley is still the sort of grumpy egomaniac who seems barely able to tolerate the human race when sober, but who gets into warm conversations with total strangers over some vodka and grapefruit juice and makes a lovable drunk. But, on the whole, events have been treating him better, and Exley's life seems funnier, sexier, and more zestful.

For a character as sensitive, irritable, and hungry for fame as Frederick Exley, the reception of his first novel, *A Fan's Notes*, seven years before seems to have provided both salve for his wounds and fresh humiliations. *A Fan's Notes*, that outrageous bellow for attention, was nominated for the National Book Award and won several other prizes. But, as Exley tells us at the beginning of this latest confession, he feared that on those infrequent occasions when his name came up at all in literary conversations he would be "summarily and disparagingly dismissed" as having shot his wad. Thus, as is the case with many a second book, *Pages from a Cold Island* becomes partly an exercise in trying to prove that the accomplishment of his first book was not a fluke. Exley provides convincing proof. In apparent anticipation of an Exley revival, in fact, Random House also published a new edition of *A Fan's Notes*.

In spite of Exley's disclaimer at the end of *A Fan's Notes* that his suffering has led him to the conclusion that it is his destiny to be forever "a fan," he shows little evidence in this new work that he wishes to accept this always-a-bridesmaid-never-a-bride way of thinking about himself. *A Fan's Notes* has clearly given him hope that, if not as a sports hero then at least as a writer, he may indeed be destined to be one of those whose fate it is "to hear the roar of the crowd."

In fact, Exley is still hungering after fame. This need expresses itself both in his sense of mission—to find some way to write the very book you are reading—and in his penchant for hero worship and sometimes embarrassing and comical celebrity-chasing. *Pages from a Cold Island* might almost be subtitled "Famous people I have met . . . or almost met." Yet most of the celebrities Exley confronts, like some bumbling Diogenes, anger and disappoint him. Gloria Steinem and Norman Mailer, for instance, seem to Exley all too human and full of pretensions to suit him.

But, like Frank Gifford in *A Fan's Notes*, who "more than any single person, sustained for . . . him the illusion that fame was possible," another personal hero of Exley's—in this case, Edmund Wilson— becomes the unifying obsession of *Pages from a Cold Island*, and, one gathers, for similar reasons. Wilson is an upstate New York "neighbor" who has lived an ascetic literary life similar to Exley's ideal; and perhaps luckily for them both, Wilson, through death, has become inaccessible to Exley's misanthropy.

Over a fourth of this book—and some of its finest moments—are taken up with Exley's lovingly researched chronicle of Wilson's last days at his old stone house in Talcottville, New York.

For most of the rest, Exley makes misanthropy and buffoonery and excess into comic virtues. Through Exley's jaundiced eyes the world is a calliope played upon his nerve endings. Isolated on his cold island, writing, he reminds us again of "the wound and the bow" and the special dignity and pain of the artist's life.

If *Pages from a Cold Island* is less prodigious than *A Fan's Notes*, it is also less overwrought, more confident, lighthearted, and under control—more a romp than a tantrum. Like *A Fan's Notes*, *Pages from a Cold Island* is digressive and episodic in structure, but as tightly and carefully put together as one of Exley's famous tuna fish, chopped hard-boiled egg, and onion sandwiches.

JOHN GARDNER

"It used to be a man took pride in his work," muses seventy-two-year-old James L. Page, the crusty Vermont farmer who is the protagonist of John Gardner's *October Light*. If he "built you a wheel or a window-sash, you could pretty well figure it would last you a while. Not now. Why? Because nobody cared a mite anymore, cared not one tunkit, *that* was why." Well, I've got good news for you, Mr. Page. Somebody does care. John Gardner cares, and he wrote this novel to prove it.

Constructed with the patience, diligence, and care of the seasoned wheelwright, and like the great Victorian classics it sometimes resembles, *October Light* is the kind of book to curl up with on long winter evenings, a hefty, accomplished, uplifting novel that is neither quick, sensationalistic, nor disposable . . . like your typical television program, for instance.

Television is one of James L. Page's problems. Poor old James L. Page is having a snit-fit during this bicentennial year, trying to cope with his increasing awareness of modern life that is brought about by the recent invasion of his eighty-year-old widowed sister, Sally Page Abbott, and her infernal television. One night, past endurance, he blasts the television set to smithereens with his twelve-gauge shotgun, and thus begins an escalating series of skirmishes between the two, a silly family feud that gets seriously out of hand. Some weeks after the television episode, James gets so mad he chases Sally upstairs to her bedroom, threatening her with a piece of stove wood, and locks the door.

But Sally, who is no doormat, decides to take her stand. Later that night, when the door is unlocked by the old man's chain-smoking daughter, Ginny, Sally won't come out. Holing up for days with only a "trashy" novel and some baskets of apples for comfort, Sally goes on strike; and James gets madder and madder.

When Sally periodically retreats into her trashy novel called *The Smugglers of Lost Soul's Rock,* we read it with her. In fact, this novel-within-a-novel takes up roughly a third of the overall space in *October Light,* and, regular as clockwork, it whisks us imaginatively a long way from rural Vermont and into exactly the sort of free-floating, amoral world that James L. Page despises and fears—a world of pot smugglers, narcs, sex orgies, and crazy Mexicans.

But in spite of vast differences, the characters in both novels seem to have similar problems—how to cope with the pain of living, how to find some acceptable justification for plodding through their lives. And the air of both novels is rife with the characters' philosophical grapplings, dogmatic posturings, and desperate metaphysical yearnings.

Gardner has been viewed by numerous readers as primarily a philosophical novelist, and that he certainly is. But in this case, it seems to me, he aims to show the limitations of systems and labels in contrast to the redeeming qualities of more instinctive human dispositions. Gardner believes in human instincts for survival, for forgiveness and fellow feeling, for craftiness, and for love—whether defined as "psycho-glandular affinity," polymorphous lust, or something else—and he delights in observing how we uncannily manage to surmount our innate irritability, morosity, and pigheadedness so that these more primitive impulses may find their expression.

The true measure of Gardner's accomplishment is in his attention to character in *October Light*. What a presumptuous and difficult task to try to dramatize the inner lives of these old, old people—James and Sally—and to try to transcend the multiplicitous stereotypes of old age and make them come alive convincingly so that we *care* about them. But Gardner succeeds marvelously—so well, in fact, that it makes one wonder why more writers haven't tried it. Among the advantages of dealing with aged characters is that there is simply more life for them to remember—almost their whole lives, complete and ripe for summary. Gardner makes us believe in their intensified need for resolution, in the particular urgency of their coming to terms—there isn't much time left.

Another strong suit in this novel, and the one characteristic that reminds one most perhaps of the Victorian tradition, is its compelling creation of the sense of community—a shared community history, identity, and allegiance among the characters. Bennington and the small Vermont villages of *October Light* seem as close to Cranford or Middlemarch as we are likely to see again in American culture. On his way down the road to the local tavern in his rickety truck, for example, James L. Page has a sudden palpable vision of the way the village had looked in his childhood, before electricity! During other moments one is impressed by the realization that some of these people have known each other for seventy or eighty years! It is a peculiar, insular world but one with special graces—people must make allowances for one another, stand by one another, deal with one another day after day after day.

The binding metaphor of the novel is October light—"that sudden contraction of daylight in October, the first deep-down convincing proof that locking time, and after that winter and deep snow and cold, were coming." It is that time of year between harvest and Halloween when "every one of them felt a subdued excitement, a new aliveness that was more, in fact, than the seasonal change in their chemistry." The themes of age, earth, community, struggle, and forgiveness are given this lyrical dimension by October light: "The old man's tractor was transformed by this stunning light, the old yellow corn-chopper tilted against the silo more distinct, more itself than it would normally be, final as a tombstone."

BEVERLY LOWRY

Lolly Ray Lasswell comes strutting down the main drag of Eunola, this small Mississippi town, and she's leading the parade in a uniform made entirely of gold dime-sized sequins that catch the sun just so as it slides above the levee. She has batons going like crazy in both hands—the crowd is bug-eyed watching her—and when she arrives at the main intersection, she executes a full split against the hot street exactly beneath the blinking red traffic light.

Lolly Ray is not your typical high school bud, you understand, but a virtuoso, a lovely freak, a veritable Nadia Comaneci of baton twirling, and all the more surprising when we find out that she hasn't had any of the advantages. Her mom gobbles Empirins, throws fits, and is more than ripe for the loony bin; and her long-suffering old man is lugging around three generations' worth of disillusionment and despair. About the only entertainment Lolly can find out in the trailer park is in practicing endless figure eights and lateral neck wraps; that is, until she meets a lonely young air force lieutenant named James Blue. . . .

Eunola, the Lasswells' hometown, is a raging, gurgling gene pool not very far from Yoknapatawpha; but the proximity is hardly a burden to the reader and frequently a delight. Beverly Lowry seems to have heeded Flannery O'Connor's warning regarding Faulkner's influence, that nobody "wants his mule and wagon stalled on the same track the Dixie Limited is roaring down." What Lowry does share with that great southern tradition of fiction is an aptitude for the dramatic, a gift for metaphor and elaboration, a vision of the past abiding in and sometimes overwhelming the present, the impulse to stake out a postage stamp of earth with measurable perimeters, and a sense of flawed and fallible human nature curtailed by its legacy but blindly and willfully struggling on just the same. Most of the time, Beverly Lowry makes this sort of literary-cultural inheritance seem no small virtue, especially for a first novelist in search of a fulcrum or a worldview.

Perhaps Eunola is a little too obviously divided between the mass of bigots, on the one hand, who Lowry enjoys pinning up like prize butterflies, and the eccentrics, drunks, idiots, outcasts, and the dreamy Lolly—the one person who seems capable of transcending it all—on the other. And occasionally Lowry becomes garrulous or inclined toward intrusive summarizing of the plot in her efforts to organize the web of implications she skillfully sets in motion in *Come Back, Lolly Ray*.

But, reservations notwithstanding, the flashes of Flannery O'Connor–like toughness are extremely gratifying. Lowry's imagination proves sound and patient, and we do anticipate Lolly Ray's downfall with real dread. For the same blood that propels Lolly to the state baton-twirling championship and to the state university on a generous scholarship donated by the town sends her back that fall of her triumphant return as "Eunola's Own" to violate their trust, vulgarize their astonishment, and prove herself a "trailer tramp" at heart. Blood will tell, sho nuf.

MAILER/MILLER

In *Genius and Lust*, Norman Mailer's passion for one of his heroes is reminiscent of John Updike's in that marvelous essay "Hub Fans Bid Kid Adieu," in which Updike tries to convince us that Ted Williams *was* the greatest hitter of all time—especially if we give him credit for four major league seasons that he lost to war, another one that he lost to injuries, and if we allow him a less heroic temperament and then go back in time and rearrange the right-field wall in Fenway Park. In this case, Norman Mailer's passionate advocacy is of the work and life of Henry Miller, whom Mailer regards as "the greatest living American writer."[1]

Because of the prudery and shortsightedness of literary criticism, Mailer argues, and the enigmatic, unclassifiable, and uneven quality of Miller's genius, Miller has been unfairly stereotyped as a minor writer of dirty books, whom no president would seriously consider inviting "to read from his work on Inauguration Day," and who has never received the sober consideration he deserves. Yet Miller is a writer who, according to Mailer: (1) has written "a prose grander than Faulkner's, and wilder"; (2) has written in *Tropic of Cancer* "one of the ten or twenty great novels of our century"; and (3) has "influenced the style of half the good American poets and writers alive today," forging the way for books as different as *Naked Lunch*, *Portnoy's Complaint*, *Fear of Flying*, and *Why Are We in Vietnam?*

To help back up his claims, Mailer presents several healthy chunks from Miller's opus, from the *Tropics* and *Black Spring* through *The Colossus of Maroussi* and *The Rosy Crucifixion*, using as his guide the principle of displaying "a feast of perception and a fireworks of energy." What we have in *Genius and Lust*, in fact, is primarily a hulking anthology of Miller's writings with time-outs between segments for a few cheers, imprecations, scenery changes, and benedictions from our host, Mr. Mailer, who seems to be dutifully going about the business of trying to perform a Malcolm Cowley.

1. Miller died in 1980.

Mailer's stance is very much that of the appreciative—not the judicious—critic, however. His eagerness to impose his taste upon us is winning, if not always convincing. Occasionally he gives the impression that he would be willing to say anything, anything at all, to persuade us to his way of seeing things, which tends to undermine confidence in his credible judgments. We come away from some passages feeling we would *not* want to buy a used car from this man. In other words, one senses that Mailer is winging it; and when Mailer wings it, it is almost invariably interesting, even if we are convinced he is writing pure baloney.

Of course, to prove that Henry Miller, or anyone, is our greatest living literary genius is a little like trying to prove that cauliflower, rhubarb, or kumquats, respectively, should be our favorite foods. Mailer seems to have taken Hemingway's metaphor of literature as a prizefight somewhat too seriously—call it Mailer's pugilistic view of art—so that we picture Miller and the big boys of American, English, and world literature slugging it out for the heavyweight title in some celestial gym.

Much of Mailer's case for Miller is based on another of Mailer's theories: the idea that to understand the place of lust in Miller's life is the key to discovering the sort of genius Miller was to become. According to Mailer, "Never has literature and sex lived in such symbiotic relation before [sic]—it is as if every stroke of his phallus is laying a future paragraph of phrases on his brain." Mailer's argument goes beyond the simple evaluation: Anybody with this much raw sexual and literary energy has got to be great—but is no less suspicious. Mailer seems to want to raise satyriasis to the level of a moral, epistemological, and aesthetic principle. "Does the man who devours the greatest quantity of ice cream know the most about the chemistry of ice cream," one wants to ask, "or is he merely obese?" If Miller is, as Mailer claims, "the Grand Speleologist of the Vagina," something more than box score alone must be involved. The M.V.P. is not always the hitter with the biggest average.

Mailer does love to think big. At times, he seems to be writing a psychosexual romance of Miller something like Freud's *Leonardo*, though in this case based on amateur psychoanalysis and breathtaking generalizations. At other points, he undertakes a scorching critical analysis of twentieth-century literary sensibility. Frequently, however, in attempting to describe *the* landmarks in the literary ocean—"Miller took off at the place where Hemingway ended"—one has the feeling Mailer is engaged primarily, perhaps unconsciously, in charting his own passage through the literary waters.

Still, if you were starting a new hockey league, Mailer is exactly the sort of scrappy, lovable, unprincipled ruffian—a triple-threat man—you would want to have on your team. Whether or not a Miller revival and reassessment is in the offing, Mailer has certainly succeeded in coercing attention to Miller's stature and reputation, introducing him to a new generation of readers and reminding us of Miller's uniqueness. Miller's right "to be regarded as a distinguished literary talent full of character and evocation" is now probably unarguable, it seems to me. And maybe that should be enough. Whether or not you would want to send him into the ring with Mr. Tolstoy will still have to be a matter of individual conscience.

JOYCE CAROL OATES

The idea of the artist as one possessed by a Muse or spirit voice is one of the most ancient and persistent in the history of aesthetics. Influenced as we are by the relatively newfangled idea that works of art are "expressions" of the artist or writer, we sometimes think of the idea of possession as quaint. But it is a tradition that has carried over even into our own time.

We know from her interviews that Joyce Carol Oates, most notably among American contemporaries, subscribes to "possession" as a way of understanding her own art or of explaining it to others. But up until now—with the appearance of her collection *The Poisoned Kiss*—we have not seen such an open and explicit statement of her belief embodied in a work of fiction.

The Poisoned Kiss is presumably a collection of tales from the Portuguese by an imaginary author, Fernandes, and "translated" by Joyce Carol Oates; and Fernandes, in fact, is given credit as coauthor of *The Poisoned Kiss* on the cover and title page. Yet Oates explains in a prefatory note that Fernandes "has no existence and has never existed," as far as she knows, though without his "very real guidance" she would not have had access to the mystical "Portugal" of *The Poisoned Kiss*. For those who have always secretly suspected that Joyce Carol Oates is actually a conglomerate of nine gifted writers writing under an assumed name, such information should prove slightly comforting—except for the possible difficulty of imagining eight more spirit voices on the order of Fernandes and what *their* names might be and what incredible realms they might be assumed to inhabit.

This particular Muse, Fernandes—unlike that of, say, Oates's comic collection *The Hungry Ghosts*—is a deadly serious fellow, and the spooky book he has given us is no laughing matter either. The fictions collected here do certainly represent a departure for Oates—in treatment, in subject, in style—though some of her habitual themes and obsessions are immediately recognizable. Most are not conventionally developed stories at all as much as they are carefully worked out (or remembered) nightmares—fragmentary, troubling, bizarre, sometimes impenetrable. Others are parables of the artist's calling ("The Poisoned Kiss," "Journey"), prose poems ("Husband and Wife"), or feats of imagination that may remind one, in style and tone, of Chekhov, B. Traven, or Hesse at their most mystical.

In two of the strangest and most haunting pieces, for instance, "Our Lady of the Easy Death of Alferce" and "The Son of God and His Sorrow," we are invited to contemplate the personal problems of deities and the metaphysical shock waves they set in motion. In the former story, we inhabit the consciousness of a wooden statue of the Virgin Mary, where, physically immobilized and helpless, we must submit to almost continual adoration and abuse. In the latter, the agonies and responsibilities of the "Son of God" are imagined in such credible proportions—the dramatization of suffering is so intense—one is simply aghast.

If *The Poisoned Kiss* proves anything, it proves that nothing seems beyond Oates's capacity for imaginative entry. She could imagine her way into the heart of a stone, make you believe it, and still uncover some fierce emotional experience to be charted there. Her imagination is so sensitive, so readily galvanized, that she frequently seems compelled to write about certain characters and events almost against her will and in a state of fright at what she must unearth.

Perhaps because of this trait she has the range of a virtuoso. She can be tender and oblique or swift and brutal, and she is a master at suggesting the most abominable or hideous implications of a scene without ever stating the awful facts, leaving you to wonder if your personal perverse imagination hasn't taken liberties on its own.

Whether or not we can accept her apparently necessary, quasi-mystical explanations regarding "possession," the extent of her accomplishment in her many, many books is now so vast and impressive, it seems likely that she may shortly have to defend herself against the charge of possession by sheer genius.

GEORGE PLIMPTON

What if you could talk to your favorite writers? Better yet, what if you could take along an urbane and well-informed and self-effacing expert on your favorite writers' work and lives who would sit there with you, or stroll casually about the garden, and who would help phrase the direct or crucial questions if the conversation seemed to be flagging? Such is the illusion and a source of the many pleasures in this, the fourth volume of the justifiably famous series: *Writers at Work: The Paris Review Interviews.*

Here we find great character portraits and astonishing autobiographical data: Anthony Burgess's revelation, for instance, that his doctors had diagnosed a brain tumor following his collapse in a Brunei classroom and had given him one year to live. Rather than pining away, Burgess began what has now become decades of prodigious literary output. There is a cheerful Nabokov claiming to be "as American as April in Arizona" and, in reply to a question about collaboration with his wife, telling how one day in 1950 she stopped him from carrying the first chapters of *Lolita* "to the garden incinerator." In reply to a similar question about collaboration, Jack Kerouac quips that he "did a couple of collaborations in bed . . . with blondes."

There is some swell silliness, to be sure: W. H. Auden saying, "I think if men knew what women said to each other about them, the human race would die out"; and his famous piece of fluff about the social and political history of Europe being no different "if Dante, Shakespeare, Michelangelo, Mozart, et al, had never lived." Arresting epigrams fairly leap off the pages.

Also abundant, as always, is the down-to-earth shoptalk, theorizing, and practical advice about writing that have made the *Writers at Work* series the best manual for young writers ever assembled.

As has always been the case, this fourth in the series is venerable rather than timely in the usual sense—more history than news—dealing solely with already canonized writers. Among the yet-living interviewees, only Updike is younger than fifty. Fewer than half are still living. Over half of the interviews are with septua-, octo-, and nonagenarians; nearly half, that is, were born in the nineteenth century. So, mostly, we are eavesdropping on talks with our elders, writers in the modernist frame of reference rather than contemporaries, all certifiable giants. And there is always something a little otherworldly about enjoying this feast, which seems like something of a cross between a dinner party and a séance.

On the other hand, the pleasures of these interviews are such that their importance may be too frequently underestimated. Critics and reviewers have been known to invent the most outlandish justifications for approving of them, feeling some guilt perhaps at admitting to a liking for a maverick form with so many low-life relatives, a checkered ancestry (since Plato), and an orbit quite distant from what is imagined to be the respectable critical enterprise.

Wilfrid Sheed, who once condemned the series as "neither better nor worse than Hollywood gossip," is seen doing a fancy dance step in the introduction to this very volume, now claiming to have discovered that, in fact, "gossip is the very stuff of literature, the *materia prima* of which both books and their authors are made." Well, I don't know about that . . . maybe so.

Alfred Kazin suggests one of the more interesting reasons for the popularity of the form in his introduction to the third series. The "biographical close-up," he says, "now satisfies us because we identify the power of art with the uniqueness of personality." Possibly the compelling reason we do not have scads of literary interviews predating Plimpton is that the ancients were not, in fact, very interested in the relation of the writer to his or her work. They truly believed in the principle of the Muse and the writer as a helpless vessel. For us, this may be difficult to comprehend because we are so strongly influenced by a critical tradition emphasizing the writer's presence in the work or the work as an emanation of the writer's personal feelings. However, this tradition did not flower until the nineteenth century with the so-called romantic movement, relatively a quite recent development.

Once we accept the position that the writer *makes* the art, an escalation in our interest in the mystery of the artist's personality is inevitably tied up with our interest in the art itself. These days we have a need to know such things—it is as simple as that—and how many scholars wouldn't barter their souls for an interview with Shakespeare, Chaucer, or Jane Austen that is as probing, astute, and ultimately revealing as one of the *Paris Review* interviews?

Surely George Plimpton has good reason to regard these interviews as history (the best sort of news?) because he has had the
foresight and doggedness to track down—with a microphone in
one hand and a copy of the *Paris Review* in the other—many of
the authentic geniuses of our time and beat them to the cemetery.
The fattest volume yet, by about a hundred pages, this fourth in the
series brings to a total of sixty the number of writers covered through
twenty years of sleuthing. And still the tape recorders whir and the
quarterly issues of the *Paris Review* turn up with new interviews—as
crisp and magical as the first ones—for, I hope, future editions.

Plimpton and his crew have become curators of live genius, marvelous literary taxidermists who have discovered a way to mount
the great minds of their day without the usual killing and stuffing,
to preserve them for all time rather than leaving such business to the
toil and uncertainty of latter-day scholar-archaeologists and the easy
adoration and distortions of as-yet-unborn idolaters, necromancers,
and excavators of all kinds. Surely this is now one of the single most
persistent acts of cultural conservation in the history of the world,
one of our great national resources.

ISHMAEL REED

Although some of this ebullient, comic novel may come "straight from the pages of history," as the jacket copy claims, most of it comes straight from the fevered, absurdist imagination of its author, and straight from the hip. *Flight to Canada* is vintage Reed, a disarming satire and an outlandish spoof in which Reed mixes fact and fiction, hilarious anachronisms, folklore and personal mythology, and caricature and idiom—all for choice comic effect.

It is the story of the demise of slavemaster Arthur Swille, a Civil War–era villain, and the takeover of his plantation by his clever black manservant, Uncle Robin, as written by the runaway and returned ex-slave Raven Quickskill. Swille, the prototypical, decadent nineteenth-century southern aristocrat, lives in a castle that is a replica of King Arthur's, where, we are told, he routinely imbibes two gallons of what he thinks is slave-mother's milk for breakfast. Actually, his manservant—having tampered with Swille's will—has been slowly poisoning the evil fellow with Coffee Mate. Swille is inadvertently burned to death at the hands of his own wife before the poison takes effect, however.

While one strand of the narrative covers these cheerful events down on the plantation in Virginia, the other follows Raven Quickskill during his flight to Canada. Imagined as an Eden for runaway slaves, Canada turns out to be a big disappointment for Raven since, with its neon signs and used-car lots, "it could have been downtown San Mateo." In a comic reversal of the you-can't-go-home-again theme, Raven returns to the South—a new South in which Swille has died and Uncle Robin has taken over.

Although characterized as a "slave's eye view of the Civil War," the satire is doled out impartially. The runaway ex-slaves who accompany the protagonist Quickskill partway on his "flight to Canada" are hardly more virtuous than the degenerate slavemaster Swille. One of them, for instance, a former chicken thief, now earns his living making porno pictures and offering himself through newspaper ads as a slave-for-a-day.

Reed's Lincoln is not the historical Lincoln, but rather an amalgam of what a century of idolatry has sometimes made of him, the product of too many worshipful Lincoln's Birthday lessons in dull grade schools, a pompous piece of calendar art.

Reed's fictional world in *Flight to Canada* is set up to allow maximum scope for wild inventions, moral skull-cracking, and the unleashing of a passel of demons. Its pleasures are derived less from its deliberately cavalier view of history than from its feats of association, improvisation, and wit. While tsk-tsking in admiration at Reed's flights, one is occasionally reminded of that Ellison character Peter Wheatstraw, from *Invisible Man*, who quips: "All it takes to get along in this here man's town is a little shit, grit, and mother-wit. And, man, I was bawn with all three."

KURT VONNEGUT

The political scientist believes in the efficacy of pragmatic solutions to human problems: Blame the system or its leaders if something goes wrong, or "events" themselves. Find better leaders or invent a better system. Gain control of "events."

The literary moralist believes human problems are the result of defects in human nature itself or in the structure of the universe that are mostly without cure: Blame the creature (or its creator). Try to reform him if possible. Try to find cause for hope.

I make this distinction because *Jailbird* will undoubtedly be described by some readers as Vonnegut's new political novel, or his treatise on the failures of liberalism, or Harvard, or the American way. Or his explanation of why Watergate was visited upon us, or his prescription for the future, or possibly even the platform for his own candidacy. Some of these characterizations are not far from the truth. (I have a feeling that Vonnegut would make a first-rate chief executive, as a matter of fact; but it seems unlikely he could ever be persuaded to run for the office.)

The narrator and protagonist of *Jailbird*, Walter F. Starbuck, is a former staff member of the Nixon White House who has been imprisoned for his "preposterous contributions" to the Watergate scandal. The historical backdrop developed for Starbuck's tale of woe covers most of the last century, from an Ohio labor riot and massacre in 1894, to a close-up of the Sacco and Vanzetti case and execution in the twenties, to views of the House Un-American Activities Committee hearings, to an inside report on the contemporary workings of the largest conglomerate in the free world, RAMJAC. It features cameo appearances by Richard Nixon, the ghost of Albert Einstein, Roy M. Cohn, Clyde Carter (fictitious third cousin to the former president of the United States), not to mention various extraterrestrials.

But the central story of how Walter F. Starbuck, the son of immigrants, goes from Harvard to the White House to jail, and then from jail to a vice presidency of the RAMJAC Corporation, and then back to jail, is a fable in the classic tradition of the great American Dream gone awry; and Vonnegut proves himself, of course, far more a literary moralist than a political diagnostician. He is, in fact, the same Vonnegut we have seen before, the thinking man's pop writer, his magnanimous soul brooding, this time over an obscene cartoon that bears too close a resemblance to the recent American past.

Vonnegut is terribly disappointed by the behavior of his fellow countrymen. His Hoosier sense of human decency and honesty is positively outraged at the mess the country is in. He is, on the one hand, an inveterate injustice-collector, appalled by the unnecessary insults life has sprung on innocent people; while, on the other, he sings a lament on the failures and the incredible posturings and ineptitude of the "damned human race."

Yet for all his cynicism and hand-wringing, Vonnegut still finds cause for hope in the human capacity for ordinary kindness. Several characters in the novel are promoted from low-paying jobs to positions as vice presidents of the RAMJAC Corporation solely for the reason that they show kindness to a stranger. The RAMJAC Corporation, we gradually discover, is not an evil conspiracy of white-collar criminals out to control the world, but merely the grandiose embodiment of the failing political dream of a former radical activist who is now a benevolent shopping-bag lady who haunts the toilets in the subcellars of Grand Central Station.

Perhaps the most surprising aspect of Vonnegut's vision of the world is that he manages to laugh, deplore, and show sympathy (even forgiveness) all at the same time. Vonnegut has become the Walter Cronkite of our literature, and we read him for his avuncular authority and charm and soulfulness as much as for the news he brings and his occasional silliness. We tend to overlook his weaknesses and mistakes as we would those of a kindly relative who is singing slightly out-of-key.

Jailbird reads at times as if put together from a goofy collection of index cards. Pet bugaboos recur, but their arrangement sometimes belies some essential culminating development. Gratuitous ironies and a few awfully tired jokes are scattered about a little too wistfully in the brew. Perhaps most distracting of all is Vonnegut's habit of punctuating a truly dramatic or exciting moment in his narrative with a fatuous banality such as "Small world" or "Live and learn"—an apparent legacy of the "So it goes" refrain from *Slaughter-house-Five*.

But we do, as I say, forgive him. His imaginative leaps alone, as seen particularly in the irreal sci-fi stories Kilgore Trout tells Starbuck in prison, are worth the price of admission and show Vonnegut at this impressive best. His far-reaching metaphysical and cultural concerns, though sometimes couched as shrugs or grimaces, are ultimately serious and worth our contemplation. We are all victims of Time and Fate. Education is no guarantee of humanity, he reminds us, any more than religious affiliation is any guarantee of moral uprightness. Hypocrisy, selfishness, and greed are everywhere across the land and are our enemies. The proper conduct of life is still a subject we have not mastered.

DAN WAKEFIELD

As in his popular first novel, *Going All the Way*, Dan Wakefield is seen here—in *Home Free*—again attempting to clothe his journalistic interest in social and cultural history in a fictional form. This time out it is a Cook's tour of late sixties lifestyles, music, bugaboos, slang, and phoney versions of salvation. Wakefield's hero, a grocer's son from the Midwest, is a likeable if pitiful victim of the times and his own innocence, vulnerability, and self-generated confusion, who learns what it means to be footloose and miserable.

In the course of Gene's pilgrimage to oblivion, Wakefield cleverly succeeds in jogging our memories about those already half-forgotten associations, landmarks, and pangs of the Age of Aquarius, from draft-dodging and dropping out, to the discovery of the generation gap, the pharmacological cornucopia, sexual license, and the suddenly necessary distinctions between hip and square.

In the end, *Home Free* proves to be an intentionally ironic title. For all of Wakefield's lost souls, petty hustlers, derelicts, and freaks are unwilling or unable to pay the price of establishing a home in the usual sense. They are all in flight from permanence, and the consequences of their rootlessness are seen to be dire and ultimately destructive. Home may, indeed, not be free, Wakefield seems to be saying, but, at whatever the cost, home is absolutely necessary; and no vague ideal of personal freedom is likely to change that irreducible truth.

PAUL WEST

Just after midnight following the events of July 20, 1944, Adolf Hitler's hoarse voice broke through on German radio to announce "a crime unparalleled in German history." An attempt had been made upon his life. A bomb had exploded in his war room, leaving him bruised and burned but "entirely unhurt," and a treasonous plot was under way to usurp authority. Hitler tried to conceal the extent of the plot, describing it as merely "a very small clique of ambitious, irresponsible and, at the same time, senseless and stupid officers, . . . a gang of criminal elements which will be destroyed without mercy." But, in fact, thousands of estimable Germans were involved in the failed coup. It was to be the only serious revolt ever marshaled against Hitler in the eleven and a half years of the Third Reich.

Paul West's novel, *The Very Rich Hours of Count von Stauffenberg*, is a fictionalized insider's account of the German resistance to Hitler from 1933 to 1945, focusing with particular sympathy and detail upon the character, temperament, and motivation of Colonel Count Claus von Stauffenberg, who assumed leadership of the abortive July 20, 1944, effort. Stauffenberg was a fundamentally good and noble man, in West's view, driven by circumstances to a desperate, last-ditch effort to save his people from what he regarded would be the judgment of history: universal condemnation and infamy.

The novel follows the transformation of Stauffenberg's allegiance from nominal support of Hitler in the early days of the Reich, to ambivalence and doubt (as he learned more), to active dislike, to loathing and hatred of everything Hitler stood for and was doing to his country, and finally to mobilization, "after which there was the whole business of an ethics that transcended ethics, culminating in a deed of homicidal saintliness, not an end in itself, but the prelude to a just polity, a decent polity, a new Germany."

As a young man, Stauffenberg was clearly prepared by his ancestry and sumptuous education for some important role, if not quite adequately for the brutal tasks his life required of him, though he did come very close to succeeding. He came from an old, congenial, and distinguished south German family, born to "a responsibility to care for others," the descendant of generals and military heroes of the war of liberation against Napoleon. He grew into a cultured, balanced, energetic man whose idealism was nourished by his friendship with poets, a man who might have become the leader Germany needed, West implies, had he had the chance; and his life poses a persuasive counterargument to the use of the example of Nazi Germany as proof of the failure of the once-assumed values of culture and the civilizing and humane influence of a liberal education. "I wanted a Germany," Stauffenberg says in the novel, "led by men from all classes of society, men committed to selfless high-mindedness."

West shows how difficult it must have been to strike out against an enfranchised authority, especially at a time of siege when the instincts of the majority of the duped populace were tuned to defending the barricades, when one was surrounded by Hitler's fanatical loyalists and henchmen, and when the foe was a maniac of such overweening dominance, decisiveness, and apparent strength who had succeeded in identifying himself as synonymous with the fatherland. The novel helps us imagine and therefore comprehend how so many reasonable and civilized German citizens could have been swept along into seeming collaboration with such an oppressive, tyrannical force.

Stauffenberg's story shows further that an idealist with convictions and an ability to act on his beliefs can change the world. Stauffenberg's main failing was apparently a lack of luck: His briefcase containing the all-important bomb was inadvertently moved after he had left the war room, thus saving Hitler. Communications snafus and the lack of commitment of some of his co-conspirators also contributed to the failure.

Most of them paid dearly, for Hitler carried out his threatened revenge with grotesque thoroughness, convening a kangaroo court for the purpose of humiliating the conspirators publicly, then having them tortured and hanged, while selected executions were committed to film for viewing by the führer and members of the military elite. Hitler vowed to exterminate even the wives, children, and near relatives of the accused. Before the purge was over, the gestapo had made seven thousand arrests and the death toll numbered nearly five thousand names. The only stroke of luck for poor Stauffenberg— then only thirty-six years old—seemed to be that he was summarily dispatched by firing squad under the auspices of a fence-straddling officer who hoped to cover his own complicity in the affair (he was later executed himself).

West occasionally seems overwhelmed by his material, or too concerned with the sheer weightiness of the turgid accumulation of names and facts. There is little attention to conventional plotting and suspense, to the aspects that could have made the novel "a thriller." But West obviously does not conceive of the work as a mere entertainment but as a serious and deep meditation on the life of a unique and altruistic man who, but for quirks of fate, might have changed the world for the better. It is not an historical novel—that is, not merely an historical novel, though it is quite convincing in its attention to historical accuracy—but rather, prose with a conscience, work that might most aptly be identified as "moral fiction."

West uncovers and explores one of the great, unheralded acts of heroism of World War II (and its attendant failings and atrocities)— to speak for dead men in an impressive feat of ventriloquism—to attempt to find out what message these wasted lives might have for us now.

INDEX

Abbott, Lee K., 5
Adams, Alice, 78
Addison, Joseph, 130
Agassiz, Louis, 48
Age of Missing Information, The
  (McKibben), 9
Ahab, 148
Alberts, Laurie, 113
Aldridge, John W., 111–12
Algren, Nelson, 113
American Energies (Birkerts), 6
American Romance, An (Casey),
  193–95
Anderson, Joy, 42–43
Anderson, Sherwood, 115
Angell, Roger, 54
Antioch Review, 37
Apple, Max, 4, 81, 179–82
Arbus, Diane, 192
As I Lay Dying (Faulkner), 143
Associated Writing Programs
  (AWP), 1, 172–74
Atlantic Monthly, The, 130
Atwood, Margaret, 19, 55–56
Auden, W. H., 211
Auerbach, Erich, 67
Austen, Jane, 78, 109, 130, 158, 212

Baber, Asa, 50, 113
Bach, Johann Sebastian, 144
Baez, Joan, 50
Balzac, Honoré de, 78
Banks, Russell, 50, 78–79, 81, 183–85
Barth, John, 2–3, 32, 64, 71, 73–74,
  80, 121–22, 142, 157, 159, 198
Barthelme, Donald, 2–4, 73–74,
  80–82, 121–22, 125, 156–57, 159,
  186–90
Barthelme, Frederick, 78–81, 83, 111

Bass, Rick, 83
Batki, John, 72
Bausch, Richard, 83, 113
Bawer, Bruce, 7
Baxter, Charles, 83
Beatles, 64, 144
Beattie, Ann, 50, 52–54, 78–79, 111
Beckett, Samuel, 81
Bell, Madison Smartt, 113
Bell, Marvin, 40, 43, 113
Bellow, Saul, 39
Benedict, Dianne, 54, 83, 113
Benedikt, Michael, 50
Bennett, William, 107, 159
Berryman, John, 113
Best American Short Stories (Foley,
  ed.), 29, 37
Bettelheim, Bruno, 101–2
Birkerts, Sven, 5–6
Black Humor (Friedman, ed.), 141–42
Black Spring (Miller), 206
Black Tickets (Phillips), 57
Blaise, Clark, 50, 113
Bly, Robert, 113
Bonfire of the Vanities, The (Wolfe),
  130, 157
Booth, Wayne, 158
Borges, Jorge Luis, 64
Bourjaily, Vance, 43, 113, 137, 142
Bowles, Paul, 69
Boyle, T. Coraghessan, 81, 83, 111,
  113, 121–25
Brademas, John, 15
Braverman, Kate, 83
Brinkley, David, 17
Brooks, Cleanth, 147
Brown, Charles Brockden, 69
Brown, Rosellen, 56, 58
Broyard, Anatole, 43

Bryan, C. D. B., 113, 137, 139, 144–46, 149–50
Buchanan, Pat, 168
Bumpus, Jerry, 113
Burgess, Anthony, 113, 211
Burroway, Janet, 113
Bush, George, 13, 15, 100, 168
Butler, Robert Olen, 113

Calisher, Hortense, 114
Canada Council, 18–19
Canary in a Cathouse (Vonnegut), 141
Cartiér, Xam, 83
Carver, Raymond, 4–5, 78–80, 82, 111, 113, 121, 191–92
Casey, John, 113, 193–95
Cassill, R. V., 113
Cat's Cradle (Vonnegut), 138, 141, 143, 148
Catch–22 (Heller), 141
Catcher in the Rye, The (Salinger), 193
Cather, Willa, 39
Caulfield, Holden, 156, 193
Centaur, The (Updike), 71
Chase, Richard, 69
Chaucer, Geoffrey, 212
Cheever, John, 80, 98, 113
Chekhov, Anton, 210
Cherry, Kelly, 54
Chilly Scenes of Winter (Beattie), 53
Christ, Jesus, 148, 166, 168
Ciardi, John, 42–43
Cisneros, Sandra, 113
Clark, Walter Van Tilberg, 113
Colossus of Maroussi (Miller), 206
Comaneci, Nadia, 204
Come Back, Lolly Ray (Lowry), 204–5
Committee of Small Magazine Editors and Publishers (COSMEP), 33–34
Conroy, Frank, 113
Cooper, Alice, 69
Cooper, Jane, 113
Coordinating Council of Literary Magazines (CCLM), 1, 33, 35–36
Coover, Robert, 65, 113, 121–22, 157, 159, 185

Cortes, 189
Cosby, Bill, 35
Cosell, Howard, 64, 181
Costello, Mark, 113
Cowley, Malcolm, 113, 206
Cox, Elizabeth, 54
Crane, Philip, 20
Cranford (Gaskell), 202
Crews, Harry, 40–41, 43
Cronkite, Walter, 16, 64, 217
Crumley, James, 113
Culture of Complaint (Hughes), 9

Dana, Robert, 113
Dante, 211
Dead Father, The (Donald Barthelme), 186–88
Defoe, Daniel, 66
DeLillo, Don, 196–98
De Mille, Cecil B., 138
DeMott, Benjamin, 139, 144, 147, 149
Descent of Man (Boyle), 122, 125
DeVoto, Bernard, 39
Dickens, Charles, 78
Dickey, William, 113
Digges, Deborah, 113
Dillard, Annie, 56, 58
DiMaggio, Joe, 13
Diogenes, 3, 200
Distortions (Beattie), 53
Doctorow, E. L., 58
Donaldson, Sam, 17, 20
Donoso, Jose, 113
Dove, Rita, 113
Drexler, Rosalyn, 114
Dubus, Andre, 113
Duke University, 88–89
Dylan, Bob, 92

Edwards, Thomas R., 129–30
Electric Kool-Aid Acid Test, The (Wolfe), 127, 129, 131, 133
Eliot, T. S., 71, 146
Elliott, George P., 43
Ellis, Bret Easton, 78–79
Ellison, Ralph, 215

Emerson, Ralph Waldo, 48–49
End Zone (DeLillo), 196
Engle, Paul, 113–14
Epstein, Jason, 149
Epstein, Seymour, 40, 42–43
Erdrich, Louise, 83
Erikson, Eric, 101
Esquire, 38, 82, 126–27, 130, 146
Esrock, Ellen, 92–93
Exley, Frederick, 113, 199–200

Fabulators, The (Scholes), 138–39, 145, 148
Falcon, The, 27–38
Falwell, Jerry, 82
Fan's Notes, A (Exley), 199–200
Faulkner, William, 67, 69, 80, 84, 109, 143, 147, 160, 185, 204, 206
Fear of Flying (Jong), 206
Fenza, David, 110, 112
Fiction International, 3, 4, 7, 29, 55
Fiedler, Leslie, 35, 66–69, 72, 139, 146–47, 149–50
Fielding, Henry, 128, 130
Finn, Huck, 156
Flight to Canada (Reed), 214–15
Foley, Martha, 29, 37–38
Fonda, Jane, 32, 64
Forché, Carolyn, 58
Ford, Gerald, 180
Ford, Richard, 78–79, 83
Frankel, Charles, 95
Frazer, Sir James George, 71
Freud, Sigmund, 71, 77, 101–2, 185, 197, 207
Friedman, Bruce Jay, 141–42
Frohnmayer, John, 1, 15–16, 167–70
From Bauhaus to Our House (Wolfe), 132, 134–35
Frost, Robert, 39, 46–47

Gallagher, Tess, 54, 113
Galvin, James, 113–14
Gardner, John, 2, 4, 70–71, 76, 113, 156–62, 201–3
Garland, Hamlin, 39
Garrett, George, 96

Gass, William H., 65, 70–71, 73, 93, 156–57, 159
Genet, Jean, 158
Genius and Lust (Mailer), 206–8
Gibbons, Kaye, 83
Gifford, Frank, 200
Gilchrist, Ellen, 83
Ginsberg, Allen, 34–35
Glück, Louise, 113
God Bless You, Mr. Rosewater (Vonnegut), 141
Godwin, Gail, 48, 50, 52, 113
Going All the Way (Wakefield), 219
Goldbarth, Albert, 113
Goodman, Walter, 43
Graff, Gerald, 87
Graham, Jorie, 113–14
Greasy Lake (Boyle), 122
Great Days (Donald Barthelme), 188–90
Great Gatsby, The (Fitzgerald), 32
Grendel, 159
Grumbach, Doris, 113
Gurganus, Allan, 113
Gutenberg Elegies, The (Birkerts), 6

Halpern, Daniel, 58
Hamilton Stark (Banks), 183–85
Hannah, Barry, 82, 114
Hansen, Ron, 113
Hardy, Thomas, 185
Harjo, Joy, 113
Harper, Michael S., 113
Harper's, 37
Harrison, Colin, 113
Harrison, Kathryn, 113
Hartman, Geoffrey, 93
Harvard University, 139, 216
Harvey, W. J., 67
Hawkes, John, 2, 50, 68–69, 80, 88, 93, 113, 121–22, 157
Hecht, Anthony, 43, 113
Hegi, Ursula, 54
Helms, Jesse, 20, 170
Hemingway, Ernest, 4, 23, 79–81, 83, 148, 160, 207
Hempel, Amy, 82

Hesse, Herman, 210
Heston, Charlton, 138
Hills, Rust, 42
Hitler, Adolph, 220–21
Hoagland, Edward, 114
Home Free (Wakefield), 219
Hoover, J. Edgar, 181
Horatio, 130–31
Howland, Bette, 82
Hudson Review, 37
Hughes, Robert, 9, 164–65
Hugo, Richard, 113
Hugo, Victor, 104
Hungry Ghosts, The (Oates), 209
Huxley, Aldous, 140

If the River Was Whiskey (Boyle), 121–25
Inness-Brown, Elizabeth, 54, 81
In Our Time (Hemingway), 23
In the Heart of the Heart of the Country (Gass), 65
Invisible Man (Ellison), 215
Iowa Writers Workshop, 1–2, 28, 108–14, 121, 137–40, 142, 144, 149–50
Irving, John, 113, 122

Jacobson, Roman, 87
Jailbird (Vonnegut), 216–18
James, Henry, 72, 77, 109, 128, 157–58, 162
Jefferson, Thomas, 175
Jen, Gish, 83, 113
Jewel Weed, The, 27–28
Job, 148
Johnson, Denis, 83, 113
Johnson, Howard, 179–80
Jonah, 138, 147–48
Jong, Erica, 48
Joyce, James, 77, 128
Jung, Carl, 70–71, 101
Justice, Donald, 113
Juvenal, 130

Kafka, Franz, 70
Kahn, Herman, 68–69

Kandy-Kolored Tangerine-Flake Streamline Baby, The (Wolfe), 126–27, 133
Kaplan, Bernie, 45
Katz, Steve, 71
Kazan, Alfred, 212
Kazantzakis, Nikos, 71
Kernan, Alvin, 8
Kerouac, Jack, 211
Khan, Genghis, 53
Kinnell, Galway, 113
Kinsella, W. P., 113
Kittredge, William, 58, 113
Kizer, Carolyn, 114
Klappert, Peter, 113
Klinkowitz, Jerome, 147
Kosinski, Jerzy, 157
Kumin, Maxine, 43–44

Lady Oracle (Atwood), 55
Land of a Million Elephants, The (Baber), 50
Larson, Gary, 122
Lawrence, Seymour, 55–57, 137
Leavitt, David, 79, 82
Leggett, John, 113
Leonardo (Freud), 207
Levine, Philip, 113
Levis, Larry, 112–14
Lewis, Sinclair, 39
Life Before Man (Atwood), 55
Lincoln, Abraham, 215
Lish, Gordon, 3, 31, 81–82
Lolita (Nabokov), 211
Long and Happy Life, A (Price), 89, 153
Longfellow, Henry Wadsworth, 48
Loon Lake (Doctorow), 58
Lot's wife, 148
Love and Death in the American Novel (Fiedler), 66–69
Lovelace, Linda, 124
Lowell, James Russell, 48
Lowell, Robert, 113
Lowry, Beverly, 204–5
Lubbock, Percy, 158
Lucas, George, 8

Macauley, Robie, 49–50, 113
Mack, Maynard, 90
MacLeish, Archibald, 39, 93
Madden, David, 48
Madonna, 104
Mailer, Norman, 179–80, 200, 206–8
Malin, Irving, 69
Mantle, Mickey, 124
Markham, Edwin, 39
Marshall, Paule, 113
Martin, Sandy, 42–43, 45–46
Martin, Valerie, 83
Martone, Michael, 82
Mason, Bobbie Ann, 54, 78–80, 111
Matthews, William, 114
*Mauve Gloves & Madmen, Clutter &
Vine* (Wolfe), 131, 133
McAusland, Randy, 167–68, 172–73
McCall's, 37
McCarthy, Mary, 67
McCartney, Paul, 145
McConkey, James, 113
McEwan, Ian, 114
McGovern, George, 32
McInerney, Jay, 78–79
McKibben, Bill, 9
McLuhan, Marshall, 6–8, 23, 145
McPherson, James Alan, 113
McPherson, Sandra, 113
Melville, Herman, 157
Meredith, William, 43
Michaelangelo, 211
Michaels, Leonard, 68, 114
Michigan Quarterly Review, 5, 83
Middlemarch (Eliot), 202
Midwood, Barton, 71
Mill, John Stuart, 28
Miller, Henry, 206–8
Mississippi Review, 5
Moby-Dick (Melville), 148, 196
Modern Language Association
(MLA), 93–94
Modigliani, 89
Molinaro, Ursule, 65
Monroe, Marilyn, 50
Montezuma, 189
Moore, Lorrie, 78–79, 81, 83, 111

Moral Fiction, On (Gardner), 4, 76,
156
Moses, 137
Mosquitoes (Faulkner), 143
Mother Night (Vonnegut), 141, 145
Motherwell, Robert, 17
Mozart, 211
Mukherjee, Bharati, 50, 83, 113
Munro, Alice, 19
Murasaki, Lady, 16
Murray, G. E., 54
Muske, Carol, 114

Nabokov, Vladimir, 87, 211
Napoleon, 221
National Endowment for the Arts
(NEA), 1, 13–24, 33, 100, 110,
163–75
New Fiction, The (Bellamy), 3, 77,
127, 156–58
New Journalism, The (Wolfe), 127–29
Newman, Charles, 80
New Yorker, The, 38, 52, 54, 78–79,
81–82, 130, 196
Nimoy, Leonard, 32–33
Nixon, Richard, 71, 216

Oates, Joyce Carol, 2, 21, 50–52, 68,
156–57, 159, 209–10
O'Connor, Flannery, 84, 113, 204–5
October Light (Gardner), 201–3
Odd Jobs (Updike), 16
O'Faolain, Sean, 37
Olsen, Tillie, 55
Onassis, Jacqueline, 34
Oranging of America, The (Apple),
179–81
Orwell, George, 140

Pack, Robert, 39–40, 42–44
Pages from a Cold Island (Exley),
199–200
Painted Word, The (Wolfe), 134–35
Painter, Pamela, 54
Pamela (Richardson), 68, 193
Paris Review, The, 32, 35, 37, 211–13
Partisan Review, 37

Peckinpah, Sam, 69
Penner, Jonathan, 113
Pesetsky, Bette, 82, 113
Phillips, Jayne Anne, 54, 56–58, 78–79, 81, 83, 113
Plato, 88, 92, 107, 159, 212
Playboy, 37–38
Player Piano (Vonnegut), 140–41, 143, 149
Plimpton, George, 33–35, 211–13
Plumly, Stanley, 114
Poirier, Richard, 144
Poisoned Kiss, The (Oates), 209–10
Polanski, Roman, 69
Poorhouse Fair, The (Updike), 153
Portable Lower East Side, 163–64, 166–69
Portnoy's Complaint (Roth), 206
Post-Modern Aura, The (Newman), 80
Pound, Ezra, 71, 87
Poverman, C. E., 54, 113
Price, Reynolds, 88–89, 153
Prichett, V. S., 114
Proust, Marcel, 77
Pump House Gang, The (Wolfe), 133
Pynchon, Thomas, 68, 121–22, 198

Rabbit Is Rich (Updike), 22
Rabelais, 199
Radical Chic & Mau-Mauing the Flak-Catchers (Wolfe), 129, 132–33, 135
Radice, Anne-Imelda, 171–74
Ransom, John Crowe, 39, 113
Rascoe, Judith, 72
Ratner's Star (DeLillo), 196–98
Reagan, Ronald, 4, 82, 168
Reasoner, Harry, 150
Reed, Ishmael, 2, 72, 157, 214–15
Richardson, Samuel, 66–68
Right Stuff, The (Wolfe), 133, 135
Roberts, Cokie, 17, 20
Robison, Mary, 81–82
Rockwell, Norman, 180
Rolling Stone, 130
Rosy Crucifixion, The (Miller), 206

Roth, Philip, 64, 113
Rubin, Louis D., Jr., 161
Russell, Ken, 69

Salter, James, 114
Sanders, Scott Russell, 90, 110
Sapphire, 166–69
Saturday Evening Post, The, 180
Scholes, Robert, 64, 137–39, 145–50
Schrag, Peter, 43
Schwartz, Lynne Sharon, 114
Searching for Survivors (Banks), 50
Segal, Lore, 43
Selzer, Richard, 82
Settle, Mary Lee, 113
Sexton, Anne, 44
Shacochis, Bob, 113
Shakespeare, William, 144, 211–12
Shaw, George Bernard, 130
Sheed, Wilfrid, 137, 139, 146, 212
Shock of the New, The (Hughes), 164–65
Singer, Jerome L., 101
Sirens of Titan, The (Vonnegut), 141, 143
Skinner, Cornelia Otis, 39
Skinner, Knute, 113
Skinner, Sam, 169
Slaughterhouse-Five (Vonnegut), 139, 146, 148, 217
Smiley, Jane, 83, 113
Smith, Dave, 96, 110
Smith, Raymond, 51–52
Snodgrass, W. D., 113
Socrates, 109
Soldiers' Pay (Faulkner), 143
Solzhenitsyn, Alexander, 8, 14, 23
Sontag, Susan, 2, 32, 144, 157–58
Sorrentino, Gilbert, 73–74
Sound and the Fury, The (Faulkner), 143
Sprinkle, Annie, 164
St. Lawrence Award for Fiction, 50, 58
St. Lawrence University, 49
Stafford, William, 113, 169
Starbuck, George, 114

Star Wars, 8
Stauffenberg, Claus von, 220–22
Stegner, Wallace, 113
Steinem, Gloria, 200
Stern, Gerald, 114
Stern, Isaac, 13
Stockhausen, Karlheinz, 186
Strand, Mark, 40, 43–44, 113
Streiber, Whitley, 58
Sukenick, Ronald, 2–3, 73–74, 80, 157
Superfiction (Bellamy, ed.), 3, 63–74, 83
Supremes, 144
Suzi Sinzinnati (Bellamy), 2, 6, 153, 170
Swift, Jonathan, 146

Tale of Genji (Murasaki), 16
Talents and Technicians (Aldridge), 111
Tallent, Elizabeth, 78
Tate, James, 50, 113
Ten Commandments, The, 138
Terminator II, 8, 24
Thackeray, William Makepeace, 78, 130
Thomas, Marlo, 33
Thoreau, Henry David, 96
Tolstoy, Leo, 78, 191, 208
Tongues Untied, 168
Tortilla Curtain, The (Boyle), 121
Traven, B., 210
Tribal Justice (Blaise), 50
Tristram Shandy (Sterne), 196
Tropic of Cancer (Miller), 206
Twain, Mark, 116, 130, 157

Unspeakable Practices, Unnatural Acts (Donald Barthelme), 159
Updike, John, 16, 22, 59, 71–72, 80, 125, 153, 157, 206, 211
Urdang, Constance, 113
Uses of Enchantment, The (Bettelheim), 101–2

Van Duyn, Mona, 113

Very Rich Hours of Count von Stauffenberg, The (West), 220–22
Voltaire, 146
Vonnegut, Kurt, 2, 64, 113, 121–22, 137–50, 157, 198, 216–18

Wakefield, Dan, 114, 219
Wakoski, Diane, 50
Walker, Margaret, 113
Warren, Robert Penn, 113
Watt, Ian, 66
Wayne's World, 24
Weesner, Ted, 113
Weil, Wendy, 46
Weingarten, Roger, 113
Weiss, Theodore, 52
Weiss, Renée, 52
Welcome to the Monkey House (Vonnegut), 65, 141–43
Welty, Eudora, 69
West, Paul, 220–22
Whitehead, James, 113
Whitman, Walt, 109
Why Are We in Vietnam? (Mailer), 206
Wideman, John Edgar, 113
Wiener, Anthony J., 68–69
Wildmon, Donald, 166, 168, 170
Will, George, 17, 82, 107
Williams, Joy, 113
Williams, Tennessee, 113
Williams, Ted, 13, 206
Williams, William Carlos, 39
Will You Please Be Quiet, Please? (Carver), 191–92
Wilson, Angus, 113
Wilson, Edmund, 200
Wilson, Robley, 56, 71, 81, 113
Without A Hero (Boyle), 121
Wolfe, Tom, 2, 32, 77–78, 122, 126–36, 157
Wolff, Tobias, 78, 83
Wolitzer, Hilma, 113
Wonderland (Oates), 160
Woolf, Virginia, 67
Wordsworth, William, 128
Wright, Charles, 113

Writers at Work: The Paris Review Interviews (Plimpton, ed.), 32, 211–13
Wurlitzer, Rudolph, 65
Wuthering Heights (Brontë), 193

Yale Review, 37
Yale University, 134
Yankee Doodle, 156, 159

Yates, Richard, 113
Yeats, William Butler, 71
Young, Al, 113
Young, Marguerite, 113

Zeus, 109
Zip (Apple), 181–82
Zola, Émile, 128

Director of the literature program of the National Endowment for the Arts during 1990–1992, Joe David Bellamy won the Editors' Book Award for his novel *Suzi Sinzinnati,* and his collection of short fiction, *Atomic Love,* was an AWP Award Series selection. He is also author or editor of ten other books, including *The New Fiction, Superfiction, American Poetry Observed,* and two collections of poetry. A former president of both the Associated Writing Programs (AWP) and the Coordinating Council of Literary Magazines (CCLM), Bellamy was the founding editor and publisher of *Fiction International* magazine and press. He has taught fiction writing and contemporary American literature for more than twenty-five years at St. Lawrence University, George Mason University, the University of Iowa, and elsewhere.